John O. Meusebach

GERMAN COLONIZER IN TEXAS

John O. Meusebach, 1852. "Freedom is not free . . ."

John O. Meusebach

GERMAN COLONIZER IN TEXAS

by Irene Marschall King

UNIVERSITY OF TEXAS PRESS, AUSTIN

To the memory of my parents,
Lucy Meusebach Marschall
and
Ernst Marschall

International Standard Book Number 0-292-74019-0
Library of Congress Catalog Card Number 67-16848
Copyright © 1967 by Irene Marschall King
All rights reserved

Printed in the United States of America
First Paperback Printing, 1987

Requests for permission to reproduce material from this work
should be sent to Permissions, University of Texas Press,
Box 7819, Austin, Texas 78713-7819.

Preface

My mother wanted desperately to write the story of her father, John O. Meusebach, who to her was a great man: never once did she see any limitations in him. Although the radius of their travels together did not exceed two hundred miles, in conversation they traversed the world. My mother was thirty-two at his death. She lived to be ninety-six years old and to the end her father remained an integral part of her life. She made many beginnings in writing his story, but she never progressed beyond his arrival in New Braunfels, where he expected to present his credentials to Prince Solms and where he found that the impatient Prince had departed for Germany.

My initial intention was to record relevant facts of my grandfather's history for my own family. I wished to carry out my mother's hope of writing about her father, but my desire was to go even further into the family's history. Standing beside my great-grandfather's grave in Germany, my husband and I were moved when told by the sexton that the folk songs collected by that Meusebach were sung annually on his birthday, at the graveside. My husband encouraged me to collect all the available material on my family. We went to the village of Meusebach in Thuringia, where the villagers preserved drawings of the centuries-old family dwelling.

When I was free to do some uninterrupted study, I began reading the seventy volumes, in German, of the Solms-Braunfels Archives in The University of Texas Library. The material relates largely to the activities of the Society for the Protection of German Immigrants in Texas. These volumes result from the efforts of Dr. R. L. Biesele, former professor of history at The University of Texas, who arranged for a transcription of the file in the Library of Congress. The Library of Congress file was transcribed from the original sources in the Fürst zu Solms-Braunfels'sches Archiv in Braunfels (Lahn), Germany.

In reading the material in the Archives my purpose was to follow my grandfather's experiences so that I could be specific about the facts of his years as a colonizer and could enlarge on these facts, with which I was already somewhat familiar. By adding this information to that which I had secured from various other sources, I believed that I could write the Meusebach story in a way to interest the family living today. Although I recognized that authenticating my account was desirable, I questioned whether a story meant only for the family needed footnotes.

My sister, her husband, my niece, and certain other friends insisted that my story would lose value unless I did document the material. I decided then to give the sources for my story so that anyone reading it could find the authority for my statements. Hence, as far as possible, I have tried to document my account. This has necessitated return visits to The University of Texas Archives, the Barker Texas History Center at The University of Texas, the Texas State Archives, and the Texas History Collection of Baylor University.

The English translations of the German sources which I used are my own.

My mother, with her keen and retentive mind, supplied primary source material in her constant conversations with me. Letters and printed materials, largely from Germany, made it possible for me to augment and authenticate what my mother related. Texas was a subject much written about in Germany during the mid-nineteenth century. I read a limited amount of this material; the books and pamphlets I used are listed in the Bibliography. I limited my study of the Solms-Braunfels Archives to Meusebach's involvement in the dramatic story that the documents revealed. Making a selection of what to include or not to include about the many participants in the drama often caused me to ponder. Material for numerous other stories is available in the Archives.

I gratefully acknowledge those publishers and copyright holders who granted me permission to reproduce material from various sources that were relevant to my study. I am especially grateful for permission from The University of Texas Archives to reproduce quotations, in translation, from the Solms-Braunfels material.

If Mr. Chester V. Kielman, archivist at The University of Texas Library, had been doing research for a publication of his own he could not have evidenced more interest and help than he did in my research, day after day. My indebtedness to Mr. Kielman is great; my gratitude to him is deep. In all my work Miss Llerena Friend, head librarian of the Barker Texas History Center, has been a valuable friend indeed. The smiles from Miss Friend's staff members brightened my days. At Baylor University, Professor Guy B. Harrison, head of the Texas History Collection, and Mrs. Walter J. Williams facilitated matters for me, as did the staff of the Texas State Library Archives.

Encouragement has come from friends outside the "halls of learning." Long before Dr. Francis E. McIntyre and I became acquainted he admired John O. Meusebach. Dr. McIntryre's enthusiasm has been like a shining light before me. A professional writer and friend, Mr. Weldon Hart, found one paragraph in the manuscript to praise; pointing it out, he remarked, kindly, "See that the rest of the manuscript comes up to that quality!" That prodding was needed and was appreciated. Mr. Jack Ward Thomas, a scientist, read between the lines of the manuscript and encouraged me to fill in the "why's" and the "wherefore's." Being adept at succinctness he deleted the extraneous, which often was "the granddaughter speaking." He set me a straight path. The circle of friendship into which he and his wife, Margaret, drew me is rewarding. On the score of deletion or amputation, my friend Mr. Robert S. Weddle was the master surgeon. He had the skill to amputate a part and then graft it at a suitable place with the final form quite acceptable. Mr. Weddle gave encouragement as well as invaluable assistance.

Two friends from my days in Pennsylvania, Mrs. J. S. Mowbray and Mrs. Waldo W. Hayes, are too kindly disposed toward me to suggest many changes, but their nod of approval made me feel that John O. Meusebach, the man who chose "to be a Texan," would have felt at home with those friends from another state. Miss Miranda Leonard is a friend whose artistic perception guided me to renewed endeavor. An architect friend who has pointed out the straightforward line of beauty in the early German architecture is Mr. John C. Garner.

A Llano high school senior, Mr. Duane Conley, has been nimble not only with his typewriter but also with his mind. His typing, even that in a language foreign to him, seldom had an error. He is a National Merit Scholarship winner; he merits, and I give him, my unstinted praise. I appreciate the typing which Mrs. O. O. Henderson did as a favor. Many friends not named have been helpful in various ways: I salute them.

Within the circle of my family, I give thanks for interest and encouragement, particularly as expressed by Mr. and Mrs. W. I. Marschall, Jr., Mrs. Marie Marschall Fuller, Mrs. Hedwig Marschall Love, Mrs. Ruby Marschall Beeley, Mrs. Esther Altgelt Riske, and Mrs. Minetta Altgelt Goyne. I am indebted to Mrs. Goyne for translating a letter written in German script in 1835.

To my sister, Mrs. Cornelia Carolyn Marschall Smith, more than to anyone else, I am indebted. Her help has been constant and unfailing. She and her husband, Mr. Charles G. Smith, have made many helpful suggestions.

I wish my husband, Mr. Clyde L. King, one-time chairman of the Department of Political Science at the University of Pennsylvania, were living to know that I have completed the study to which he gave his blessing.

Irene Marschall King
Llano, Texas

Contents

Illustrations

PART I

Germany, 1812–1845

The Family Circle: Dillenburg

CHAPTER 1

S tanding in his father's library, within the shadow of Berlin, thirty-two-year-old Otfried Hans Freiherr von Meusebach let his thoughts range the world. His thoughts quickened as they came to rest on the Republic of Texas because the new book about Texas intrigued him. The critics said the book was creating a furore all over Germany. This intellectual, however, preferred to make his own evaluation of the book. As he removed *Life in the New World* from the crowded library shelves, he noted particularly the chapter "The First American in Texas or the Squatter Chief." From that section he turned again to the opening pages to read the dedication:

... Free Citizens of a Free State ...

Was that reality or only the dream that Goethe had put into words:

Aye! Such a throng I fain would see
Stand on free soil, among a people free.[1]

Although Charles Sealsfield, the author of the new book, may not have actually set foot on the soil of the Republic, the idea of the freedom which had been attained in Texas was so enticing that the book was hailed by all. It pictured a place, a situation, that many Germans were seeking.

From the library window young Meusebach could see in the distance the old imperial city of Potsdam—thoroughly Prussian. Near at hand in the village of Baumgartenbrueck were his father's well-tended grapevines. The orderly arrangement of both the city and the vineyard, man-made, seemed to him a symbol of the mold into which Germany was being shaped.

To his father, Baron Carl Hartwig Gregor von Meusebach, Otfried read Sealsfield's description of the hundred-foot-high grapevines in Texas, so

[1] J. Wolfgang von Goethe, *Faust* (George Madison Priest, trans.), p. 340, 11. 11579—11580.

wild and varied in shape that the most skillful gardener would try in vain
to imitate them. The cultivated and well-trimmed vines in Germany were
in decided contrast to the native plants across the sea.

The father, a bibliophile, had previously noted the imprint, "Zurich,
Switzerland, 1837," in the German version of the book, and "New York,
1844," in the English translation. He was distressed that a book addressed
"to the German Nation" had to be printed outside of that country because
German laws prohibited the printing of books more than twenty pages in
length. The father shared his son's interest in "nature's bounty" in Texas.
He looked askance, however, at the idea of being a squatter in a cabin.
How could anyone who had lived in houses mellowed by centuries, who
was accustomed to the amenities of life, give serious consideration to such
a primitive existence as this book pictured? The father pointed out sections which to him seemed fanciful. The son agreed with his appraisal.
But the younger man was interested in the farflung acres and their produc-
tivity, and in a place where formality and restrictions gave way to self-
government. Sealsfield wrote, "The American is scarcely conscious of his
advantages; they surround him as water surrounds the fish."[2] Every page,
beginning with the dedication, reflected the glory of freedom. Otfried
read:

> To the German Nation
> roused to the consciousness of its power and dignity
> these pictures of the domestic and public life
> of the Free Citizens of a Free State
> destined to Historical Greatness
> are respectfully dedicated
> by the author.

Here was an admonition! The author, a German, suggested that the
German nation examine itself, hold the mirror to its face. What kind of
image would be seen? What lay unobserved behind the facade of castles
and vineyards along the Rhine? Was there an inner substantiation to the
glory of Germany? Were the people *free citizens of a free state*? The
mirror held up to Germany would show princes and peasants. If intellectuals were reflected, their ideas would be only theories—as transient as a
reflection. Theories alone would never "rouse a nation to the consciousness
of its power and dignity."

What would arouse the nation? questioned the young aristocrat. Not a

---

[2] Charles Sealsfield, *Life in the New World; or Sketches of American Society*
(Gustavus C. Hebbe and James MacKay, trans.), p. 268.

revolution in Germany, where obedience to authority was never questioned; surely reforms could come in an orderly manner. Yet as Otfried, standing in his father's library that summer day of 1844, reflected on the horizons of freedom, he knew quite well that the changes in the world were not always wrought in an orderly fashion.

As the eighteenth century came to an end, the winds of change were beginning to blow. It had been the century of the American Revolution and the French Revolution.

The success of the American uprising in 1776 owed a debt to a German, General von Steuben, for the military training he gave Washington's army. On a Valley Forge hill stands a monument to von Steuben, a symbol of America's appreciation. As a nobleman, the general could determine his choice of action. But the subjects of a ruler had no choice but to obey. Such was the situation when the autocratic landgrave of Hesse-Cassel sold his subjects as mercenaries to fight for the British against the American colonists. The landgrave, stung by a pamphlet denouncing his action, bought up every copy of the pamphlet and issued a rebuttal upholding his feudal right to sell his subjects. These Hessian mercenaries, derisively called the "Dutch" by the Americans, brought back stories of promise and opportunity in the "land of the free"; and von Steuben wrote glowingly of the country which had no kings or feudal lords.

The thesis of "inalienable rights" proclaimed by the American colonists' Declaration of Independence fell on indifferent ears among the average Germans. The ears of the intellectuals, however, were receptive. The ideas of "liberty, equality, fraternity," engendered by the French cataclysm in 1789, would require more than half a century to effect a reaction among the German people, but the intellectuals were receptive in the early nineteenth century to these ideas also.

These liberal principles became an integral part of the legal procedure on the west bank of the Rhine; on the east bank and on into the adjacent interior, the French legal ideas were looked upon with approval. Such was the case in Dillenburg, one of the chief cities of the province of Nassau. Here Baron Carl Hartwig Gregor von Meusebach was assistant judge of the regional court in 1804, and it was in that year that he brought his bride, the former Ernestine von Witzleben, to live in the official residence. This impressive structure had been built from the stones of the province's ancient royal castle. The arch over the entrance was adorned with the Meusebach coat of arms. As they stood before it the young man told his wife about the village named Meusebach and the fortresslike *Schloss*, or castle, that had been in the family's possession since the tenth century. [3]

The couple then turned from the past to the present and set about beautifying their walled garden. They added to their orchard and gave special attention to a small vineyard on the land rising to the hills. Walking with his young wife, the husband recited his hymeneal poem, "The Constancy of Love." Two years before her marriage Ernestine had met Jean Paul Richter, a poet of recognized standing, for whom both she and her husband had great admiration. Richter, while passing the Witzleben home in Kassel, heard one of his own poems being sung. The poet was so delighted that he followed an impulse and went to the door to introduce himself and his wife. They were welcomed by Ernestine; it was she who was singing, to her own piano accompaniment. [4] This pleasing experience naturally deepened Ernestine's admiration for the poet. Her reaction was shared by her husband, who for many years had recognized Richter as an accomplished poet.

The Meusebach family at first appeared destined only for heartbreak. The couple's first child, Sidonie, born on April 6, 1805, lived less than two years. A son, Otfried Isidor, born in 1806, lived just to the beginning of 1808. Two daughters followed: Ludowine, born in 1808, and Caroline, born in 1811. A son was born May 26, 1812, whom the parents named Otfried Hans in memory of the first son.

This second son seemed to give them back the child they had lost. But his independent nature quickly gave him a place of his own in his parents' hearts. With his reddish-gold hair he was like a ray of sunlight. The little fellow was soon following his father around and begging to be taken to the sun. The boy's first spoken phrase was "More light." After another son, Carl Bernhard, arrived in 1814, the Meusebachs had their family complete: two daughters and two sons.

Singing together gave delight to the family. They sometimes sang the poems the father had composed. Or the gifted mother would interpret an ancient folk song found by the father in a remote district. Meusebach searched far and wide for these ballads, centuries old. Some were trans-

---

[3] Ernst Heinrich Kneschke, "Freiherren Meusebach," *Neues allgemeines deutsches adels-lexicon*, VI, 271.

[4] Karl Schwartz, "Karl Hartwig Gregor von Meusebach, Lebensnachrichten" (Part II), *Annalen des Vereins für Nassauische Altertumskunde und Geschichtsforschung*, XXI (1890), 67.

mitted orally; others were written. They stemmed always from a deeply felt emotion. Some represented an individual's feeling; others reflected the feeling of a group. Meusebach had intense pleasure in collecting this folk literature because it enhanced his interest in the sentiment of racial unity. It was the custom for friends to gather in the Meusebach home in the evening, and one such friend, Dr. Friedrich Hofmann, vied with his host in making the myths and folk sayings take on renewed life. To write his own poems, Meusebach often retired to the terrace house.

The family enjoyed outings, and some excursions took them to the valley beside a nearby stream, where the girls gathered flowers while little Otfried peered into the crevices for loose stones. Returning home, they sometimes sat on the terrace for a while. Then as they entered the house, the father often read aloud the words *Tenax Propositi* on the family crest above the door. The girls would call, "Say it in our language." The father would translate, "Perseverance in Purpose." The mother would then smile at Otfried and explain, "Finish what you begin, Son."

In addition to the requirements of his official position, Meusebach was called upon to participate in several civic societies. He was also named as counsel to the military department responsible only to the general procurator in Düsseldorf. This appointment necessitated visits to that city, where he quickly acquainted himself with the procedure of French courts of law. On the occasion of Emperor Napoleon's visit to Düsseldorf, Meusebach wrote in his diary of 1811, "On October 18, a glorious trip by boat on the Rhine from Koblenz to Cologne, and on to Düsseldorf. On November 2, presentation to the Emperor Napoleon and the Empress Marie Louise." [5]

This event was celebrated with high pomp and ceremony, but the young judge was more interested in the opportunity to learn the fine points of French law, which now were coming into force in the German courts. Meusebach's competence in legal matters gave him the reputation of being the best-qualified judge in the province. Younger officials came to him to learn. From this period of study in Düsseldorf arose his preference for oral procedure and the jury system, a preference which he held all of his life. [6]

On his return to Dillenburg he related to his associates his new ideas pertaining to the law; he shared the story of his personal experiences, as usual, with his wife.

[5] *Ibid.*, p. 74.
[6] *Ibid.*

Official as well as family relationships were so pleasurable in Dillenburg that the Meusebachs were loath to give them up. Yet a promotion having wider responsibility could not be ignored. With a degree of reluctance, but with high hopes, Carl Hartwig Gregor von Meusebach in 1814 accepted a new assignment in Koblenz.

The Circle Widens: Koblenz

CHAPTER 2

To Koblenz, the thriving city on the east bank of the Rhine, Meusebach came as president of the Court. Koblenz was named the seat of the general government of the province in May, 1814, a month after Napoleon, upon his defeat, had abdicated the throne of the French Empire. One of the many factors that had contributed to the monarch's downfall was the joining of the princes of the Confederation of the Rhine with the Allies, who opposed the French. Now, following their military success, the German authorities had certain rights, one of which was the regulation of the courts. Meusebach had suggested a court of appeals in Koblenz to replace the French-controlled courts. His final plan was to establish a court of justice in that central city. In recognition of his accomplishments as a judge and of his plan of organization, he was appointed president of the Court. His tenure in that position was marked by signal achievements.

The headquarters office for the Court was in the building in which Prince Clemens Wenzel Lothar Metternich-Winneburg was born. That prince's name already carried authority with it and continued to do so for many years. Metternich, Chancellor of the Austrian Empire, called a congress to convene in Vienna in 1814 to determine many problems that arose from Napoleon's triumphs and defeats. The decisions of this Congress of Vienna were a determining factor in the future of much of Europe and certainly of that part in which Meusebach was officiating as president of the Court.

Meusebach's ability to coordinate the military and civil authorities was widely recognized. He had learned methods of approach from his work in Dillenburg and had used these methods to advantage in bringing accord with the authorities in Düsseldorf and Trier. Consultations with many persons were necessary; from among the group two men continued their warm friendship with Meusebach beyond the Koblenz association: Generals Count von Gneisenau and Karl von Clausewitz. The latter was host to a festive party which began a tradition of social gatherings among several friends. President Baron von Meusebach showed such wit and humor at these gatherings that Clausewitz and his wife (née Countess Bruhl) called him the "President of Koblenz Amiability."[1]

For one party the friends came in masquerade. The elder Meusebach was in gala costume and wore a wig. His son Otfried was a small duplicate except that he held a loose bouquet instead of wearing a wig, and his reddish-blond hair revealed his identity amid the laughter of the elders.

Distinguished visitors to Koblenz, among them Goethe and William Humboldt,[2] were guests at these gatherings from time to time, and on such occasions the group engaged in a stimulating exchange of ideas. When Humboldt once was asked for his opinion on revolutions he gave an answer that arose from careful observation. He had spent some years in Paris and had seen there both the beneficial and the harmful results of a revolution. A man of wide learning, particularly in political science, he had an answer for these inquiring friends: " 'Do not subscribe to the revolutionary; that course of action may too easily result in the many shackles of government. Request of your ruler not better government but less government'."[3]

To join the group of friends, Joseph Goerres, the publicist, came across the Rhine River from his home in the Rhineland Province on the west bank. During the ascendancy of Napoleon that province had been exposed to French ideas; the people, essentially feudal and given to petty restrictions of caste, became familiar with the idea of equality of rights. The diverse laws prevalent in the various German provinces adjacent to France were unified under the Codex Napoleon, with its fundamental principles that every subject is a free man and that all subjects are equal before the law. Meusebach and Goerres agreed on the necessity of establishing unified legal systems, the backward East to follow the advanced West. When the Rhinelander argued once that " 'Nature made the Rhine the frontier of France',"[4] there was quick disagreement. These Eastern Germans were

---

[1] Karl Schwartz, "Karl Hartwig Gregor von Meusebach, Lebensnachrichten" (Part III), *Annalen des Vereins für Nassauische Altertumskunde und Geschichtsforschung*, XXI (1890), 4.

[2] Camillus Wendler, *Briefwechsel des Freiherrn Karl Hartwig Gregor von Meusebach mit Jacob und Wilhelm Grimm*, pp. vii and xv.

[3] Humboldt is quoted in George Peabody Gooch, *Germany and the French Revolution*, p. 111.

[4] Goerres is quoted, *ibid.*, p. 484.

accustomed to the boundary of their land as they had always known it, that is, extending west beyond the Rhine. In fact, the river was an integral part of their country. To reduce the extent of their land, to allow French territory to touch the Rhine, was an intolerable idea.

The Rhine River gave the Meusebach family many happy hours. Young Otfried was attracted by the water and begged for a chance to swim. Despite the increased demands of the father's profession the family did not forego its practice of making excursions into the countryside. The picnic baskets they took with them were frequently brought home filled with wild strawberries. Their arms were laden with flowers, some to fill vases, others to be studied as botanical specimens. Otfried made a collection of minerals, which the family helped identify. On one excursion the children asked why their father's collection of poems had been named *Kornblumen*. Cornflowers grew so profusely that the boys were allowed to gather them to make garlands for their blue-eyed sisters. They observed that this particular flower grew all through the rows of grain and they remarked to their father, "You write so many poems. Did you name them for the flowers that grow so easily everywhere?"

The elder Meusebach was awake to the beauty about him—the spiritual as well as the material. Sensitivity to poetical values was deep within him. During one homeward journey the family stopped at a little church containing a figure of Christ hewn roughly from stone. The father asked, "Do you know any mortal man who has as many memorials as Christ has? Can we see anything tangible that He left on earth? But when we look in our hearts, we know His work." That night the father wrote in his notebook, "Man's spirit is too seldom directed to that which is holy. A prayer that is egotistical is not heard; the prayer uttered in humble simplicity is more likely to be heard."[5]

In 1817 Baron von Meusebach wrote his dedicatory poem at the birth of Adolph von Nassau, princely heir to the duchy of Nassau.[6] In addition to his creative work in poetry, Meusebach continued his collection of fifteenth- and sixteenth-century folk songs that came in time to total 350. Prized among these was Martin Luther's songbook of the year 1545. In appreciation of these folk songs the inhabitants of Alt Geltow, a village near Potsdam, today annually sing selections from them at the graveside of the elder Meusebach on his birthday. He and his wife are buried in the Lutheran churchyard of the village.

[5] Schwartz, "Karl Hartwig Gregor von Meusebach" (Part III), *Annalen des Vereins*, XXI (1890), 64.
[6] *Ibid.*, Part II, p. 73.

The dictum of Jacob and Wilhelm Grimm that "Only folk poetry is perfect" shows a bond of interest between them and Meusebach. The brothers Grimm sent compilations of their immortal fairy tales to the Meusebachs when the children were young. The children's enjoyment of the fairy stories was unbounded, as it has been ever since with children the world over.

Meusebach and his two sons took long walking tours together. Otfried and his father shared their thoughts, particularly when the son showed aptitude in the study of jurisprudence. That subject in itself was not discussed formally until a later time, but the son's interest was evident early. The father quoted appropriate aphorisms, hoping thereby to pinpoint some idea. An oft-repeated maxim was *Gedanken sind Zoll frei* ("Thoughts are toll or tax free") ; another, *Gegen Dummheit kämpfen die Götter selbst vergebens* ("Against stupidity the gods themselves strive in vain"). The counterpart to many such ideas had been pithily stated by Benjamin Franklin.

The father explained that Goethe sometimes compared Justus Möser, the historian-critic, to Benjamin Franklin, and then he expounded some of Möser's political ideas to his son. The conclusion to the little exposition was given in Möser's own words: " 'One can *say* much that our fathers hardly dared to think'."[7] A related statement which meant little at that time to the child was very significant to the older generation: " 'Before the French Revolution nobody *thought* of a constitution'."[8] By the time the Congress of Vienna met in 1814–1815 constitutions were not only *thought* of, but demanded.

The French Revolution had left its mark so decisively that the south German states were furnished with parliaments within a reasonable time; Prussia had to wait until 1848. After the many triumphs and the final defeat of Napoleon the alignments in Europe needed to be recorded. A new map of Europe had to be drawn. This, and more, was done when representatives from the Continent and from England met in the Congress of Vienna. The preceding twenty-five years had been so turbulent that peace and order were welcome, especially to the older generation. The Congress was made up of the greatest dynasts and diplomats of the time; Prince Metternich, Chancellor of Austria, presided. The door to liberalism and nationalism, twin offspring of the French Revolution, was closed by Metternich. His own Hapsburg realm was composed of so many diverse nationalities that if each had gained status the realm would have fallen

---

[7] Möser is quoted in Gooch, *Germany and the French Revolution*, p. 507.
[8] Welcher is quoted, *ibid.*, p. 514.

asunder. The Chancellor's policy, therefore, was to keep things as they were. The ruling princes of Germany were amenable to these conservative policies, since many of them still held feudal rights over their subjects. The number of sovereign princes had been reduced from several hundred to thirty-nine during the Napoleonic period. These princes, made stronger by annexed territory, did not see fit to sacrifice their sovereignty to form a unified state with one ruler. The glory of Germany may have animated them, but even the lesser principalities or dukedoms considered their particular territory essential to that glory.

Prussia, loosely bound to Austria, was not yet strong enough to lead, so the jealous princes allowed Prince Metternich of Austria to dominate and to become the permanent president of the Confederation of Princes. By birth that dominating prince was German; he himself said that the Rhine River flowed in his veins. With his consent the German Confederation, or the Bund of 1815, was formed, made up of princes rather than of peoples. The Bund set up a federal diet, which had the power to enact laws. All this was decided over the heads of the people: they had fought the wars, but no victories came to them.

The Confederation gave the people no feeling of unity, nor did it engender the idea of nationalism. But the idea grew in force and could not be thwarted, particularly because it was supported by the youth and by the intellectuals. The action that the Congress of Vienna directed against liberal tendencies caused great discontent, with the protest centering in the universities. The students began a movement to form one large student association (*Burschenschaft*). This was to be the model for a united German nation, with the watchwords "liberty, honor, fatherland."

A series of events during which the students became involved in political activities culminated in an extremist action by a student at the University of Jena. Metternich determined to institute severe reprisals. He had the German states pass reactionary measures, the Carlsbad Decrees of 1819. The Decrees put the universities under surveillance, instituted censorship of the press, and prohibited secret organizations. The hands on the clock of progress were not only stopped; they were turned back.

In that fateful year of the Carlsbad Decrees the elder Meusebach was transferred from Koblenz to Berlin to be president of the Court of Review there. The Decrees were abhorrent to him, but he hoped that an awakened spirit of nationalism would open the door to liberal ideas. Since his early life belonged to the period of romanticism, he felt that a glorification of the Middle Ages—when the German emperors determined the destiny of Europe—was one approach to arousing a spirit of nationalism.

Other men in official life harbored similar ideas. Baron vom Stein, one-time Chancellor of Prussia, spent many years in producing a collection of documents of the Middle Ages, the Monumenta Germaniae Historica. Each volume carried the inscription, "The sacred love of the fatherland animates us." Baron vom Stein had contempt for the petty German princes whose pretense stood in the way of a strong, unified nation.

Meusebach's contribution to the search for indigenous medieval culture was a collection of the works of the sixteenth-century satirist Johann Fischart. This writer leveled satire at perversities in the public and private life of his time. Meusebach's interest in Fischart began early in life and never really ended. He acquired much of the material by correspondence with libraries and individuals. Agents sometimes acted for him at auctions. On an occasion when the agent failed to obtain the book being auctioned, Meusebach's wife consoled her husband by baking a cake and decorating it in the style of the desired book.

His own father, Christian Carl, whose chief interest was botany, also had patronized auctions. His interest, however, was Meissen china, and he ended with thirty-nine cabinets full of Meissen. His children scoffed at this predilection for china. The Meusebach who collected the works of Fischart fared better, for he had sympathy from his children. His daughter Caroline often helped him with the collection. The Fischart Collection is recognized as definitive and is deposited with the 350 folk songs in the Royal State Library of Berlin.

For Meusebach the whole of past German life called for explanation and interpretation. The science of law was subjected to historical scrutiny by F. K. von Savigny. He and Meusebach had frequent conferences on the interpretation of legal theories. Another friend, Karl Lachmann, made a critical study of the Nibelung epic and likewise examined the songs of the minnesingers. The Germans found patriotic stimulus in contemplating their own heroes. They invoked the past to kindle the spirits of the living. They made use of scholarship to fan the sacred flame of the love of the fatherland.

There were obligations to the Germany of the present and the elder Meusebach expressed them with the words:

> "Oh you Germany, I must march
> Oh you Germany, I must depart."[9]

The reference is to is departure to Berlin, where he moved with reluctance in 1819.

[9] Wendler, *Briefwechsel*, p. ix.

The Expanding Horizon

CHAPTER 3

Baron Carl Hartwig Gregor von Meusebach gave his full attention to his new assignment as judge of the Superior Court in the capital city, Berlin. Great stacks of case documents were brought to him for rulings. He worked at them with thoroughness and conscientiousness, night as well as day.

Poetry, manuscripts, and catalogs of antique books were put away for future enjoyment. Social life was postponed except for family gatherings; these were never denied. But friends still gravitated to Meusebach's house, where the pursuit of the intellectual was uppermost in importance. The great library of 38,000 volumes,[1] which this bibliophile had been gathering all his life, attracted visitors. Caroline characterized her father as being patient and helpful, and as being generous enough to give hours at a time to his callers. Yet one critic stated that the "eccentric" Meusebach turned the key on all but the brothers Grimm.[2]

The Meusebach sons were sent to the parochial school at Rossleben, where their father also had been a student. The two brothers carried fond memories of their experiences at this school. In 1828 the boys attended the Mining and Forestry Academy at Clausthal in the Harz Mountains. Here they studied geology and natural sciences. With the mountains nearby Otfried had an excellent opportunity to probe into one of his favorite subjects, geology. He shared with his grandfather, Christian Carl von Meusebach, who lived in Vockstedt, an interest in botany, and the two of them took long walking tours to study nature at firsthand. On these ex-

---

[1] Karl Schwartz, "Karl Hartwig Gregor von Meusebach, Lebensnachrichten" (Part IV), *Annalen des Vereins für Nassauische Altertumskunde und Geschichtsforschung*, XXI (1890), 48.

[2] Heinrich Gotthard von Treitschke, *History of Germany in the Nineteenth Century* (Eden and Cedar Paul, trans.), IV, 551.

cursions the grandfather frequently gathered herbs, from which he made
tea. He shocked his grandson by drinking a dozen cups in succession. The
family enjoyed vacations together when the other members came to this
region.

Otfried's father had interested his children from childhood in the heroes
of their land. A favorite was Hermann, the victor over the Roman legions
at Teutoburger Forest in A.D. 9, during the time of Augustus Caesar. Otfried recalled in later years how vividly his father told the stories of the
heroes. Engraved in his memory was an excursion the family took during
a vacation in 1829 to Castle Voigtstaedt and their feudal estate in the
golden Aue of Thuringia, a section designated as "golden" since the
year 1200. It derives its name from the fertility of the land, which is un-
surpassed by any region in Germany and yields abundant harvests. The
experiences during excursions into that valley glowing with beauty were
the source of lifelong nostalgia to Otfried. He remembered that he and his
brother always held high the lighted torches while their sisters walked
between them and their parents followed. As they wound their way homeward in the twilight the family sang together the ancient songs of the minnesingers. Then their father told them the saga of their forefathers.

The first ancestor of whom there is record lived in the eighth century,
during the time of Charles Martel,[3] grandfather of Charlemagne. When
Charles Martel, on the field of Mars, called the roll of his supporters
against the invading Moors a Meusebach was among the defenders. The
sovereign ordered that a laurel wreath, a symbol of Meusebach's fidelity
to the cause, adorn the family coat of arms and that a Moor's head sur-
mount the shield. The Moor's head is sometimes replaced by that of a
Negro, indicating that the Moors had conquered the natives of North
Africa. *Tenax Propositi*—"Perseverance in Purpose"— was the motto
given the family. Baron Otfried von Meusebach found a source of strength
in this motto at every crucial moment in his life. The father mentioned another Meusebach ancestor, who participated in one of the Crusades, as his
tomb in the church near Roda bears witness.

The son respected his father's predilection for the past glory of Germany, but it was the present that called to the younger man. Life was making its demands at that moment. Their mutual interest in the field of law
made father and son agree that the University of Bonn was the place to
pursue that study. Law, cameralism, and finance were the subjects which
the student put on his roster when he entered the University in 1832.

[3] C. M. von Witzleben (comp.), Geschichte der Freiherren von Meusebach. MS.
Meusebach Family Files.

Since young Otfried had a burning desire to learn, it was not difficult for him to give full attention to his academic work.

One thing for which he turned aside from his studies was swimming, a recreation which he pursued avidly. When his fellow students dared him to swim to a certain point in the Rhine River within a specified time he accepted the challenge. He had not taken into account the wheels of industrial plants that churned the water of that great river and made swimming difficult. Despite the difficulties, however, he reached the goal on time and won the bet, as well as the admiration of his fellows. His excellence as a marksman added to his standing in the group. His classmates admired his tall, well-knit physique and his agility. He carried a look of accomplishment, but there was no braggadocio about him.

Bonn, from its proximity to France, reflected the concerns of the French. The deposition in 1830 of the French King Charles X was still a vital subject for discussion by the students two years later. But talked about even more than the event in France was the forced abdication of two rulers in Germany. The University students were concerned about the gathering earlier in 1832 of 25,000 persons at Hambach Castle in Bavaria. The hope of a united fatherland had been revived at that meeting. The discussions centered around democracy and revolution. One speaker asserted that all the German princes were traitors. A former government official, P. J. Siebenpfeiffer, offered his solution to the struggle for democracy: the formation of the "United Free States of Germany." He prophesied a time "when the princes will exchange the ermine mantle of feudalist rule by divine right for the *toga virilis* of German national dignity."[4]

This outburst of democratic aspirations was followed by severe reprisals in the form of a renewal of the 1819 Carlsbad Decrees. Restrictions were applied not only to publications but to public assemblies. The most drastic of the Decrees forbade German rulers to do anything that would reduce their sovereignty. All points were shaped in the interest of the rulers, the princes, the lords; the people were simply pawns.

The injustice of these Decrees rankled in young Otfried's being. He was an aristocrat, but such disregard for the rights of men was abhorrent to him. The restriction on the printing of books beyond a certain length stifled new ideas. The men at the head of the government were looking backward, not forward.

The apparent path of Otfried's life was set for him by birth. As yet he did not see a way to break the pattern. He had obligations to his parents,

---

[4] Treitschke, *History of Germany*, IV, 263–264.

to his own future. His university work must proceed. Because of a long-time interest in the natural sciences he transferred to the University of Halle, where the teachers had excellent reputations in scientific fields. The friendship with these professors, which had began while Otfried was a student, continued for many years. One professor, Dr. Johann Gottfried Gruber, a friend of Otfried's father, said that the elder Meusebach was bringing about a sense of nationalism by endorsing the customs union (*Zollverein*). The first treaty to help effect this union had been signed by Prussia and a tiny sister state in 1819. In time such agreements would bind all the princely states together as one nation. Yes, thought Otfried, but what would happen to liberal ideas? There would be a semblance of equality, but this generation did not want shackles; it wanted liberties—within the law. If King Frederick William IV would grant the constitution the people were clamoring for, the chance at liberalism would come. When Otfried expressed such thoughts to his professor the reply, in substance, was, "Young man, first take your bar examinations. Thereafter you can approach the idea of the constitution through legal channels."

Would Metternich's domination never cease? questioned Otfried. It seemed that in the Austrian Chancellor's mind a liberal, a thinker, belonged in only one place: a jail.

After Otfried took the bar examinations at Naumburg in 1836 the examiner sent this letter to Otfried's parents:

Your son has passed the entire oral examination with brilliance: I have seldom encountered an examinee who was so at home in the principal areas of jurisprudence. I especially admired his sagacity and memory with reference to the land rights of the kingdom. Your son has rightly earned the reputation of a promising young man. He has, as well, the reputation of being a lovable young man in the few groups he associates with.[5]

The son Carl likewise made a creditable showing in his bar examinations. When the two young men jubilantly returned to their parents' home in Berlin many friends came to help them celebrate. Among them Otfried found congeniality with those discussing William Humboldt's ideas on the subject uppermost in his mind: freedom. The friends reported Humboldt's theory to be that a statesman must allow all restrictions on freedom to remain untouched; that ripeness for freedom was best promoted by freedom itself; furthermore, that by the fetters on freedom being removed one by one, progress would be hastened at every step. They

[5] Unidentified letter, 1836. Meusebach Family Files.

pointed out that earlier a great fetter had been removed when Chancellor Stein liberated the German serfs.

Another friend who came to join the celebration was General Gustav von Below. He and the elder Meusebach were rivals at auctions in bidding for rare books. This particular evening von Below carefully selected a book from the shelf and, simulating an auction, mentioned a price. Meusebach also named a sum. Then he called to his sons to put in bids. Von Below declared himself the winner of the auction and with Meusebach's blessing took the book. Caroline was near at hand to rearrange the books on their shelf.

Caroline was a favorite with all the family. Since the sudden death of Ludowine in 1822 she had been the only daughter. In 1833 she had married August Freiherr von Witzleben, a member of a family that had served Germany with distinction.[6]

The von Witzlebens brought with them this evening a dear friend. She was Elizabeth von Hardenberg, a young woman reserved in manner. She contributed little to the conversation, but what she said had significance. When Otfreid looked at her, she returned his glance gravely. He saw in her eyes a luminous light that seemed to come from within.

---

[6] General Erwin von Witzleben took a leading part in the bomb plot to assassinate Hitler and as a result was hanged.

A Meeting of Minds

W hen the position of administrative assessor in Trier was offered to Otfried in 1836 he gladly accepted it. The proximity of Trier to France made him believe that the people in that city, like the French, were convinced that they should control their own destinies. No foreigner, no Frenchman, remained on the German land, but the foreign leaven of liberal ideas did remain. Young Meusebach, walking among the Roman ruins in Trier, the outpost farthest north of ancient Rome, meditated much on Roman law, the foundation stone for all jurisprudence.

Legal matters, neither old nor new, however, claimed all of the time of this jurist. The young men in his circle, seeing how well-groomed he was, suggested that he go with them to call on some young French women in Aachen (Aix-la-Chapelle). The idea had special appeal because en route he could stop at Koblenz, that city of unforgettable associations for his family. Following the dictates of polite society, Otfried had his calling card engraved, ready for presentation to the young lady and her family. When the evening was over his friends inquired what date was fixed for his return. Otfried replied that the young lady was fine, but one evening had used up all her conversation; a second visit would avail nothing.

The Meusebach family had enjoyed the advantages that Berlin offered: music, art galleries, museums. But the merits of the countryside outweighed those of the city for them. They had contemplated moving to the country for some time; in 1836 they made the change. They retained their Berlin residence for some time after this, however. Otfried used it after his transfer in 1838; the father also used it when occasions made it necessary to remain in the city.

Repression, made legal by the renewal of the Carlsbad Decrees, reached its high point when in 1837 seven professors at the University of Göttingen were dismissed for protesting against the flagrant breach of Hanover's constitution by the sovereign of the province. Among these seven professors were Jacob and Wilhelm Grimm, who gave up their positions rather than their political rights.

The Meusebach brothers were glad that one result of the repression was to bring the Grimms to Berlin. The two professors were invited by the elder Meusebach to come as his guests to the capital city where they could find scope for their talents. Meusebach, through his position in the High Court, helped them officially to an extent, but nothing could have given them more satisfaction than the circle of friends into which he drew them. The brothers Grimm did not relish being proclaimed political heroes; they declared that they had merely held to the oaths they had sworn at the University and thereby kept their consciences clear. Meusebach, the father, punctiliously performed his duties as ranking jurist and thereby kept *his* conscience clear. As an aristocrat, a nobleman, he owed loyalty to his king. That fact did not blind his eyes to royal shortcomings. But the king had promised a constitution; and when it came there would be parliaments for each principality. The principalities would unite; then the unified Germany that his sons were talking about would be realized. Meantime the former greatness of Germany would be renewed by bringing to light the literature of medieval days. The world, to Meusebach, to the brothers Grimm, to Humboldt, was a shelf of books, wherein they saw the future as well as the past glory of their beloved country.

Folk songs and poetry were also mutual concerns of these men. When Carl Hartwig Gregor von Meusebach received an honorary degree during the 1837 jubilee celebration at the University of Göttingen, Wilhelm Grimm saw to it that music accompanied the citation. In the Preface to his great dictionary *Deutsches Wörterbuch* (1854), Jacob Grimm pays a tribute to Meusebach for his investigation of the language of the sixteenth and seventeenth centuries. Wilhelm Grimm's dedication of his monumental book on Germanic heroes, *Die deutsche Heldensage* (1829), was a significant courtesy to Meusebach, for the two men felt that this book implemented the cause of nationalism. Wilhelm Grimm declared that nothing was dearer to him, as a historian, than the love of the fatherland as shown by these heroes. The Grimms and Meusebach exchanged letters[1] for a

---

[1] These letters, with introductory remarks, notes, and a supplement on the Grimm brothers' stay in Berlin, are published in Camillus Wendler, *Briefwechsel des Freiherrn Karl Hartwig Gregor von Meusebach mit Jacob und Wilhelm Grimm* (Heibronn, Germany: Gehr, Henninger, 1880).

quarter of a century. The letters relate primarily to their common interest in philology, but their warm friendship shines through the pages.

In 1836 the elder Meusebach had secured a residence in Baumgartenbrueck, a village not far from Potsdam. To live in the country, removed from the noise and strain of the city where he had lived for seventeen years, relieved Meusebach from the tension increased by a hearing difficulty. He wanted undisturbed time to work in his library. A number of projects were planned—one was to trace the Faust motif in early manuscripts.[2]

Now there was opportunity to indulge in outdoor life again. As a family the Meusebachs enjoyed developing their grounds overlooking the Havel River. Swans glided over the water and under the bridge leading to a little grove of spruce and fir trees. The family built up the sandy soil, and the cherries, plums, and grapes grew in abundance. They cultivated boxwood to be used in landscape planting. Fresh grapes from the greenhouse were a treat during the Christmas season.[3] From their apiary they obtained beeswax—from which they made their candles—and honey. The mother liked fresh flowers for the house. It was more important to have flowers on the dining table than to use the banquet cloth of hand-loomed damask and the yard-wide napkins or even the beautiful heavy family silver. The sons said, "We'll grow flowers for you, Mother; just put that ornate silver in the museum. It belongs there."[4]

After two years at his post in Trier, Otfried was invited in 1838 to assume a legal position of more responsibility, with headquarters in Berlin and Potsdam. Carl was to succeed his brother in Trier. But first the brothers planned a visit home, where they would surprise their father by bringing him fruit grown on their estate in Dillenburg. Often the father had spoken longingly of the orchard the family had tended there. The brothers met at Dillenburg and packed the apples, pears, and nuts, labeling each item to indicate the tree from which it came. On their arrival home in Baumgartenbrueck they placed the fruit on prized family plates and presented it to their father. His delight knew no bounds.

The brothers talked long into the night. Aside from reviewing their experiences, they manifested in their conversation a deep love of their country and a growing concern for its future. The Meusebachs of early

[2] Meusebach did not complete the Faust project nor any of the others that he considered at this time. His primary contribution to the study of early literature was his definitive collection of Fischart's works.

[3] Wendler, *Briefwechsel*, p. xx.

[4] Lucy Meusebach Marschall, Notes and Memoranda. MSS. Meusebach Family Files.

times had not failed their homeland. What of the present? Was this country that tolerated the renewal of the hated Carlsbad Decrees really *their*
Germany? More appropriately it could be called Austria, for it was the
Chancellor of that country, Metternich, who pushed these restrictive Decrees through the Confederation of German Princes. Germany was in
truth only a geographical term; she had no true citizens, for there were
really only citizens of provinces—Bavarians, Rhinelanders, Prussians—
but no Germans. The country called Germany was a patchwork of nearly
forty pieces, with each principality clinging to its sovereignty, not willing
to give up any prerogative in order to make a German nation.

Since Otfried's work as assistant judge took him to Berlin and Potsdam
he could be with his parents in Baumgartenbrueck quite often. Friends
came frequently to this home, where a distinguished circle engaged in
erudite conversation. One evening when Carl was home from Trier, the
brothers decorated the house for the visitors by filling vases with branches
which they had brought in from their tramp in the woods.

Bettina von Arnim, a writer who undauntedly espoused worthy causes,
came often to the Meusebach home, for she admired the family—the son
Carl in particular. Accompanying her this evening were Elizabeth von
Hardenberg, who was like a second daughter to Bettina, her own daughter, Gisela, and Hermann Grimm. Hermann brought greetings from his
father, Wilhelm, and showed the group one of his preliminary sketches of
their host. All agreed that Hermann had depicted the typical Carl Hartwig
Gregor, Baron von Meusebach, bibliophile, sitting at ease in his smoking
jacket, oblivious to everything but his manuscript.

Elizabeth von Hardenberg, with artistic discrimination, suggested that
Ernestine, the mother of the household, be the next to sit for a portrait,
possibly on the terrace with the grapevine as a background. During this
conversation Otfried's and Elizabeth's eyes met often. Between them a harmony which made words unnecessary seemed to exist.

When poetry was mentioned, Caroline and Bettina vied with each other
in quoting from Goethe, for whom they both had deep admiration. When
Bettina was a child she and her mother had visited Goethe in his home.
This was the beginning of an interesting correspondence between Goethe
and Bettina. The elder Meusebach had arranged for the publication in
1835 of *Goethe's Correspondence with a Child*. Bettina saw the poet as the
liberator who through his life and personal example encouraged artists
and all men to live according to the dictates of their innermost free nature
and to create out of this freedom of nature. When this small group spoke
of Goethe they felt as if a hand had been stretched out in benediction to

give them grace and strength. The lines the group never tired of hearing were from *Faust*:

> Of freedom and life he only is deserving
> Who every day must conquer them anew.[5]

These lines brought to mind Karl von Rotteck's ideas on freedom and life that had struck responsive chords with the students at the University in Bonn. Von Rotteck emphasized having liberty above national unity. If one of these desires had to be sacrificed, it should be unity, not liberty. The intellectuals gathered in the Meusebach home were disturbed that anything should take precedence over the guarantee of liberty. They recognized the importance of the love of one's fatherland, but they felt this love could be attained by strengthening national morale. Meusebach read von Rotteck's terse statement, " 'I do not desire [national] unity without [political] liberty, and I prefer liberty without unity to unity without liberty'."[6]

During the ensuing conversation about liberty Bettina took the lead and occasionally left openings for Elizabeth's opinions. Bettina's political convictions were far ahead of her time. She later accepted a prison sentence rather than suppress her findings about the lamentable living conditions of the weavers in Silesia.

After the group of friends had dispersed, Otfried read to his brother two additional lines from von Rotteck: " 'I reject unity under the wings of the Prussian or Austrian eagle; I desire a unity of the German peoples that will protect them against the union of the princes and of the aristocrats'."[7]

The nationalistic movement that was developing in the early 1840's emphasized the power of the state, the nation. Otfried objected to this type of nationalism which exalted the state; he desired a type of liberal humanitarianism, which placed emphasis on the individual and his freedom to make choices. Two main currents opposed the reactionary policy of Prince Metternich. These were the overwhelming desire to see the many German states united under one government in one fatherland; and the fervent wish for individual freedom, for unhampered opportunity for each person, and for a minimum of governmental control. Meusebach valued the dictum of less governmental and more individual responsibility. He let this idea supersede that of a united Germany.

[5] J. Wolfgang Goethe, *Faust* (George Madison Priest, trans.), Part II, p. 340.
[6] Von Rotteck is quoted in Heinrich Gotthard von Treitschke, *History of Germany in the Nineteenth Century*, V, 321.
[7] *Ibid.*, p. 322.

The young aristocrat Otfried Hans Freiherr von Meusebach knew of von Rotteck's admiration for the United States. This fact, among other things, kept that country in Meusebach's mind, if only subconsciously. The Meusebach brothers talked about America, and Texas in particular. They read the books on that subject which had passed the censor. They mentioned emigration societies, particularly the one at Giessen. Some intellectuals, Otfried noted, had emigrated to Texas. Leaving the country, however, did not solve the problems. Now, at this moment, here in Berlin, it was important for him to understand Prussia from every angle, and perhaps in that way to find a solution to the problems, or at least personal adjustment to them. Therefore he decided to continue his professional employment in Berlin and remain there for a time. This would give him an opportunity to study the situation at firsthand.

Meusebach admired the cultural nationalism that his father espoused. To his regret he saw evidences that this espousal was giving way to a purely national political consciousness. The younger generation, sometimes called Jung Deutschland, had respect for liberalism; the intellectuals actually embraced it. If the two ideas of nationalism and liberalism could have gone hand in hand, all would have been well. Liberalism stood out against the privileges of the old ruling class; it wanted the citizens to have a part in political responsibility. Its prime concern was for the freedom of the individual. Naturally a written constitution had to record these rights. The nationalists, who desired a democratic unified Germany —one nation—could be identified with the liberals in the sense that they both opposed the old order of conservatives.

According to the theory of the nationalists all German princes and states would have to be subordinated to a common emperor and a unified nation. One corollary of the theory was that a small state would foster pettiness in political thinking while a large state would foster political magnitude. Such an excessive feature was objectionable. When the patriotic German became the militant Prussian partisan, he was intolerable to Meusebach— Prussia must not become the power state. German liberalism, or democracy, was showing signs of being willing to accept the leadership of Prussia and barter its idealism for the power which the Prussian autocracy might give to the liberal cause.

One writer has described the German political movements of the period as follows:

Soon the new nationalism stressed collective power and unity far above individual liberty; it tended to mean independence from outside rather than freedom within. In time power was overestimated and liberty underestimated. Nationalism changed in the middle of the nineteenth century from liberal humanitarianism to agressive exclusivism, from the emphasis on the dignity of the individual to that on the power of the nation.[8]

Recognizing trends of change, Otfried and his brother felt that a discussion of current topics would help them understand the political situation; so they arranged for a symposium in their home. An evening must have a lighter vein also. *Sylvesterabend,* New Year's Eve, was an opportune time.

The friends admired the Christmas tree bedecked with gilded walnuts. Hidden in each walnut was a brief poem or proverb written by the father, who signed himself "K. H. G. v. M." He derived his initials from the New Year's wish *Komm Holdes Glück verjunge Mich* ("Come lovely luck, rejuvenate me"). No names were attached to the walnuts, so amid laughter each guest took a turn at fitting the poem to the right person. Carl regaled the friends in telling how his father transported a Christmas tree to Otfried's apartment in Potsdam. The father had put on snowshoes, tramped to the woods, brought out the fir tree through the deep snow, then persuaded the engineer of the train to allow him to fasten the tree to the front of the engine; and decorated thus, the family had merrily arrived in Potsdam. There a sleigh had taken them and the tree, decorated by now with natural icicles glistening in the moonlight, to Otfried's residence, where the merriment continued.

The circle of friends gathered in the Meusebach home derived strength from each other. Although close to the constant stress of the Prussian capital, this home, in spirit, was far removed from Berlin. Here the emphasis was on the pursuit of the intellectual; everyone was acquainted with the topics of the day, at home and abroad. The ideas of a young intellectual named Karl Marx were receiving some attention. Political authorities called his ideas radical, and there was the possibility of his being expelled from the country. Marx was writing articles for an American newspaper, *The New York Tribune.* Some theorists at that time advocated communal organizations; these Marx scornfully summed up as "utopian socialists."

With their thoughts focused on America members of the group asked each other how a land like the United States could proclaim liberty so loudly and yet tolerate slavery. Elizabeth wished Otfried to reconcile the two ideas. His answer was that they were irreconcilable; liberty for one

[8] Hans Kohn, *Nationalism, its meaning and history,* p. 50.

bespoke liberty for all. He quoted De Tocqueville, lately returned from the United States, where he had found a working democracy. De Tocqueville advocated liberty, but he did not feel that liberty implied equality.

The young woman questioned further: by what means did a man gain recognition in that new land? Was it by academic accomplishment, money, or proven ability? And what was the basis of power? Young Meusebach answered, "Most likely the basis of power in governmental affairs is the vote." Bettina, who had an "educated heart," had been working for the improvement of the slums in Berlin. She was glad to quote De Tocqueville again as saying, "Politics should be directed to the happiness of the little man."

The group of friends in that village suburb of Potsdam heard echoes of a socialistic experiment called "Brook Farm" in faraway America. The Germans wondered whether that community would become permanent. Otfried quoted the line that was said to describe the tenets of the Brook Farm adherents: "high thinking with plain living." If plain living meant Spartan food, the appeal of the venture lost some ground with the Meusebachs, for they had epicurean tastes. One time a visitor to the many-volumed library had been invited to dine with the Meusebachs, who served sauerkraut for dinner. The guest had previously regarded sauerkraut as quite ordinary, but after partaking of it with the Meusebachs he considered sauerkraut an extraordinary dish.[9]

This guest was the poet Hoffmann von Fallersleben, who found great congeniality in the Meusebach household. He had read much about the Republic of Texas and had entertained ideas of going there. That distant land seemed to stand for many of his ideas; hence he wrote poems on the subject. One of his compositions incorporated the concepts about which the group had been talking that evening. At their invitation he read an excerpt:

> The world with its joys
> Is a spring gone dry
> Without freedom—the fountainhead
> Of virtue and of light.

When the poet let the friends know that he was composing a poem to use as a salutation to Texas when a group of travelers took their departure

[9] Karl Schwartz, "Karl Hartwig Gregor von Meusebach, Lebensnachrichten" (Part IV), *Annalen des Vereins für Nassauische Altertumskunde und Geschichtsforschung*, XXI (1890), 34.

for that fair land, the German friends at Baumgartenbrueck asked to hear it. He then read "The Star of Texas":

> Off to Texas! Off to Texas!
> where the star in the blue field
> proclaims a new world ...

On this *Sylvesterabend* the traditional dessert for New Year's Eve was served: *Springerle,* anise seed cookies with interesting designs imprinted on them. To toast the New Year, 1842, Ernestine brought in wine distilled from their own grapes, and marzipan, a favorite confection made from crushed almonds.

Before the group joined in the songs to welcome the New Year, Elizabeth sang as a solo a medieval folk song. Everyone was moved by it; and Otfried saw that she was more lovely than he had ever dreamed. He wondered: could he take her from her environment? If he followed his present inclinations his future might take him to distant lands.

Love finally spoke above every consideration. When they realized their love for each other they became betrothed. Life took on new dimensions.

The Leaven of Liberalism

CHAPTER 5

Until about 1840 the conservative forces held the liberal-national forces in check, with no discernible breakthrough. Efforts to bring about constitutional changes seemed futile. It was important to keep liberalism to the forefront, through constitutionalism, abolition of privilege, freedom of expression, the founding of imperial courts to provide prompt and exact justice. It was this last phase to which Meusebach applied his ability. He wanted to help waken Germany out of a "political coma." The coma of political inactivity had developed into what might be called a death sleep. This description applied particularly to Pomerania, where public claims indicated that no improvement in the administration of justice had been effected for two hundred years. An opportunity to help remedy the political doldrums of Pomerania came to the young jurist in 1841 with the proffer of a legal position in the city of Stettin. This assignment in a region of Germany pleased Otfried's friends who had heard of his interest in moving to a foreign country. These friends felt that the young intellectuals of the aristocracy should remain at home to contribute their talents to the cause of a unified Germany.

Municipal self-government for a number of the cities in Prussia had been secured by Chancellor Stein. The Chancellor had been unable to obtain the King's approval for similar privileges in rural areas, but he did put into effect the Town Ordinance, which revived communal life after a retrogression of two centuries. In the course of time this amounted to giving liberty and independence, property, and the protection of the laws to what Stein called the "submerged" part of the nation.[1] Difficulties arose in the application of this measure, particularly because of the authorities' differentiation between the semiliberal towns and the conservative rural

[1] George Peabody Gooch, *Germany and the French Revolution*, p. 524.

areas. Such a dichotomy existed between Stettin and Anclam, a neighboring rural town. Anclam had certain grievances, and when authorities in
Stettin found that Meusebach was level-headed they sent him there to
mediate between authorities and citizens. Within a short time he was
named *Bürgermeister*, or mayor, of Anclam.

When his family and friends at home heard that he had been designated as *Bürgermeister* they joked about it. In his younger days Otfried
had been dubbed "*Bürgermeister* of Saardam"[2] because of his ability to
take charge of a situation. At last he was a *Bürgermeister* in fact—with
perplexing problems to solve.

As a guideline for negotiation the new *Bürgermeister* used Humboldt's
dictum, "The state should be no more than an agent to secure protection
and freedom for its citizens." This axiom had been ignored in Anclam:
the citizens felt that in their town the individual had no voice in public
affairs and the bureaucratic system dominated the individual even to the
point of official intrusion. Further grievances related to remnants of feudal
obligations. Remembering Humboldt's ideas and proceeding on the basis
of his own liberal outlook, Otfried was able to reconcile the old order with
the new. Here was a demonstration of communal living: a community
working together was asking for recognition of the existence of the individual.

Fiscal matters in Anclam needed attention. Feudal dues were certainly
outmoded at mid-nineteenth century. Remnants of a past age were set
aside to make way for completely new forces. Meusebach's university
training in finance, as well as in cameralism, was used here to advantage.
He put his hand to all phases of the city's needs. At the end of two years at
Anclam he could see some results from his efforts. A new day seemed to
be dawning. Yet the sunlight of liberalism did not actually break through
the clouds of traditionalism. After the community was again moving forward higher authorities felt that Anclam must be organized within the accepted pattern. The city returned for a time to the traditional.

The immediate need had been met. But must the final answer of traditionalism always be superimposed on the present? Must the individual always fit himself into the pattern set by officialdom? Meusebach decided
that for himself he would break the pattern. Perhaps he could help others
to do the same.

The authorities in Stettin were reluctant to accept his resignation. They

[2] Karl Schwartz, "Karl Hartwig Gregor von Meusebach, Lebensnachrichten"
(Part IV), *Annalen des Vereins für Nassauische Altertumskunde und Geschichtsforschung*, XXI (1890), 25.

pointed out that his abilities were being recognized and that broader opportunities would inevitably follow. For the love of Germany, they asked, could he not stay and support his native land? These men, long established in their regime, recognized that a spirit of liberalism was moving through the land, but they were not yet able to give up their adherence to the old institutions. They represented a dualistic blend—half official and half independent.

Reform in the direction of equality was in the air. But to equality must be added liberty.

What was happening in Germany? King Frederick William IV, who "held an order in one hand, a counter order in the other, and disorder in his head,"[3] was assenting to measures which made Germany a "political graveyard." "And yet," wrote one historian, "already there were in America so many German refugees that in some quarters fears had been expressed lest the German language overwhelm the English. During those years the German government did nothing to help those of German speech beyond the seas, save to swell their numbers."[4]

Could Otfried help those of his countrymen who felt impelled to emigrate? In what respect could he help? This young man, at thirty-three, turned his face westward.

[3] Heinrich Gotthard von Treitschke, *History of Germany in the Nineteenth Century*, VI, 537.

[4] Poultney Bigelow, *History of the German Struggle for Liberty, 1815–1848*, I, 42.

The Noble Experiment Begins

CHAPTER 6

Meusebach was familiar with the emigration societies which directed people to New Zealand and to Guatemala. America appealed to him more; there men were unfettered. They had proved their independence in the year 1776. In America lay limitless stretches of land not bound in by man. Literally mile after square mile awaited development. There were no overlords; each man must rise to meet the challenge of his own responsibilities. The potentialities for the individual shone like a great beacon of welcome.

On October 24, 1844, Meusebach wrote: "For several years I have been considering going to America to obtain a large enough property to be the basis of nature study and furtherance thereof in those rich fields. I have had my eyes especially on Texas."[1] He kept up with all the current books on Texas. Some he had read in his father's library; most of them he had in his own possession. When he loaned them to his friends, they declared that they received vicarious warmth from the semitropical land of Texas, so different from the frigid Baltic coast. Carl recommended to his brother the book on that new republic written by William Kennedy, British consul in Galveston.[2] Kennedy characterized the success of the Texans in maintaining constitutional government as one of the most remarkable passages in the history of associated man. As an official Kennedy described places with exactitude and authority. The very name of one landmark, Enchanted Rock, added fascination to the beckoning land. Meusebach hoped to probe for a scientific explanation of the mysterious sounds that were said to issue at times from the 640 acres of solid granite. He marveled that such an immense outcropping of mountainous rock was located in an area bear-

[1] Meusebach, Berlin, October 24, 1844, to Castell. Solms-Braunfels Archives, LI, 1.
[2] William Kennedy, *Texas: the rise, progress, and prospects of the republic of Texas.*

ing the name "Llano," the Spanish word for "plain." He wanted to know the reason for this contradiction.

When Carl mentioned the accounts in the newspapers of March, 1844, concerning the Verein zum Schutze deutscher Einwanderer in Texas, or Society for the Protection of German Immigrants in Texas, a door seemed to open; there, felt Otfried, was the place to focus one's thoughts.

This *Verein*, or society, originally had consisted of twenty noblemen, five of whom were reigning princes, who had formed an organization in 1842 to direct emigration to Texas. They met at Biebrich on the Rhine in a castle belonging to the reigning Archduke of Nassau, who later was named protector of the Society. Count Carl Castell was the moving spirit of the organization. He was an officer in the Austrian garrison in Mainz, where he relieved the tedium by reading travel books, particularly those on Texas. These men had great expectations for their organization. The presiding officer, Count Christian von Neu-Leiningen-Westerburg, said: "We want to create something grand, noble . . . . We want to be able to say, 'That is my work.' The names of the founders will belong to world history."[3]

The gentlemen meeting at Biebrich signed the following document on April 20, 1842: "We, the undersigned, hereby make known that we have today constituted ourselves as a society for the purpose of purchasing lands in the Republic of Texas."[4]

This "galaxy"[5] of princes and noblemen dispatched Prince Victor von Leiningen and Count Joseph von Boos-Waldeck to Texas to purchase land and to make recommendations about colonization. Leiningen's request for tax concessions were refused by Sam Houston, the President of the Republic. The Prince failed to secure a land grant; neither did he arrange for the purchase of land, although thousands of acres were available at ten and fifteen cents per acre. Prince Leiningen, however, did report favorably on large-scale colonization. For $3,321 Count Boos-Waldeck bought for the Verein in Fayette County a farm of 4,428 acres, a league, which he named "Nassau" to honor the Duke of Nassau. Boos-Waldeck advised against colonization on a large scale because the expense would be too great. When his advice was disregarded he withdrew from the group.

[3] Minutes of Verein, n.pl., n.d. SB Archives, XXX, 148.
[4] Rudolph Leopold Biesele, *The History of the German Settlements in Texas 1831–1861*, p. 67.
[5] Moritz Tiling, *History of the German Element in Texas from 1820–1850, and Historical Sketches of the German Texas Singers' League and Houston Turnverein from 1853–1913*, p. 60.

Castell had hoped that the Prussian government would approve his colonization plans and that following that example other German states would likewise approve them. It was anticipated that some financial assistance would be included in the approval. One specific appeal was for the governments to aid the *Verein* in sending one thousand unemployed families to Texas. Because Alexander von Humboldt, a world traveler and adviser to the King, did not agree to this appeal or to other proposals related to the emigration ideas, none of the other states gave their sanction to the idea.

No phase of Castell's plan was accepted officially. He was not deterred thereby; he met the rejection by making an appeal for a larger membership. All who came into the organization were members of the nobility, among them several reigning princes, who, in respect to taking official action, were regarded as private individuals.

The subject of governmental sponsorship of the Verein's undertaking was mentioned at times by members of the Verein, but no action was taken.[6]

While Boos-Waldeck was still in Texas the group reorganized into a stock company with a capital of $80,000 divided into forty shares of $2,000 each. On March 25, 1844, a new society, or Verein, was formed taking the name "Society for the Protection of German Immigrants in Texas." The threefold purpose of the Society was announced as: (1) improvement of the conditions of the working classes and a decrease of pauperism; (2) opening of new markets for the products of German industrie; (3) the development of maritime commerce.[7] These purposes were altruistic; no speculation or political goals were contemplated.[8] However, financial gains were expected, because the distribution of profits was provided for.

Prince Victor Leiningen was elected president and Count Carl Castell was elected vice-president and executive secretary, or business director.

It is possible that Prince Leiningen's report favoring large-scale colonization was based on his recognition that an existing colonization contract could be acquired. One such contract had been negotiated by Henry Francis Fisher and Burchard Miller. Fisher, a native of Kassel, Germany, had been a resident of Texas since 1838. In association with Burchard Miller, Fisher received a colonization contract from the Republic on June 7, 1842. This contract was renewed on September 1, 1843; after further

---

[6] Resumé of Verein business, Wiesbaden, July 28, 1845. SB Archives, XXX, 149–151.

[7] Verein zum Schutze Deutscher Einwanderer in Texas, *Gesammelte aktenstücke . . . nebst einer karte*, Article I, Paragraph 3.

[8] Minutes of Verein, Biebrich, July 23, 1847. SB Archives, XXXI, 56–57.

renewals the final date of expiration was fixed for August, 1847. It is possible that Fisher evaluated the situation and interested Prince Leiningen, during his visit to Texas, in the land granted by the Republic to Fisher and Miller.[9]

The second existing contract that might be available had been negotiated with the Republic by Alexander Bourgeois, associated with Armand Ducos, on June 3, 1842, with the expiration date of December 3, 1843. Such contracts with the Republic of Texas stipulated that the contractors were to receive generous amounts of land in return for bringing in colonists, who would likewise receive grants.

Because the Verein's plans for colonization had crystallized but no arrangements for land in Texas had been made Alexander Bourgeois was able to persuade the members of the Verein, on April 7, 1844, to acquire the colonization rights of the Bourgeois-Ducos contract. Bourgeois, a Frenchman who lived in Texas and claimed President Sam Houston as his personal friend, added the suffix "D'Orvanne" to his name, presumably to influence the members of the Verein, all titled men. Since the time limit on Bourgeois's grant was December 3, 1843, and the colonization contract had not been fulfilled, the grant was already forfeited when the Verein acquired it on April 7, 1844. Bourgeois, however, believed he would be able to have the time extended by the Congress of the Republic.

The Verein arranged for the acquisition of Bourgeois's grant of land and elected him to membership in the organization. Futhermore the members named him colonial director and named Prince Carl of Solms-Braunfels commissioner-general for the colonial establishment in Texas. These two men went to Texas to make preparations for the colonists. They arrived in Galveston on July 1, 1844, and proceeded to the area of Bourgeois's grant. Bourgeois, after communicating with Texas officials about the renewal of his land grant, felt encouraged by their responses. Prince Solms felt similarly, as his report of July 15, 1844, indicates.[10] Bourgeois's appeal for a time extension was presented through accepted channels, namely communication with Anson Jones, Secretary of State. The Frenchman also expected to call on President Houston, but found that he was away from the capital.

Bourgeois had information which gave him basis for thinking that Fisher was able to have his request to Congress for the renewal of his grant

---

[9] Biesele, *History of German Settlements*, p. 78.

[10] "Berichte des Prinzen Karl zu Solms-Braunfels an den Mainzer Adelsverein" (Nassau Farm, July 15, 1844, to Verein), *Kalender der Neu-Braunfelser Zeitung fuer 1916*, pp. 17–18.

advanced to the third reading by an unusual procedure. Fisher's petition came to the floor of the House on the ninth of January. After a very lively discussion, the vote showed eighteen for and eighteen against. When the result was made known, something seldom heard of took place. One of the members, the representative from Milam County, stated that he had voted mistakenly and now wanted to vote for the bill. The House acceded to the request. The petition was then read for the third time and Bourgeois believed it would be discussed on the following day and then go to the Senate.

Bourgeois saw the possibility of a setback for all of the land contractors, including Fisher. As it turned out, the extension of time for fulfilling the requirements of Fisher's grant was extended; that of Bourgeois was not.[11]

Fisher had himself appointed by President Houston as consul to the Hansa free city of Bremen. He was there on May 20, 1844, and a month later, on June 26, he had consummated the sale of an interest in the Fisher-Miller land grant to the Verein. The price was $9,000 cash, with $2,000 payable at New Orleans on September 1, 1845. A number of stipulations to the advantage of Fisher and Miller were put into the agreement.

This deal with Fisher was entered into by the Verein, although the members had made a commitment on April 7 to Bourgeois. Prince Solms and Bourgeois were en route to Texas to inspect Bourgeois's grant, located northwest of San Antonio, when Castell, the executive secretary, informed Prince Solms of the acquisition of the Fisher-Miller land and of the appointment of Fisher as colonial director. On August 28 Bourgeois announced his own resignation as colonial director.

Prince Solms stated in his third report that Bourgeois would not accept any of the Verein's offers of further employment connected with the colonization of the Fisher-Miller Grant, but that he intended to return to Europe to bring his suit of accusations to the Verein. Previous to Bourgeois's dismissal, the Frenchman had reported the Prince's shortcomings, emphasizing his extravagances and saying that he looked at business with closed eyes. The Prince was relieved at the departure of Bourgeois.

After Castell notified Solms of the acquisition of the Fisher-Miller Grant, the Prince reported that a large amount of desirable undeveloped land could be found in the Grant, but that the northwestern part was the hunting grounds of the Comanche Indians.[12] He proposed to extract a treaty that the Comanches would abide by or to inflict such a decisive defeat on them that they would become harmless. Colonel Jack Hays, the

[11] D'Orvanne, n.pl., n.d., to Castell. SB Archives, XLVIIa, 223.

[12] "Berichte des Prinzen Karl zu Solms-Braunfels" (San Antonio de Béxar, August 26, 1844, to Verein), *Kalender fuer 1916*, p. 31.

Indian fighter, said that Fisher believed the Grant to be too far from the coast (about three hundred miles) to be suitable for the first settlement of the colonists. Solms gave Fisher great credit for this opinion.

Such an opinion was advantageous for both men: neither felt obliged to make a settlement in that distant homeland of the Indians. Fisher knew well the disadvantages of the Grant when he sold it to the Verein. The members, as well as Prince Solms, soon learned that Fisher's tactic was to look to his own advantages in disregard to their effect upon others. Solms's later complete disillusionment is shown in his report of February 8, 1845:

Mr. Fisher had difficulty in getting together the necessary money for a trip to Europe, and he spared no effort, Heaven knows, to make something out of his contract. When he reached Mainz, he saw immediately how poorly informed the Verein was about Texas, and at the same time he saw that confidence would perhaps be placed in him. As soon as this happened, his head swelled. He saw himself in possession of means (for the first time in his life) and spent freely. . . . Furthermore, he wanted to assume to himself the employment of all officials and agents, so that he could have his subordinates everywhere who could fill their own pockets; or, in any event, certainly see to it that Mr. Fisher's pockets were filled.

. . . In order to make himself and his partner, Mr. Miller, seem important, Mr. Fisher declares . . . that he and Mr. Miller put $60,000 into the colonization project and that five ships with five to six hundred immigrants on board have arrived in Galveston Harbor. Yet every person here, from the President of Texas to the smallest Negro lad, knows that if Messrs. Fisher and Miller both were put under a cotton press, not one dollar, let alone $60,000, could be pressed out of them both.[13]

Even before that report was sent in, immigrants had arrived in Texas; 439 came in November and December of 1844. Prince Solms wrote that he was in the embarrasing situation of having hundreds of persons arriving with no place in which to locate them. He worked heroically to make provisions for them and succeeded in finding a favorable location, Las Fontanas, or Comal Springs, which was approximately 150 miles northwest of Indianola, the point of disembarkation for the immigrants. With the Springs as the central point, Solms bought, on March 15, 1845, two leagues of land for a consideration of $1,111.

While Fisher was in Germany the Verein had given him the sum of $11,000[14] with which to buy supplies, particularly transport wagons, for

---

[13] "Berichte des Prinzen Karl zu Solms-Braunfels" (Galveston, February 8, 1845, to Verein), *ibid.*, pp. 51–52.

[14] Castell, n.pl., October 9, 1844, to Verein. SB Archives, XLIX, 161.

the project. In Texas, Solms gave him an additional $2,360 with which to purchase draft oxen. Fisher failed to obtain the larger portion of the necessary supplies: he collected only fifteen of the fifty wagons needed; he had not bought any of the draft oxen and cattle needed; he had not provided any beef cattle or corn meal. Instead of attending to these responsibilities, Fisher spent time advancing his own interests with the Texas Congress. Meanwhile, Solms, acting through his colonial Administrative Council, sent Captain F. W. von Wrede to obtain the necessary supplies in New Orleans. Solms stated emphatically that the administration of Verein affairs should not be entrusted to Fisher; that such an appointment would not promote the interests of the Society.[15] The Prince asked pointedly that a highly capable individual be sent to replace himself as commissioner-general, a request he had made in every report after his first one. He added, "I will make all preparations for my successor in such a manner that he will have to fit himself into the situation with zeal and determination in order to be able to accomplish all that I shall have instituted."[16]

[15] "Berichte des Prinzen Karl zu Solms-Braunfels" (Port Lavaca, December 23, 1844, to Verein), *Kalender fuer 1916*, p. 47.
[16] *Ibid.*, p. 46.

Decision

CHAPTER 7

The brothers, Otfried and Carl, spent hours talking about this organization, the Verein, and its work. Reports in the newspapers were frequent; not all were favorable to the Society, but new ideas often had detractors. The name of the Society was reassuring; the idea of protection appealed to Otfried. Those who were leaving their country were often the inexperienced; direction and protection were needed at such a time.

Meusebach felt that the men forming this Society bore names of high worth. They were all of the nobility; in fact, the Verein was already being called the *Adelsverein,* a union or society of noblemen. A man with an inherited title owed something to his fellow man. How else could *noblesse oblige* be interpreted? Certainly nobility obligated its possessor.

Meusebach wanted this question answered: what motivated these men to put their energy to this undertaking? His brother knew personally some members of the Society whom he expected to recognize the magnitude of their undertaking. Carl helped his brother evaluate the Society's program, for it had far-reaching implications: (1) What was the reaction of the German government to this Society's project? (2) What sort of person was to be solicited? (3) What kind of land had the group procured, and was its location desirable? (4) Did the Society have financial stability? Unless the answers to these questions were favorable, reasoned the brothers, certainly those forty aristocrats would not spend their time with this project.

Meusebach gave the matter intense thought. As he pondered the question he realized that his profession promised security and advancement for him at home in Germany. On the other hand, perhaps he could give security and protection to his less-favored countrymen by leaving Germany. In such event he could not hope for a continuation of the cultural advantages he now took for granted. Many of these he would have to forego in a frontier life. Yet there was much to be learned from the pioneer people, whose wisdom was sharpened on the whetstone of experience. He visualized a great opportunity for studying nature in every aspect, its plant life and geology in particular. Texas, located near the juncture of the temperate and tropical zones, would abound in interesting vegetation. He was challenged by the prospect of improving certain plants, or even of introducing new plants, such as the olive tree. The younger pioneers would be attracted by experiments in every line. In due course an exchange of products would enlarge the trade of the mother country.

But to leave his fatherland—there was the rub! He was a German to the marrow of his bones. He loved his beautiful country, so far ahead of the world on many counts, albeit so far behind on others. What minds it had produced, minds universal in scope. Among the famous musicians, Beethoven stood out as a man who knew no boundaries. Then there was Goethe, rising above nationalism; could there be a person more universal, more Olympian in stature? Meusebach thought the song should not proclaim, *"Deutschland über Alles"* ("Germany above Everything"); it should say, "Brotherhood above everything; equal opportunity for all." He could not subscribe to Germany's glorification solely of things German. Despite his love for his native country, he felt he must leave.

The general program of the Verein was in line with Meusebach's thinking; therefore he agreed to consider his brother's suggestion that he become associated with the Society. Carl had communicated with Count Carl Castell in October, 1844. Castell remarked that if Otfried joined the company and bought a $2,000 share the possibility of his becoming commissioner-general might develop.[1] Otfried replied that he would not refuse to join, but he added frankly, "I dare not conceal the fact that the designated land appears worthless if the conditions do not justify a large working capital."[2]

Meusebach and Castell exchanged several letters relative to the conditions of his contract as commissioner-general. Meusebach expressed the desire for time in which to acquaint himself with certain phases of medicine that could be helpful in the colony.[3] He received a $2,000 allowance for buying scientific equipment and for adding technical books to his own already significant library. His salary was to be $790 annually plus a commission of two per cent of the net profits of the Verein and an alloca-

[1] Meusebach, Berlin, October 24, 1844, to Castell. Solms-Braunfels Archives, LI, 3.
[2] Meusebach, Berlin, December 4, 1844, to Castell. SB Archives, LI, 11.
[3] Meusebach, Berlin, October 24, 1844, to Castell. SB Archives, LI, 9.

tion of five hundred acres of land. If the Verein should dissolve within five years he was to receive an indemnity of $5,000.[4] Meusebach also would be given the privilege of selecting his attendant to serve him in Texas.

In conclusion to the contract, Meusebach wrote Castell on Demember 4, 1844, that as the new commissioner-general he must keep his eye "on an economical administration to prevent too rapid depletion of the funds of the Verein."[5]

When Meusebach, after careful deliberation, decided to leave Germany, the decision was final. He did not waver. He would return to visit his family, but not to take up residence again. It hurt him to leave his parents. Nor was it easy to leave a brother who was a friend as well. Then there was his fiancée, Elizabeth von Hardenberg, for whom he was coming back when his situation in Texas was settled enough to receive a bride. She was eager to go with him but remained behind lest she add to his burdens.

Meusebach and his fiancée talked over many facets of his life ahead in the utter strangeness of a pioneer land. He would find crudities which could pass into amenities only through the passage of years. Customs, daily routine, even animal and vegetable life would be different from what he had known. Would there be someone to care for him if the need arose? Negro slaves were there, and the whole idea of slavery—no matter what the color of the enslaved—was abhorrent. Otfried was seeking freedom for one and all. This young aristocrat was leaving behind the idea of class distinctions. He knew quite well that money should not elevate one person above another; position should depend on individual accomplishment. The two discussed it all. This young woman, sensitive to the world and its conditions, and the young man, steeped in tradition but aware of its shackles, weighed all the considerations. When the scales were read the advantages in Texas outweighed the disadvantages. The decision was made, the answer was without equivocation: "Texas forever."

What bright hopes that land named Texas called up! Meusebach and Elizabeth knew that the Republic was named for an Indian tribe, the Tejas, and that Indians still inhabited it—were perhaps rampant at times. Could not the Indians be approached with a fair proposition? And the uncrowded land, thousands of acres, was it not said to be pregnant with riches? Every map had the marking "silver mines."Neither the riches nor the Indian affairs, however, provided the lure that the prospect of the

[4] Meusebach's report, Wiesbaden, September 9, 1851, to Verein. SB Archives, LXV, 27.

[5] Meusebach, Berlin, December 4, 1844, to Castell. SB Archives, LI, 13.

scientific investigation of the geology and flora and fauna held out to them. To have acres to cultivate and to make productive: that was truly an incentive to journey to a new land.

But beckoning beyond any other call was the knowledge that Texas was a republic—a land where "each man daily won his freedom anew." Freedom was not really free, it was costly.

As if to emphasize his decision to go to that land of new beginnings, Otfried determined to relinquish his hereditary title of baron. So his father would not feel that the son desired to break the family relationship, Otfried decided not to announce the relinquishment until he was actually on his way to America. What better declaration of democratic intent could he make than this, a deliberate turning away from centuries of ensured status? "Texas Forever" he added to his family coat of arms, but he did not abandon his family motto, *Tenax Propositi*. Tenacious of purpose, perseverance in all undertakings: that idea was bred into him. It was part of his being.

While Meusebach was still in Berlin, Count Castell had asked him to call on Prince Friedrich of Prussia at the Royal Palace. The Prince was a member of the Society and he showed great interest in its proposals. Meusebach had come away from the interview that cold January day in 1845 with a special regard for His Royal Highness; he felt that the Society had the good will of the Prince.

Leaving Berlin in February, Meusebach stopped in Leipzig, en route to the headquarters of the Society in Mainz, to try to win the editor of the magazine *Herolds* to the side of the Society. If ignorance of the principles of the Society caused the opposition of the liberal papers, the papers should be enlightened. In Munich in 1844, George Franz had published a pamphlet in which he attacked the Society. His attack, directed especially against the German princes and noblemen, charged that the German press did not dare to question the motives of these men. Franz said that had the plan been formulated by commoners rather than by princes and noblemen the press would have taken great pains to attack the absurdity and speculative nature of this project.[6]

A second stop for Meusebach was at Halle, where his friends among the university professors were the lodestone. The professors were pleased that he had ordered scientific instruments to be sent to Texas, and that he promised them mineral specimens from the new land. They recalled that

---

[6] Franz (*Die Auswanderung der Deutschen nach Texas, Nordamerika, und Ungarn* [Muenchen, 1844]) is quoted in Rudolph Leopold Biesele, *The History of the German Settlements in Texas 1831–1861*, p. 99.

he had always had a wide horizon—now he was traveling toward it, as it were, and they gave him encouragement.

In Mainz Meusebach met the enthusiastic Count Carl Castell, who related some particulars about the organization. Since Texas desired settlers no money was paid to the government by Fisher and Miller for the land grant. The stipulation, however, was that six thousand families were to be settled on the Grant by August, 1847. Each settler was to receive 640 acres if married, 320 if single. The contractor, in this case the Society, had the right to retain one half of the land granted to the settler. Therefore, each married immigrant brought the Society 320 acres. That number multiplied by six thousand families amounted to almost 2,000,000 acres.

Castell showed unbounded delight over the prospect of that much land. He passed lightly over further details of the contract with the Republic of Texas, for example, that the Society was to pay surveying costs on all land, including alternate sections reserved by the Republic, and that the first six hundred families were to be settled within eighteen months. As for finances, Castell was confident that the deposit of $240 by married men and half that amount by the unmarried was adequate to cover what the Society promised, namely: ocean passage, transportation of family and unlimited baggage from Galveston to the settlement, a cabin, and sustenance until the first crop was raised. Half of this first deposit was credited to the immigrants, who could draw on it for farming implements or extra rations from the company's stores.[7] The emigrants were allowed also to deposit funds additional to the required amount. On this money, which could be withdrawn at will, they were to receive interest. Each individual was given a deposit book in which accounts were recorded by officials. Those wishing to buy supplies on credit from the Society store had that privilege.

The Executive Secretary emphasized only the vast acreage; he said to Meusebach, in effect, "You will learn all details in Texas, where you will be able to care for all needs. The contract for you to become commissioner-general is ready for your signature."

Thereupon Meusebach signed the document; the date was February 24, 1845. He deposited $2,000, the cost of a share, with Count Castell, who remarked that the payment was merely an evidence of Meusebach's union of interests with those of the Verein.

[7] Moritz Tiling, *History of the German Element in Texas from 1820–1850, and Historical Sketches of the German Texas Singers' League and Houston Turnverein from 1853–1913*, p. 73.

Meusebach wondered who was paying for the expenses. He noted the various outlays: the cost of Farm Nassau; the investment in the Fisher-Miller Grant; the purchase of the site of the colony at New Braunfels; and now the daily sustenance for the 439 colonists. The total of these expenses was a large sum; the addition of the salaries and travel allowances for the personnel in Germany and in Texas would put an obvious strain on the capital. A quick summation of these outlays was the basis of Meusebach's statement to Castell that insolvency of the Verein was in sight. Castell replied, "The members will not allow that to happen; they will not leave it in the lurch."[8]

Castell gave Meusebach a letter of credit in the amount of $10,000. In light of the probable financial difficulties this sum should give a measure of relief, thought Meusebach.

Meusebach's solution for refilling the treasury was to assess each member of the organization, or to take in more members. On an earlier occasion Castell's answer to a similar suggestion had been, "If the door were opened, the forty members would appear within an hour."[9] But Castell did not act on either of Meusebach's suggestions. One reason was that the members wished to keep the Society exclusive—as it was often expressed, *inter pares*.[10] Membership was restricted to the nobility. An employed person, even a financier, would not be received.

In many respects the Society resembled a club or fraternity made up of like-minded individuals. Although the printed material stated that the purpose of the Verein was philanthropic, a speculative motive also could be discerned by some. A prospective member, Count von Walderdorf, said that the statutes of the Society did not show the protection of the immigrants to be the focal point of the organization; therefore, he did not join. No member attempted to refute the accusation.

Meusebach concluded that the Society did not take in additional members because it wished to conceal its actual financial straits. Since Prince Solms was on the ground in Texas, it was reasonable to expect him to have plans that would suggest a way out. The new Commissioner-General relied on getting a report before the retiring executive left New Braunfels.

Count Castell attempted to conceal from Meusebach the dire financial situation of the Verein. Nor did he mention other matters which troubled

8 Meusebach, Mainz, September 8, 1851, to Verein. SB Archives, XL, 55.

9 Castell, Mainz, September 16, 1843, to Boos-Waldeck. SB Archives, I, 106.

10 W. von Rosenberg, *Kritik der Geschichte des Vereins zum Schutze der Deutschen Auswanderer nach Texas*, p. 9.

him, as his letter written to Prince Solms just a month earlier, on January 20, 1845, revealed:

> You will certainly wait for von Meusebach since it is necessary that you instruct him personally. Also it would make a bad impression on the Verein if you, like Boos-Waldeck, departed and left things to strangers, especially since you promised to stay two years. Because of the infamous newspaper articles, we have lost over 400 emigrants who were accepted. We helped on the payment of many in order to hold them. In March we are sending twenty-five young men at our own costs. More we could not do, because otherwise our funds are at an end. We had to pay the cost of Meusebach's trip and outfitting him—he became a Verein member.
>
> We shall have to pay your return trip as well as that of d'Orvanne, and certainly we'll have to pay d'Orvanne for his writings. With all of this we cannot do more. Therefore, I beg of you not to make your return voyage too expensive, for I tell you in confidence, we will otherwise be bankrupt before we earn.
>
> Bourgeois d'Orvanne is in Paris; he is coming here shortly to indict us for $100,000 damages.
>
> Bring some Texas rarities along, also silver out of the San Saba Valley to show as an exhibit to the general meeting of the Verein.[11]

This beginning with uncertainties presented difficulties, yet Meusebach determined to proceed. From Mainz he traveled via Aachen, Cologne, Ostend, Dover, and London to Liverpool, which was his port of embarkation for the journey to America. His heavier baggage, including chests, a secretary, and many books, had been sent from Bremen by a sailship. His attendant had already embarked for Texas.

Meusebach turned to look at the English shore, full of hurry and bustle, yet well ordered from years of established seaside procedure. The afternoon sun pierced the overhanging fog; to the west an occasional bright stream of gold could be seen. He looked sharply in that direction. Then he walked up the gangplank, carrying his own bag. To himself he said, "At this point I relinquish my title. From here on I stand in my own shoes, John O. Meusebach."

---

[11] Castell, Mainz, January 20, 1845, to Solms. SB Archives, LIX, 191–196.

PART II

Colonization, 1845–1847

Texas on the Horizon

CHAPTER 8

L ike Janus, the double-faced Roman god, who could look in opposite directions at the same time, Meusebach now viewed the past and the future. For him Germany represented the past, which he must fold up and tuck away in some isolated compartment of his mind and heart. The future was represented by new work in a new world—Texas.

During the voyage Meusebach studied the material Castell had given him in Mainz. He discerned that the sums to be charged the German emigrants whom the Society was bringing to Texas did not cover the cost of their move; twenty-four dollars would not build a house. And who would transport a family and unlimited baggage from Galveston to Indianola in Matagorda Bay and on to the colony for four dollars? Castell's geographical location of the colony hardly seemed to fit the map. The Count had told Meusebach that Prince Solms had bought land for a settlement 165 miles northwest of the disembarkation port, and had named the settlement New Braunfels. Why had the Prince settled at this point, 150 miles short of the Fisher-Miller land, which the Verein expected him to occupy? Meusebach certainly would ask Prince Solms this question when he met him in New Braunfels. The new Commissioner-General feared that the members of the Verein had been overpersuaded when they placed their entire undertaking into the hands of the man who was selling them the land—Henry Francis Fisher.

The problems of the Verein, however, did not consume all of Meusebach's thoughts during the two-week voyage across the Atlantic. Since English was the language spoken aboard *The Cambria*, Meusebach gave close attention to the conversations going on. His practice of the use of English was somewhat academic; hence he was glad to hear the idiomatic. He was told that the English spoken in Texas would sound quite different from that which was spoken by a person native to England.

His fellow passengers were curious about Texas. Those acquainted with world affairs, knowing that the Republic was close to becoming a member state of the United States, wondered if that event had come to pass. They questioned whether Mexico would give up all the territory that Texas embraced without some protest, and if war between the two nations would follow annexation. The discussions continued about the merits, relative to England, France, and Germany, of Texas as a state and as a republic.

As his ship neared icebergs off the shores of Newfoundland Meusebach calculated the measurements of the huge masses.[1] He thought of the immigrants sailing the warm southern route and hoped that the eight-week voyage was pleasant for them. His steamer had to put in at Halifax for repairs. In that city he walked for the first time on the soil of the New World. He felt as if he were opening a book with blank pages, and he wondered if his actions would give something worthy to be recorded. Such was his intention.

The steamer reached Boston on March 14, 1845. Meusebach wanted to visit the scenes of the patriotic struggles in the United States: Boston, New York, and particularly Philadelphia. While in that area he wanted to see what Germans had done for their adopted country. The urge, however, to reach the Germans in Texas, lately come to these shores, hurried him to Pittsburgh and thence by boat down the Ohio and Mississippi Rivers to New Orleans. [2]

On April 10, 1845, he arrived in New Orleans. The new President of the United States, James K. Polk, had been in office not much over a month, and the inauguration still was the topic of conversation. Many people in New Orleans were discussing the proposal of the United States to annex Texas. In this city, predominantly French, the citizens took pride in the fact that France had given recognition to the young Republic. They knew that France, as well as England, hoped that Texas would remain independent and ultimately would give those countries commercial advantages and other benefits.

These French Americans recalled that in 1844 President Tyler had failed to get a two-thirds vote in the Senate for ratification of the annexation bill, but that in the closing hours of his administration he put the proposal through by a joint resolution. On March 1, 1845, President Tyler, in one the last acts of his administration, signed the resolution.

[1] Lucy Meusebach Marschall, Notes and Memoranda. MSS. Meusebach Family Files.
[2] Meusebach, Baltimore, March 21, 1845, to Castell. Solms-Braunfels Archives, LI, 51.

Map of the Grant and Verein settlements, 1851. Original in Fürst zu
Solms-Braunfels'sches Archiv, Braunfels, Lahn, Germany.

Courtesy University of Texas Archives

Meusebach again wondered about the reaction of Mexico, which, having lost Texas, had never acknowledged her independence. In fact, the annexation of Texas was the last in a series of episodes that eroded the Mexican empire. [3]

Becoming a citizen of the Republic of Texas was a privilege that Meusebach had anticipated with pleasure. Annexation settled the farfetched speculation that Texas could be developed into a German state, as Prince Solms had hoped. Meusebach harbored no such idea. He had left his native country to seek a new, free world, not to establish a new German state. In the Republic of Texas everyone was his own master; it would be the same when Texas became a state in the United States—that indissoluble union!

Why could not the German states have joined themselves together in a similar fashion? Meusebach asked himself.

But his business was at hand; the Commissioner-General of the Society for the Protection of German Immigrants in Texas introduced himself to Ambrose Lanfear, the New Orleans banker who represented the Society. He deposited with the bank his $10,000 letter of credit and his personal funds. From the banker he learned that a representative of the Society in Texas, F. W. von Wrede, had recently made significant purchases for the organization.

The boat that Meusebach had expected to take for Galveston had sailed before his arrival. He, therefore, had time to visit the German consul, W. Vogel, who candidly expressed his unfavorable view of Henry Francis Fisher and his activities. Vogel's appraisal of Fisher certainly differed from Castell's evaluation of the man. Meusebach was troubled to hear that Prince Solms and Fisher were at odds over Fisher's failure to buy the necessary supplies with the funds he had received from the Verein. This report of Fisher's business manipulations was Meusebach's first inkling of the trouble which lay ahead.

Meusebach hoped that the difference could be resolved by careful handling of the situation. Eager to reach Texas, he took the first boat available for Galveston.

[3] Bernard De Voto, *The Year of Decision: 1846*, p. 13.

Texas in Reality

Meusebach first touched Texas soil on a May day of 1845. He squared his shoulders—six feet, two inches tall he stood—and faced a new world. As he contemplated the surprising strangeness of the brilliant landscape he was startled to hear himself addressed in a familiar accent, "*Wilkommen, Herr Baron.*" He returned the greeting of the Verein's agent and soon let it be known that he was no longer using the title of baron and that he wished to be known simply as John O. Meusebach. This new Texan wished to be on equal footing with other citizens of the land.

Meusebach asked about the condition of the Society's affairs. D. H. Klaener, the agent of the Society in Galveston and Houston, replied at first with hesitation, but responding to Meusebach's informal manner, Klaener revealed the situation candidly: Prince Solms lacked business acumen; the drafts and overdrafts that came through the Agent's office at times proved this. Klaener criticized Henry Francis Fisher because he had failed to provide the supplies that he had been commissioned to obtain, for example, transport vehicles. This shortage would hinder future operations, the Agent pointed out. Klaener knew that Fisher did not lack funds, for the Verein had supplied $11,000 for these purchases before his departure from Germany.

Klaener quickly gave Meusebach details of the operations of the Society, the general plan of which Meusebach had been studying carefully all along. After a voyage of eight to ten weeks from Bremen or Antwerp in sailing ships, the emigrants landed at Galveston. From there they were transferred by schooner to Indianola in Matagorda Bay. The name of that port had been changed to Carlshafen by Prince Solms to honor the three men bearing the given name of Carl: Prince Leiningen, who, according to Solms, had been christened Carl, not Victor; Count Castell; and himself. The trip by schooner took from one to three days, sometimes even five, depending on the weather. The accommodations for the immigrants in Carlshafen were tents; a two-room frame building served as headquarters for the officials of the Society. Provisions were sent with each ship so that food would be at hand on the immigrants' arrival in Texas. The supplies brought by the ships were supplemented by meat and corn meal secured in Texas. The plan was that the immigrants would be taken to the settlement by wagons or ox carts immediately after arrival.

Klaener reported that five Bremen brigs, landing in July, November, and December, 1844, had brought a total of 439 persons to Galveston and Carlshafen. On March 21, 1845, about two hundred of the number had reached the place soon to be called New Braunfels. The remainder had followed during the next month. Most of the immigrants had thought it was too late to prepare the soil and sow grain. They had felt no urgency to raise food because the Society had promised provisions until the first crop was harvested, or even until the second crop came in if no harvest was made in the first. Thus Klaener painted the picture with quick strokes. The Agent had many ideas for improvement and many reports of complaints, which, for the most part, were directed against Fisher.

On his arrival in July, 1844, Prince Solms had been welcomed by the citizens of Houston with a salute of twenty-one guns. Since that time, however, his popularity had declined sharply. Klaener, though appointed by Solms, felt that the Prince's attitude had been unrealistic on many points. For example, he had chosen to disembark the immigrants at Carlshafen, which, being located in the uninhabited region of Indian Point, offered only meager accommodations. Meusebach saw that Galveston would have been more advantageous as the disembarkation port for the Agent, as that was Klaener's home; therefore, certain arguments were to be discounted. In the meantime Meusebach made preparations to investigate matters for himself. He wanted to get the facts from the Prince, and, of course, once in New Braunfels, Meusebach expected to present his credentials to the Prince.

So that he might know from firsthand experience just what the immigrants underwent, Meusebach determined to follow the exact route they traveled from Carlshafen to the new settlement. He took a schooner to Carlshafen, where he arrived at twilight on May 8, after a three-day trip. The lantern carried by the local agent of the Society, Ludwig Willke, shed a welcoming light over the beach. Willke greeted Meusebach warmly, but gave warning immediately that rattlesnakes might be crawling about the area. The men entered the poorly constructed headquarters building, where Willke related the events of the last three months. The story of the privations suffered by the immigrants disturbed the new Commissioner-General; of immediate concern, however, were the mosquitoes, which settled so heavily on him that he felt he must go outside to distract the insects. Walking under the Texas stars made him forget, momentarily at least, all but the beauty of the heavens. Yet Meusebach remembered to have mosquito nets sent to Carlshafen to protect future immigrants.[1] Meusebach, interested in the cultivation of every kind of plant life, was pleased that Willke's tobacco plants were thriving. Looking ahead, he hoped for the possibility of marketing the tobacco.

Early the next day, with Willke accompanying him, Meusebach set out on horseback to ride the 165 miles to the settlement, New Braunfels. At the first of the six overnight stops the brand-new Texan had his first typically Texan meal—corn bread and bacon, mainstays of every meal. Novelty gave zest to Meusebach's appetite that first meal, but a year later the German immigrant yearned for a slice of firm rye bread. As the two riders covered the miles the newcomer marveled that so few villages were to be seen. Were there no centers of population on this route?

Willke explained: Prince Solms had deliberately chosen to avoid American settlements; he wanted his people to remain German and not to mingle with Americans. At that moment Meusebach longed for the roads of Germany, paved with stones laid centuries before. His companion explained that wagons were often mired in the morass. The Prince, he said, had plans to lay out a road on which a railroad could be built in the summer of 1845. The railroad was to have live-oak rails, and until locomotives could be brought over, horses were to draw the cars.[2]

Meusebach the naturalist was alert to the kind of country they were traveling and to every geological formation. Leaving the barren waste of the coastland, he was relieved to find better vegetation. Not long thereafter trees became part of the landscape. The live oaks intrigued him. He liked their name; and their "alive" quality compensated for the evergreens—the pines and spruces—of Germany. The cacti and the yucca attracted him,[3] and the fragrant wild flowers were enchanting.

Meusebach wanted to linger at many places. The "flower-spangled"[4]

---

[1] Meusebach, Houston, June 10, 1845, to Bracht. Solms-Braunfels Archives, LI, 162.

[2] "Berichte des Prinzen Karl zu Solms-Braunfels an den Mainzer Adelsverein" (Port Lavaca, December 23, 1844, to Verein), *Kalender der Neu-Braunfelser Zeitung fuer 1916*, p. 45.

[3] Meusebach, Galveston, May 31, 1845, to Castell. SB Archives, LX, 204.

[4] William Kennedy, *Texas: its geography, natural history and topography*, p. 40.

prairies seemed to call to him. William Kennedy, in his book on Texas, used that beautiful phrase. Perhaps he took it from a song that had been widely distributed on broadsides, "The Star-Spangled Banner."

Texas had its own flag, the Lone Star, but after annexation it would be superseded by the flag of the United States. Everyone appeared pleased that the annexation of Texas had been approved in Washington, D.C. The Republic of Texas had existed only ten years. The citizens of the Republic were to vote on the question of annexation soon. No doubt the vote would favor annexation; in Meusebach's opinion that was the proper course. He determined to arrange immediately for naturalization papers and voting privileges.

He was brought harshly back to reality by the presentation of due bills drawn on the Society, which people along the route presented to him when they found that he represented the group. The number of such confrontations grew as the travelers neared the settlement. When Meusebach saw New Braunfels lying before him, he brushed aside the harrassment of the creditors, the minutiae of the moment. Before him lay his new home —and the freedom he was seeking.

Soon the travelers were in the colony, with the settlers gathered around them. As Meusebach heard the native tongue of Germany again, his thoughts returned to the Old World. But a new world was all around him. He had to pierce the frontier, for his countrymen as well as for himself. The Society had a noble idea, one worthy of princes. But the idea alone was not sufficient; it had yet to be directed to fulfillment. With that thought he went to present himself to Prince Solms.

Meusebach walked briskly to what had been pointed out as the headquarters building. He held firmly to his slender briefcase as he greeted the attendant and asked for Prince Solms. To his amazement, he was told that the Prince was gone. The agent of the Society informed the new Commissioner-General that his predecessor was already on his way to Galveston and thence to Germany. The agent then introduced himself as Lieutenant J. Jean von Coll, the treasurer of the settlement. He made apologies for the Prince, saying that he was restless and eager to catch his ship. He could probably be overtaken in Gonzales.

For a moment shadows enveloped Meusebach. He had relied confidently on getting the benefit of the Prince's experience. The bills in his pocket reminded him that he needed all the help he could get. When he asked the agent for an explanation of these bills he was told that the Prince did not require a record of promissory notes because so many different individuals issued them. When Meusebach further questioned the financial situation the Treasurer answered, "The Prince's theory was that no accounting was necessary until all funds were used up."[5]

Meusebach lost no time in handing von Coll the notes that had been thrust upon him. Von Coll said he surmised well enough that the treasury held no balance, yet he was under orders and had to work according to instructions. Meusebach better understood this man's failings as treasurer when he learned that he had been a lieutenant in the service of the Duke of Nassau, the "protector" of the Society. This service had taught the Lieutenant unquestioning adherence to the dictates of his superiors. Whether it qualified him to be a bookkeeper or treasurer was open to question.

Meusebach, trained in business, felt it was urgent to know the state of the finances. He therefore made a quick survey and found the indebtedness to total nearly $20,000. Such a huge debt was a staggering handicap with which to start work. His $10,000 letter of credit reassured him somewhat. Meusebach asked whether the Prince could have foreseen such an indebtedness. The Treasurer felt that he could have if at any time he had added up the disbursements. He confided also that the Prince's provision for daily food was one big expenditure. For example, fresh meat was provided three times daily. The colonists mentioned this fact when they wrote home, because in Germany on many days they had had no meat at all.

What the new Commissioner-General learned about the state of the Society's finances gave him great concern, but he hoped that the Prince could clear certain matters. He decided to hurry back to Galveston in the hope of overtaking Prince Solms. At the end of his 230-mile journey to the port city he found the Prince eager to see him as well. Creditors of the Society had taken out a writ of attachment; Prince Solms was being detained by law. Meusebach, drawing on his letter of credit, lifted the attachment. The Prince expressed gratitude, but he had another favor to ask. He needed more funds to deal with creditors who might overtake him in New Orleans. Meusebach supplied the money; practically all of his $10,000 letter of credit was now used.

Meusebach pressed Solms for an explanation of the colony's finances, but Solms only referred him to the Treasurer. Meusebach countered with what he had already learned from von Coll—that the treasury was empty —and added that his own quick survey showed heavy indebtedness. Prince Solms agreed to take Meusebach's report of the financial needs to the

[5] D'Orvanne, San Antonio, August 22, 1844, to Verein. SB Archives, XLVIIIa, 187.

Verein directors in Germany. He promised to leave any unused funds in New Orleans.

The Prince turned east. He must return to Germany and to Frau Sophia, the widowed Princess of Salm-Salm, née Princess of Lowenstein. Before his departure from the settlement, the Prince had deposited the Princess' picture, with her array of names attached, as the principal item in the cornerstone of Sophienburg, the fortress he was having built in New Braunfels. To make it official he had stamped the picture with his seal and had signed it with his own name, Prinz Karl zu Solms-Braunfels, and added twenty-two names and titles belonging to him.[6]

Meusebach turned his face west. He had much to see about in the colony of New Braunfels; among other things he must find a solution to the financial dilemma into which Prince Solms had plunged the Society. The Prince himself had claimed no knowledge of business. His reaction to financial matters is shown by his report written after ten months in Texas:

I can assure you that the disposition of the funds, the accounting of them, as well as the anxiety that there would still be money to see me through so that I would not suddenly be "on the rocks" with so many people, gave me more fear, distress, and sorrow, and called forth more drops of sweat than the July sun and the Indian tribes of Texas were able to draw from me.[7]

Although Meusebach had sympathy for the Prince, a cavalier, in his lack of business ability, he felt the importance of letting the Verein know immediately how matters stood. His report of June 3, 1845, which Solms had agreed to take with him, began with a frank statement: "I regret to be able to send only bad news. I put urgently the thought into your hearts that the existence of 400 people is threatened unless we quickly get significant funds."[8] The report added that $20,000 was needed to cover existing debts. He did not report the indignity of the attachment for debt that had been put on Prince Solms or the partial use of the letter of credit to extricate the Prince.

Prince Solms took this report to the executive headquarters in Germany. He made a report himself to the Verein on July 28, 1845, but probably made no mention of financial difficulties in the colony. He wrote laconically, "I sailed June 4 for New Orleans after telling my successor orally

---

[6] Robert Penniger (ed., comp.), *Fest-Ausgabe zum fünfzigjährigen Jubiläum der Deutschen Kolonie Friedrichsburg*, pp. 43–44.

[7] "Berichte des Prinzen Karl zu Solms-Braunfels" (Galveston, February 12, 1845, to Verein), *Kalender fuer 1916*, p. 58.

[8] Meusebach, Galveston, June 3, 1845, to Castell. SB Archives, XXX, 163.

and in writing the condition and details [of the present, after giving ideas] as well, in regard to the future."[9]

Castell received encouragement from Meusebach's reporting that the large sums named earlier by the Prince were not needed. Meusebach thought he was justified in reducing Prince Solm's requests, since the latter was accustomed to extravagant expenditures. Meusebach had added three definite stipulations to his first report: (1) that debts be paid, (2) that the situation be looked at realistically, and (3) that funds available be taken into account.[10] These ideas were enlarged in Meusebach's report mailed from Houston just seven days after the dispatch was sent along with the Prince. Meusebach reviewed the financial plight and recommended that the contract with Fisher and Miller be revised. After only a few days' experience, Meusebach said, "Association with these men can only be pernicious."[11]

This evaluation of Fisher confirmed what Prince Solms had already seen and experienced in various situations. In matters other than financial concerns, Fisher had been a cause of continual irritation to Prince Solms. In a letter written from New Orleans on June 11, 1845, the Prince wrote that he had Fisher to thank for the indignities suffered there. In utter exasperation he declared that Fisher was not worth "the cord it would take to hang him and Miller."[12]

While the new Commissioner-General was still in Houston, he again pondered why the Carlshafen route to the settlement had been chosen over the route via Houston and the established roads. He had learned the answer as he had ridden the lonely road from Carlshafen to the colony: the Prince did not want his people to lose their German characteristics by mixing with other nationalities. This answer confirmed what Meusebach had read in the newspapers while he was still in New York: "German colonists under Prince Solms have no more intercourse with the inhabitants than is absolutely necessary."[13]

[9] Solms's report, Wiesbaden, July 28, 1845, to Verein. SB Archives, XXX, 162.

[10] Meusebach, Galveston, June 3, 1845, to Verein. SB Archives, XXX, 163.

[11] Meusebach, Houston, June 10, 1845, to Verein. SB Archives, XXX, 166.

[12] Solms, New Orleans, June 11, 1845, to Honored Sir [Meusebach], in Franz J. Dohmen (trans.), *Life and Memoirs of Emil Frederick Wurzbach, to which is appended some papers of John Meusebach,* p. 35.

[13] Meusebach, Baltimore, March 21, 1845, to Castell. SB Archives, LI, 52–53.

Echoes of Prince Solms

CHAPTER 10

The new Commissioner-General's first official act in New Braunfels was to post a notice printed in English and signed "John O. Meusebach."[1] This notice directed that only designated officials were empowered to sign drafts and to transact business for the Verein.

As he looked out on the embryonic colony before him Muesebach meditated on his predecessor's accomplishments. He gave the Prince full credit for breaking the barriers that attend a new undertaking.[2] Furthermore, Solms did not shun difficulties, and he was well-intentioned. Castell called him the *grand seigneur*.[3] This cavalier gave himself and his fellow Verein members a full share of glory, as is revealed in his report of February, 1845:

The eyes of all Germany, no, the eyes of all Europe are fixed on us and our undertaking: German princes, counts, and noblemen stand at the head, and no doubt can remember the historical glory of their ancestors and bring new crowns to old glory while they at the same time are ensuring immeasurable riches for their children and grandchildren.[4]

Now that he was back in the colony, Meusebach thought about ways to integrate the Germans and the Americans. Prince Solm's idea of establishing the settlement as an isolated island, with little or no communication with Americans, was not in line with the thinking of his successor. An interchange of ideas would certainly be helpful; Meusebach hoped to make

---

[1] Official notice signed "John O. Meusebach." Solms-Braunfels Archives, LI, 100a.
[2] Meusebach, New Braunfels, September 8, 1845, to Castell. SB Archives, LI, 170.
[3] Castell's report, n.pl., 1845, to Verein. SB Archives, LIV, 92.
[4] "Berichte des Prinzen Karl zu Solms-Braunfels an den Mainzer Adelsverein" (Galveston, February 8, 1845, to Verein), *Kalender der Neu-Braunfelser Zeitung fuer 1916*, p. 57.

friends with the Americans at once and to be counted as one of them. The difference in language formed a barrier, of course, but Meusebach knew English and was improving his command of the language each day. Meusebach believed in love of country, but his patriotism was not so extreme as that evidenced by either Bourgeois d'Orvanne or Prince Solms in their conversation. When the Frenchman said disdainfully, "Pah, nationality, that is only a word," the Prince answered, "Yes, for you perhaps, but not for me nor for the Verein."[5]

Meusebach's attempt to integrate the two nationalities took the form of an invitation to the Americans to settle in the Verein's colony in Texas. Baron von Ehrenkreuz, a writer on emigration, protested Meusebach's policy. Ehrenkreuz maintained that upon the execution of Meusebach's ideas,

" . . . the colony will cease to be a national German settlement . . . It is my opinion . . . that if the attention of the German emigrant is drawn in every way, and more than heretofore, to Texas, that state will within ten years be overwhelmingly German and thus must become a true colony of Germany as a whole . . . and remain permanently connected with the Fatherland, with mutual interests binding the one to the other."[6]

Another writer on emigration, Traugott Bromme, took a different view when he said, " 'The settlement itself can never bring any direct consequences for Germany, now that Texas is a state of the Union, standing on the same basis as all the other states'." He added, " 'I am extremely pleased that [Meusebach] has opened the western part of [the] grant to Americans, as they are more suited to such a remote settlement than are our Germans'."[7]

Meusebach did not hesitate to express his antagonism to Solms's scheme of forming a feudal state in Texas. He revealed his sentiments to Nicolaus Zink, the Verein's engineer. Zink informed him that the Prince had exchanged letters with the English ambassador about a German occupation of the country. This seizure was to be accomplished by throwing a mass of German immigrants, unnoticed by the authorities, into the country and placing them in fortresses on commanding heights.[8] The Prince prob-

[5] "Berichte des Prinzen Karl zu Solms-Braunfels" (San Antonio, August 20, 1844, to Verein), *ibid.*, p. 21.

[6] Ehrenkreuz is quoted in John A. Hawgood, *The Tragedy of German-America*, p. 166.

[7] Bromme is quoted, *ibid.*, p. 167.

[8] Meusebach, New Braunfels, September 8, 1845, to Castell. SB Archives, LI, 171.

ably considered that arrangement as the beginning of a German state, which would hold back the "Yankees, that go-ahead nation" and would facilitate Germany's commercial access to the Gulf of Mexico. Certain Englishmen also believed that a German state adjacent to Mexico would restrain the power of the growing United States. Prince Solms wrote to Anson Jones, Secretary of State of the Republic of Texas, that the Society preferred to see Texas remain independent.[9] In a second letter to the Secretary, in December, 1844, the Prince offered to confer with Santa Anna and to promote the sovereignty of Texas.[10]

Such ideas were a detriment to the Society and, had they become generally known, would have compromised its standing. Prince Solms declared that Santa Anna was striving for peace and that he intended to wear the imperial crown again. The vice-presidency of Mexico was offered to Prince Solms, who no doubt was tempted to accept. Had this fact become public, matters would have become even more complicated.

Evidence is lacking that the Verein was given any form of official support by the British government. There are, however, indications that the British government knew what the Verein was doing and kept informed about the group's intentions, since the foreign policy of Britain opposed the annexation of Texas by the United States. Prince Solms appealed to William Kennedy, the British representative of the Republic, to support his ideas against annexation.[11] John A. Hawgood in *The Tragedy of German-America* notes that "the overtures of which we have any knowledge all came from one side and that was not from the side of the British government. Solms . . . might have offered the tempting fruit, but there is no proof that even the smallest bite was taken from it."[12]

An allegation sometimes made is that British interests were connected with the founding of the *Adelsverein*. Since both Great Britain and Prince Solms desired to prevent annexation, the rumor naturally arose that "British Gold" was back of the Verein. August Siemering, a journalist, made such a statement in a manuscript, fragments of which were published serially in the weekly magazine *Texas Vorwaerts* in 1894. A direct answer to this allegation was given by W. N. Rosenberg in his *Kritik:* "The official documents to be found in the State Archives, prove that the English

---

[9] Anson Jones, *Memoranda and official correspondence relating to the republic of Texas, its history, and annexation*, p. 392.

[10] *Ibid.*, p. 407.

[11] Hawgood, *Tragedy of German-America*, pp. 176–178.

[12] *Ibid.*, pp. 182–183.

government never gave out money to bring German immigrants to Texas."[13]

Reports on Prince Solms came from many sources. A. H. Sörgel in his book *Latest News Out of Texas* related that the Prince once refused to partake of a meal set for three guests at an inn; he chose to dine in state, alone. As a mark of honor the wife of the innkeeper arranged the table a second time, including a place for herself. The Prince declined that arrangement also. The innkeeper, instead of throwing the Prince out the door, added to his bill.[14] This the Prince interpreted as American inhospitality.

Prince Solms had spent a night at the residence of Sam Maverick in Decrow's Point. Maverick reported that laughter could be heard roundabout when a valet was seen helping the Prince draw on his tight-fitting breeches.[15] That evening the Prince's band of musicians played for the Mavericks. One of the instruments was a guitar which the Prince was taking to his Lady Sophia. The old codger who sold the guitar raised the price considerably but excused himself with the remark, "You won't mind paying a little extra if it's going to a princess."[16]

Prince Solms did not fail in his attentions to his betrothed. Even on the uninhabited prairie land of Texas he wished to celebrate the birthday of Princess Sophia—and to do it worthily. As a salute to the Princess he ordered twenty-one shots from his cannon. To distribute largesse was his way of showing good will on this auspicious day. No persons were at hand except the followers of Henry Castro, the Alsatian colonizer; so those immigrants were the enthusiastic recipients of the gift money. Castro, on hearing their jubilant hurrahs, became so incensed that he immediately wrote a letter to the officials at Washington-on-the-Brazos, in which he accused the Society of seducing the immigrants with money and enticing them away from him. Alexander Bourgeois, who was escorting Solms to the Bourgeiis Grant, hurriedly dispatched an explanation to Anson Jones.

Salvos of cannon shots were fired to mark the laying of the cornerstone of the fort Sophienburg. Prince Solms raised the black-and-yellow flag of Austria, as if, said Fisher, to raise a "government within a government."[17]

---

[13] W. von Rosenberg, *Kritik der Geschichte des Vereins zum Schutze der Deutschen Auswanderer nach Texas*, p. 31.

[14] Alwin H. Sörgel, *Neueste Nachrichten aus Texas. Zugleich ein Hülferuf an den Mainzer Verein zum Schutze deutscher Einwanderer in Texas*, p. 37.

[15] Sam Maverick, Reminiscences. TS. Maverick Papers.

[16] Charles Elliot, Houston, March 15, 1843, to My dear Count. SB Archives, I, 51.

[17] Fisher, Washington-on-the-Brazos, December 28, 1844, to Castell. SB Archives, LIX, 96.

The Prince at the time was an officer in the Austrian army. To counter this breach of courtesy to the country where he was presently a guest, the settlers assembled in the market place and on an improvised flagstaff raised the flag of the Republic of Texas.

When Meusebach, on his arrival at Carlshafen, had noted that the Verein official was called a commandant, he had thought that the title was out of place, and that the existence of breastworks was certainly inappropriate. From the beginning Meusebach had seen that the military company, wearing hats bedecked with a cockade of rooster feathers, gauntlet gloves, and long clanking sabers, was the laughingstock of the Americans as well as of the immigrants. The company really formed a bodyguard for its captain, von Coll, who resigned when Meusebach changed the military company into a work battalion.

Since the Prince had favored a military organization, a number of officers were in the settlement when Meusebach arrived. Various reasons had brought them: members of the Verein had recommended some, either to repay a favor or to get rid of an undesirable individual. Others were no longer welcome in their native land, as was the case with Lieutenant Leopold von Iwonski, who was described as the "expelled Prussian."

Meusebach wrote Castell that in the free land of America no standing military organization was needed; hence the sending of officers was superfluous. He mentioned that the Prince was surrounded by a suite, or staff—something out of place in rugged Texas. When the Prince, who was now in Germany, read the report about his "suite" he was indignant. He filed a protest and required as an "act of justice" that the directors of the Verein reprimand Meusebach. If his request was not carried out, he declared, he would have to publicize the matter. He asked for a written acknowledgment of his request and for an answer to be given by return mail.[18] There is no record of a reprimand's having been pronounced by the directors of the Verein. Instead Castell advised Meusebach from Germany that it was important that he not antagonize Americans as the Prince had done. He wrote also to the President of the Republic of Texas with the hope of putting the Society in the proper light.[19]

As the thirty-three–year–old official looked about the settlement he realized that his need was not for military personnel but for men experienced in business and for a trained secretary. The lack of adequate funds and the designs of Fisher hindered the success of the undertaking. Fulfilling the promise of acreage for the settlers depended on the availability of land in

[18] Solms, Montpellier, February 19, 1846, to Castell. SB Archives, XLIII, 48.
[19] Castell, Mainz, April 19, 1845, to Meusebach. SB Archives, LI, 46.

the Grant. Meusebach hoped that in future dealings with Fisher he might show the advantages of cooperation.

The financial muddle posed the greater obstacle. The embarrassment that Meusebach had felt in Galveston over the legal attachment on the Prince still rankled him. If the hand of the law had been put on the leader of the Society for debts, was the treasury really nonexistent? In conversation with Castell before leaving Germany Meusebach had pointed out how imminent insolvency was; now it was Meusebach's own responsibility to rectify matters, although Castell had written him, "After [Solm's return to Germany,] we must get busy getting money so that the undertaking doesn't go on the rocks."[20]

To bring order into the accounting Meusebach set up a system of bookkeeping. His university training in finance was the basis of the system; at a later time von Coll said that Meusebach dwelt in a "world of ideas and ideals."[21] Meusebach realized, however, that the Treasurer, recently on the staff of a duchy's army, much preferred the military field to books and figures. Prince Solms had allowed von Coll to put the treasury aside while he drilled the peasant lads of the colony.[22]

To have found debts and no money was disheartening enough, but more disheartening was the extent of bookkeeping that was necessary because no records had been kept of the hundreds of promissory notes.[23] After careful study Meusebach asked himself, Can this organization, the Verein, really continue to function? The easy answer for himself would have been to resign, but for the sake of the immigrants the business must be upheld.

As Meusebach meditated on the precarious situation he realized that he must bear the burden alone. He resolved to keep the state of the finances to himself; if his associates even suspected how near the Society was to insolvency he feared they could not conceal their uneasiness.[24] And if the public suspected there would be panic. At that moment the public relied little on promises, as evidenced by the pressure exerted by the creditors every day. Gradually, confidence was restored by sound business methods and by careful management. Holding the creditors' confidence, however, was a difficult task. Although the treasury was empty, Meusebach knew he must speak about money matters with assurance. Only by such methods was credit renewed. Had Meusebach not accomplished this task the daily

---

[20] Castell, Mainz, May 19, 1845, to Meusebach. SB Archives, LI, 41.
[21] Meusebach, Galveston, January 20, 1846, to Castell. SB Archives, LII, 74.
[22] *Ibid.*, p. 76.
[23] John O. Meusebach, *Answer to Interrogatories*, p. 14.
[24] *Ibid.*, p. 19.

Ink drawing by Elizabeth von Hardenberg on wooden cover of notebook which she sent to Meusebach, depicting her impression of life in Texas and Germany, 1845.

From Meusebach's journal, a copy in his hand of lines from Goethe's *Faust*, including his favorite "Stand on free soil among a people free."

Otfried Hans Freiherr von Meusebach, 1832. Pencil sketch. Sketches of shells
later added by Otfried's family in recognition of his proclivity as naturalist.

Carl Hartwig Gregor Frhrr. von Meusebach,
vulgo: Der Malte.

Carl Hartwig Gregor Freiherr von Meusebach, 1846. Pencil sketch by Hermann
Grimm.

Meusebach Family Files

Official residence of the judge of the Court of Appeals in Dillenburg. Above door is the Meusebach coat

Meusebach family estate in Thuringia. Pencil sketch.

Anteilschein des Vereins zum Schutze deutscher Einwanderer in Texas
Steindruck von F. Klimsch um 1844

A typical advertisement of an immigration company, 1844. Originally published in Hermann von Freeden and Georg Smolka, *Auswanderer* (Leipzig, 1937).

Prince Carl of Solms-Braunfels in military dress. Reproduction of oil portrait in Braunfels, Lahn, Germany, presented to Sophienburg Museum, New Braunfels, by the family of H. V. Dittlinger.

Treaty of Peace by John O. Meusebach and Colonists with the Comanche Indians, March 2, 1847. A copy of the oil painting by Lucy Meusebach Marschall, daughter of John O. Meusebach, in Pioneer Memorial Library, Fredericksburg

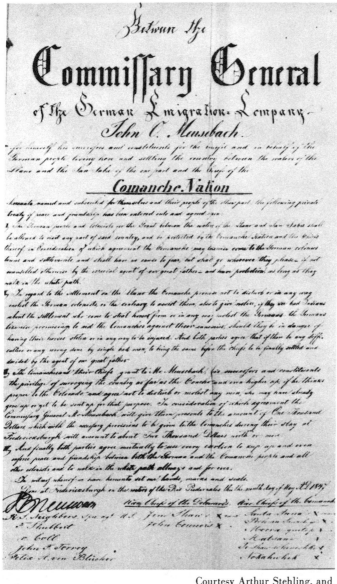

English version of the peace treaty between John O. Meusebach
and the Comanche Indians, signed on May 9, 1847. Original in
Fürst zu Solms-Braunfels'sches Archiv, Braunfels, Lahn, Germany.

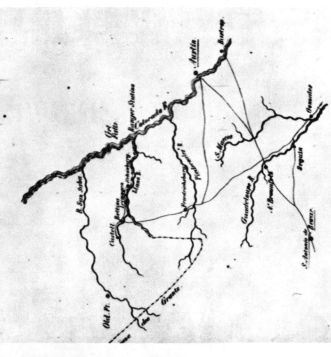

Enchanted Rock, a solid granite boulder covering 640 acres in Llano County.

Early drawing of Verein settlements within the Fisher-Miller Grant. Of the four colonies, established in 1847, Castell, later moved to the south bank of the Llano, is the only town in existence today. Original in Fürst zu Solms-Braunfels'sches Archiv, Braunfels, Lahn, Germany.

Courtesy Kilman Studio, Fredericksburg

Two-wheel ox cart, typical of the kind used to transport early colonists from the coast to the settlements.

Vereins Kirche, the octagonal church in Fredericksburg. Detail from pencil
sketch by Seth Eastman, 1849. From *A Seth Eastman Sketchbook, 1848–1849*
(Published for the McNay Art Institute by the University of Texas Press).

The Nimitz Hotel in Fredericksburg. First structure erected by Charles H.
Nimitz replaced in 1855 by two-story building of lumber and adobe resembling
a steamboat. Preserved as a historical museum. From a postcard printed by
Fredericksburg Publishing Co., Texas.

Courtesy Arthur H. Kowert of
the *Fredericksburg Standard*

The Peter Tatsch home in Fredericksburg, built of native stone in the typical
German architectural style of 1850's. Copy of design and dimensions preserved
in Library of Congress, Washington, D.C.

Courtesy George Pechacek,
Llano, Texas

Ruins of "roman" bathtub and water reservoir, which Meusebach built in 1875
at Loyal Valley.

Agnes Coreth Meusebach, wife of John O. Meusebach, 1875.

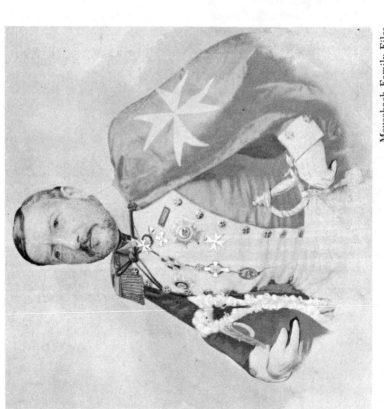

Carl Bernard Freiherr von Meusebach, brother of John O. Meusebach, 1851. German consul general to Bucharest.

John O. Meusebach, 1887.

Courtesy George Pechacek,
Llano, Texas

Historical marker commemorating the signing of the
treaty between the colonists and the Comanche Indians.
In roadside park thirteen miles north of Fredericksburg on Highway 87. Erected by the Gillespie County

Courtesy Arthur H. Kowert of
the *Fredericksburg Standard*

Memorial to John O. Meusebach in front of Pioneer
Memorial Library, Fredericksburg. Monument de-
signed by Louis C. Page, of Austin. Bronze bust executed by Charlotte August Tremper, of New York

sustenance for the 439 people in the colony would not have been delivered. The Society had promised maintenance until a crop was harvested, but they had thought that the immigrants would plant a garden immediately upon arrival. As a result of untoward circumstances—the immigrants arrived in New Braunfels too late to start a garden, and garden tools were not always available—food had to be brought in. To secure sufficient food in a sparsely settled land took planning, then arrangement for storage.

Making provision for adequate shelter was a second requirement. Fisher's estimate of $24 as the cost of a house was obviously far too low, because in Texas the minimum cost of a house or cabin was found to be $100. The promises of the Verein had to be kept; therefore, the organization suffered a loss of $76 on each house. Fisher's estimates, in every case, had been designed to persuade the members of the Verein that their capital of $80,000 was adequate to supply all the needs of the undertaking.

The Society also had promised to advance each settler the material for cultivating and fencing fifteen acres, as well as the necessary oxen, cows, and horses to start a farm. These items were difficult to obtain in a frontier land; so a period of waiting was required of the settler. Although such delays often brought Meusebach close to despair, he received encouragement from many of the colonists who manifested sympathetic understanding of the conditions or expressed gratitude for the new life which was being opened for them. He thus was able to face the task with fortitude.

The Commissioner-General strove constantly to build the morale of the colonists by trying to answer their questions and to assuage their misgivings. Many colonists were severely disappointed at not being located where their promised 320 acres lay. Some accepted their town lot and ten-acre plot with great reluctance, although the Society specified that these land provisions were not to take the place of the 320-acre tracts described in the immigration agreements.

With perseverance Meusebach was able to conclude a financial report covering Prince Solms's term of office and to dispatch it to Germany on August 7, 1845. He worked five days and five nights on the report, since only at night could he escape interruptions. He found that the debts of the Society at the time of the Prince's departure came to the staggering amount of $19,460.02. Not only was the original principal of the Society, $80,000, used up, but now a sum close to $20,000 stood as a debt. And the colonization project had barely begun!

Prince Solms had left New Braunfels in May. There was no end to the expense in the colony; expenditures for provisions had to be made every single day. These amounts added to the standing debt brought the total indebtedness to $24,000 by the time Meusebach sent in his itemized report in August. His letter of credit had been largely used up to rescue the Prince in his dilemma upon departure. Meusebach relied on the Prince's promise to report the financial needs to the Society and to see that remittances were sent to Texas without delay.

The headquarters where the reports were calculated was only a makeshift log structure. The wind whipped through the cracks, frequently scattering the papers. When engineer Zink was asked to improve the structure, he replied that all of his helpers were busy fencing in their plots, while he was concerned with surveying. Meusebach's residence was a log house, the only furnishings being two rough tables and a sofa.[25] In view of the frequent mention of Sophienburg, Meusebach had expected to see something memorable. What he actually saw atop the little hill was a cornerstone with a furrow drawn to indicate the dimensions of the structure; not a stone or a single log was at hand for building.[26]

The settlers enjoyed lighter moments in the course of daily living. Hermann Seele, who became the teacher for the first German-English school, which opened on August 11, 1845, gives this word picture of the colonists' adaptation to circumstances as they arose:

The swollen Guadalupe prevented crossing, so the possessions of the colonists were piled high, watched over by soldiers of the Verein. They wore long riding boots, grey blouses, black velvet collars decorated with brass buttons, broadbrimmed hats trimmed with black feathers, tilted back on their heads, swords buckled on. Armed with rifles, they made a good impression and called forth a feeling of security; one felt that he was no longer dependent wholly on himself.

The transfer of baggage across the Guadalupe in leaky boats took several days and several men were needed on each side. The guarding soldiers changed posts frequently, so that often there were several people in the unsteady vehicles.

On the occasion of the transfer of a barrel of sherry, halfway across the Guadalupe, the men pulling the ferryboat noticed the wine spilling and stopped the boat mid-stream until their thirst was slacked. Shouts from either side had little effect. When at last the boat and cargo reached the far side of the river, the remainder of the wine was quickly disposed of. The question of further work that day was not raised.[27]

The Prince's predilection for things military was manifest in the com-

25 Meusebach, New Braunfels, September 8, 1845, to Verein. SB Archives, LI, 134.
26 Meusebach, Galveston, January 20, 1846, to Castell. SB Archives, LII, 65.
27 Hermann Seele, "Meine Ankunft in Neu-Braunfels," *Kalender der Neu-Braunfelser Zeitung fuer 1914*, p. 36.

pleted stockade, a palisade of logs. Close at hand were the two outmoded cannons, which Solms had brought from the Braunfels principality in Germany. The firing of the cannons night and morning perhaps had kept most of the Indian tribes at a distance from the settlement. The Waco tribe, however, had evidenced friendliness. To strengthen that relationship Meusebach decided to pay the Indians a formal call. The chief greeted the stately man in a noncommittal manner, but the squaws and children looked with wonder at the flowing beard of the white man. When he took off his hat and the rays of the setting sun burnished his hair and beard the squaws were astonished even more.

The Indian chief indicated that he desired a second meeting the next day under a widespread pecan tree near a bend of the Comal River. At the appointed time Meusebach appeared, walking a little ahead of his own delegation. Swift as an arrow twenty squaws sprang from the bushes, caught the white chief quite unceremoniously, held his hair and beard to the water's edge, and rubbed them vigorously in the crystal-clear water. When they had convinced themselves that the reddish-gold color would not wash off they disappeared into the woods like wild deer. This encounter was finished quickly, and Meusebach remained calm throughout. The conference proceeded as planned. Soon Meusebach and the Indian chief were smoking the peace pipe.

The Waco Indians remained the steadfast friends of the Germans. They named Meusebach "Ma-be-quo-si-to-mu," "Chief with the burning hair of the head."[28]

A few tribes were friendly toward the white people, as the story of the Waco Indians' relationship with Meusebach illustrates. But on the whole, white men always had to be wary of the Indians, for their lives could be at stake in dealing with them. The true picture of the Indians was unlike those presented in the advertisements of the Verein, in which the Indians were shown only in charming, friendly colors. "What fraud!" said Alwin Sörgel in his book of advice to immigrants.[29] Count Castell had not mentioned the word "Indian" to Meusebach during their conference in Mainz. It is likely that Fisher had carefully avoided bringing the Indians to the attention of the Verein when he was negotiating the sale of his land in 1844. While Meusebach was still in Germany the Count had said that the Society was making plans to send a contingent of emigrants late in 1845.

---

[28] Anonymous, "Der Häuptling mit dem brennenden Haupthaar," *Kalender der Neu-Braunfelser Zeitung fuer 1905*, pp. 59–60.

[29] Sörgel, *Für auswanderungslustige: Briefe eines unter dem schutze des Mainzer vereins nach Texas ausgewanderten*, p. 2.

No confirmation of this plan had come, but Meusebach felt that his primary responsibility was to get to the Fisher-Miller Grant, the land under the control of the Society. The acreage which the Society had contracted to give each colonist lay within the boundary of the Grant. The prospect and promise of that land had brought most of the immigrants to Texas. Nothing should stand in the way of the colonists' reaching and having their promised land. That was Meusebach's deep conviction.

But something *did* stand in the way. The most formidable obstacle was the Comanche Indians. The mere word "Indians" struck people with horror; to say "Comanche" doubled the horror. The word "Comanche" comes from the Ute and means "enemy." The designation for "Comanche" in the sign language is a backward, wriggling motion of the index finger, signifying a snake, which connotes stealth. The Comanches came to be associated with the ideas of wildness, fierceness, and savagery. And it was their territory which lay athwart the Fisher-Miller Grant. This was their heartland, their hunting ground, theirs by right of possession; for 150 years they had dominated all other Indian tribes in the plains area, and for 50 years they had been able to stop the advance of the Spanish from the south, the French and Americans from the east.

The Frontier

CHAPTER 11

The Comanches had checked the forward march of American colonists in Texas. The Indians had been in undisputed possession of the area encompassed by the Fisher-Miller Grant since the Spaniards had withdrawn from the Presidio of San Saba about 1770, after having contested the Comanches some thirteen years. According to legend, the Spaniards had left behind valuable silver mines. But the story of the wanton slaughter of the people of the Mission Santa Cruz de San Sabá by the Comanches and their allies in 1757 held other would-be settlers at bay.[1] Meusebach hoped that he would be able to break that barrier, although the Anglo-Americans were said to be intolerant of the Indians. If his people, lately Germans but now Texans, were to live in the Comanche territory, an accord must be reached.

Henry Francis Fisher was one American who had made it appear, albeit only on paper, that the Indians had not deterred him. Facts soon proved otherwise. As agent for the San Saba Colonization Company, whose land was encompassed by the Fisher-Miller Grant, he had issued statements that he would explore the San Saba River country. He had canceled the plan on May 13, 1843, because, he said, " 'the government was negotiating for amity with the Indians. The presence of an exploring party might frustrate the objective of the government and perhaps endanger the lives of the commissioners'."[2]

Having just issued the statement about the danger of the Indians, Fisher had good reason to know that his land could not be occupied by the colonists of the Verein. Despite his recognition of this danger, he consum-

[1] Robert S. Weddle, *The San Sabá Mission: Spanish Pivot in Texas*, pp. 178–181, 198, 201–209.
[2] *Telegraph and Texas Register*, May 24, 1843, p. 3, col. 2 is quoted in Rudolph Leopold Biesele, *The History of the German Settlements in Texas 1831–1861*, p. 78.

mated in 1844 the sale of his land, which not only included the San Saba River territory but extended far beyond. The Grant consisted of 3,878,000 acres lying between the south bank of the Colorado and the north bank of the Llano. It began at the confluence of the two rivers and spread to the vicinity of the Pecos River on the west. When the Society obtained the area for colonization Fisher did not tell them of the danger of the Indians or of the isolation of the land. The Society accepted without question Fisher's description of the area and did not see fit to have the land inspected before purchasing the rights to it. The unfortunate results of failing to inspect in advance the Bourgeois Grant seemingly had taught the Society no lesson.

No doubt the idea of a "grant" intrigued these guileless noblemen, who were inexperienced in business matters and who allowed the promise of things to come to outweigh the immediate and the practical. They sat at ease in their inherited castles, far removed from daily responsibilities. Prince Solms in Texas, as impractical as his fellow Verein members, was disillusioned, nevertheless, with the giving of land grants:

> What, after all, are all grants, one just like the other—nothing but a farce, a bad joke; they might even be called a deception, whereby one could deceive others.
>
> The government gives out an enormous amount of land, by which the recipients get, under troublesome stipulations, much poor and little good land, all located at a great distance.[3]

Prince Solms, though, was attracted by the storied San Saba mines in the Fisher-Miller region, which early came to his attention. In fact, a Mexican offered to guide him to the "rich mines."[4] Solms immediately suggested to the Verein that miners be sent to the colony, and the sooner the better. The possible wealth to be found fascinated the Prince, but did not induce him to face the Indians in the area of the rumored mines.

After his arrival Meusebach felt that personal inspection of the Grant was of primary importance. A restlessness stirred among the colonists because they had not come into possession of the land which was to be theirs permanently. Only the most industrious were making good use of the ten-acre plots assigned them until they could reach their tracts lying in the Grant. Meusebach was determined to spare no effort to put the colonists in possession of their land.

[3] "Berichte des Prinzen Karl zu Solms-Braunfels an den Mainzer Adelsverein" (San Antonio, August 20, 1844, to Verein), *Kalender der Neu Braunfelser Zeitung fuer 1916*, p. 24.

[4] *Ibid.*, p. 33.

Before he could absent himself from the colony, however, he must endeavor to make the settlement stand on its own feet.[5] Prince Solms had ingratiated himself with the colonists by approving a credit system. With supplies thus available the settlers relied on the Verein to fill their needs. Now in an attempt to make the immigrants self-sustaining, Meusebach sought out labor assignments for them. Making preparations for the transportation and reception of more than a hundred new immigrants arriving at Indian Point during the late summer furnished some employment opportunities. The transfer was accomplished in such a fast and orderly fashion that it was described by officials as exemplary.

Careful management had inspired creditors to continue furnishing supplies; but after three months passed without the arrival of money, Meusebach was at a loss as to where to turn. His impulse was to resign his post, but he reasoned that the Society's contract with the immigrants must be kept, regardless of personal disadvantage. He turned to the work before him and waited expectantly for the next mail from Germany. When no financial help had been received by September 8, Meusebach wrote, "There is exactly zero [and he drew a "0"] in the Treasury." In fact, money was so scarce that a collection had to be taken among the officials to pay messengers to take out letters.[6]

In the face of this financial crisis, another problem of equal importance weighed upon him. Where was he to settle the immigrants that Castell planned to send later? The logical answer was to make the settlement on the land purchased for that purpose, the Fisher-Miller Grant. Meusebach decided to make an inspection tour of that land without further delay. He had recognized from the beginning the necessity of this inspection, but the urgencies of each day had deterred him. Fisher could certainly be expected to go as guide to the land he had sold the Germans. At Meusebach's urging Fisher started with him, but did not venture beyond Twin Sisters Creek, sixty miles northwest of New Braunfels.[7] Meusebach continued with a few companions, using his compass to advantage. He pierced the wilderness far enough to know the nature of the territory and to see the imminence of the Indians. He reported that nomadic, unfriendly Indians were found within the Grant.[8] He found the distance from New Braunfels to the nearest boundary of the Grant to approximate 150 miles. The inter-

[5] Meusebach, Galveston, January 20, 1846, to Castell. Solms-Braunfels Archives, LII, 105, 109.

[6] *Ibid.*, p. 50.

[7] Meusebach, Fredericksburg, January 19, 1847, to Castell. SB Archives, LXIII, 44.

[8] Meusebach, Galveston, January 20, 1846, to Castell. SB Archives, LII, 60.

vening country was entirely uninhabited by white people. Although the distance to the Grant and the isolation of it made a settlement there impractical for the time being, Meusebach did not abandon the idea of settling within the boundaries; he definitely planned to accomplish such a colonization.

On their return the little exploring party camped on the Pedernales River and lived on nature's bounty. Nearby they shot a bear literally enveloped in fat,[9] and buffalo stragglers from the herd. The buffalo were not fat and the meat was poor, but the bear-rib steaks, broiled over coals were delicious. Soft-shelled turtles caught in the pools of the river and honey from bee trees enriched the meal.

Meusebach's interest was aroused by this region. He took careful notes on the geological formations and on the petrifactions and stated that he wanted to examine everything in detail when time was not limited. Beyond the Pedernales region he saw mineral-bearing hills and mountains, which he longed to explore. Enchanted Rock was within a short distance, but he could not get to it because the horses were exhausted. That section composed the granite formation; nearer at hand was the limestone outcropping, which he viewed as a source of material for future dwellings. The countryside was covered with abundant pasture grasses, with deep humus underneath, which would produce excellent farm products. Meusebach visualized sugar, indigo, and tobacco crops, noting that the climate was favorable for fruit growing and for horticultural experiments. The native grapes could be used as rootstock for improved varieties. Meusebach's father had previously sent cuttings to be used for grafting.[10]

Meusebach made a point of stating that slaves were not needed for agricultural success. "But," he added, "the slow Germans must take the caps off their eyes and ears; otherwise the ever-wakeful Americans will reap the benefits."[11] With farseeing vision this man pictured commerce with Mexico extending to the Pacific Ocean; he thought that even a railroad was conceivable.

Experiences on his trip convinced this explorer that a way station to the Grant had to be selected. This Pedernales area, halfway to the desired goal, gave promise of being a fortunate location. It offered the advantages of water, good soil, and wooded areas.

On a hill within sight of the Pedernales River, Meusebach halted his

[9] *Ibid.*, p. 122.

[10] H. Lettorff, Berlin, July 13, 1846, to unidentified recipient. SB Archives, XVI, 287.

[11] Meusebach, Galveston, January 20, 1846, to Castell. SB Archives, LII, 119.

white horse to survey the land. It was a beautiful valley, with grass knee
high and fine trees in abundance, especially along the river. As he came to
the water's edge, he found a large pool, in which fish and soft-shelled
turtles abounded. A short distance downstream the water cut through
high banks to a ten-foot-high waterfall, which spread into a crystal-clear
basin.[12] At one point the river was one hundred feet wide. Grapevines
festooned high in the trees reminded Meusebach of Sealsfield's book, *Life
in the New World*, from which he had read to his father with such wonder-
ment and eagerness. He was now in Texas, the place so idyllically pictured
by Sealsfield. The idyllic features he could see, but he could not take time
to enjoy them, because responsibiiities held him like a vise. Not for a
moment since his arrival in Texas had he been free from heavy responsibility. He did not allow himself time for writing personal letters, though
thoughts of home filled his heart.

Encouraged by the sweep of his thoughts, that autumn day in 1845 he
chose the exact site for the depot-settlement. He selected the area between
two flowing creeks. The land drained to the Pedernales River, five miles
distant. Meusebach had desired a site by that river, but ten thousand acres
would be needed to settle a colony, and the land, being privately owned,
was not for sale in that quantity.

The business transaction involved buying headrights in the desired
amount. With no funds available, the purchase had to be made on credit.
The plan for the depot-settlement was to be similar to that used in New
Braunfels—a town lot, one-half acre in size, and a ten-acre plot for each
family. This allotment was in addition to the tracts promised within the
Grant. Residence on the small tracts was to be temporary; the Grant was
to be occupied as soon as it was made safe from the Indians.

The possibility of developing a thriving community—perhaps even a
city—was inherent in the plans. The future city must have a worthy name.
Meusebach thought of Prinz Friedrich of Prussia, who had evidenced true
interest in the colonization program when Meusebach had consulted with
him in Berlin. Furthermore, the Prince was the highest ranking nobleman
in the Society. This colony should be named for the Prince—Friedrichsburg.

That valley, encircled by seven hills, had a natural beauty. When the
colonists came to live there, they would preserve nature's gifts and add a
quality which was uniquely their own. Some persons had said that this
section of the country resembled Switzerland, or perhaps the Black Forest

---

[12] *Ibid.*, p. 121.

of Germany. Why could not the handcraft industries of those regions be introduced in this new area? "Picturesque" was the word Meusebach applied to the locality; he added that the romantic mountain parties that could be held there would rival those of Germany.[13] In thinking over his surveying trip to the northwest, Meusebach declared the section he had chosen for the new settlement "the most beautiful part of the entire country."[14] That was the place his people deserved, but plans to make it habitable were necessary.

After Meusebach returned to New Braunfels preparations for receiving the thousands of new immigrants occupied his time almost entirely. But that way station in the Pedernales Valley had to be opened. His first step was to organize a surveying party of thirty-six men under the command of Lieutenant Louis Bene, whom he instructed to lay out a road from New Braunfels to the site of the proposed settlement. The Bene group reached the location late in December, 1845. There they used the tools that had been provided to build a headquarters blockhouse. The surveyors divided the land into plots. On leaving they buried their tools under a spreading live oak so the Indians would have no cause to suspect an attack and so the settlers would have tools at hand. Since supplies necessary for further work could not be replenished in the wilderness, the expedition returned to New Braunfels in February, 1846.

Two months later, on April 23, 1846, under the direction of Lieutenant Bene and accompanied by eight men of the Society's military company, the first immigrant train of twenty wagons and two-wheeled Mexican carts left New Braunfels. The 120 men, women, and children in the train said a poignant farewell. After an arduous trip of sixteen days, they reached Fredericksburg on May 8, 1846.

Near the end of their journey some Indians gave the Germans great fright. The settlers were soon relieved to find that the Indians were making only peaceful overtures, since they were of the friendly Delaware tribe. As the leaders of the caravan neared the Pedernales River one of their number saw a bear and quickly felled him with a ringing shot. Those at the end of the train presumed that the shot was fired against Indians. Said the eleven-year-old daughter of the Heinrich Strackbeins: "Mother, we should have eaten our eggs yesterday instead of saving them to set for chicks in our new home. Who knows now that we'll ever get there?"[15]

---

[13] *Ibid.*

[14] *Ibid.*, p. 123.

[15] Robert Penniger (ed., comp.), *Fest-Ausgabe zum fünfzigjährigen Jubiläum der Deutschen Kolonie Friedrichsburg*, p. 62.

When the long caravan reached its destination in the evening on that May day in 1846, a great fire was built, over which was roasted the bear meat and the meat of a panther that also had been killed on the approach to the Pedernales. The immigrants drew courage from each other as they partook of that communal meal. When the next day dawned, and with it the requirements of starting a life in the wilderness, the test of courage came.

Soon after the immigrant train had left New Braunfels, Governor J. Pinckney Henderson sent the authorities this message:

I am led to believe that the Mexican Government will add to its invasion of the soil of Texas an attempt at formenting the hostility of the Indians on our frontier . . . I would suggest the prudence of abstaining from a movement in that direction untill time schall prove that it can be made without a reckless exposure of human life.—I do this . . . because circumstances may render it impossible to afford the military protection which was intended to be given to the expedition on the part of the state.[16]

The New Braunfels colonists hurried the messenger on to Fredericksburg. They expected their fellow Germans to return. Not one did so. Three days later the colonists again spurned the opportunity to return to New Braunfels with the teamsters and the Society's soldiers.

Esther Mueller, a resident of Fredericksburg, gives the following account of the colonization in her paper, "How Fredericksburg Came To Be":

Once the German emigrants had arrived, the region between the town creeks resounded with axe blows on oak trees, as they set up temporary homes with brush shelters and tents of linen sheets.

A commissary and a wooden stockade were built at the Adelsverein head-quarters and became the business center.

In June a second wagon train arrived. Others followed in quick succession. In July the surveyors were giving out town lots, and numerous log cabins appeared along Ufer Strasse and Haupt Strasse. By the end of 1846 five hundred emigrants had reached Fredericksburg. In the fall an epidemic of fever and dysentery swept the colony and many settlers died. Ninety-four found resting places in the *friedhof* [cemetery].[17]

Meusebach had selected the site and made the plans for the founding of Fredericksburg. He was responsible for the lives of thousands of immi-

[16] J. Pinckney Henderson, Austin, May 2, 1846, to authorities in New Braunfels. SB Archives, XXVIII, 29.

[17] Esther Mueller, "How Fredericksburg Came To Be," *The Edwards Plateau Historian*, I (1965), 1–5.

grants—at Indian Point, New Braunfels, and now Fredericksburg. He was bound by responsibilities, as evidenced in a letter to Count Castell: "I rode up and down the Colorado and farther into the country in order to arrange for an uninterrupted flow of wagons. But always money is short. Everything that was still possible to assemble I directed to New Brannfels, in order finally to start the second expedition to Fredericksburg under the leadership of the Col. Director Dr. Schubbert."[18] Meusebach projected his thoughts far into the future, seeing the fruition of his high hopes for the new colony, Fredericksburg.

[18] Meusebach, Nassau [Farm], April 17, 1846, to Castell. SB Archives, LII, 169–170.

Swarm of Immigrants

CHAPTER 12

After an absence of two months on this reconnaissance trip to the Fisher-Miller territory, Meusebach had returned to New Braunfels early in November with the hope and the belief that letters with money or credit would be at hand. Letters he found. The first one that he opened stated with apparent satisfaction, almost triumphantly, that more than four thousand immigrants were to arrive soon. Meusebach expected the second letter to give word about the financial provision for that large contingent. Instead, it revealed the establishment of a credit of $24,000 in New Orleans. That amount merely cleared the indebtedness as of the moment.

He turned hopefully to the next letter from the Executive Secretary. It gave details about the 4,304 emigrants who were soon to be on their way to Texas; no mention was made of money to care for them. Meusebach reread the letter. His eyes saw the four digits, yet his mind, his reason, told him that the Society could not be sending ten times as many people as were already in New Braunfels. He was preparing the valley of the Pedernales to receive a contingent equal to that of New Braunfels. Prince Solms had certainly recognized the settling of New Braunfels as an all-consuming task; he had on-the-spot experience. He surely would not allow such a responsibility to be magnified ten times.

Fisher was waiting for Meusebach in New Braunfels. Upon Meusebach's return early in November they drew up a new contract to replace the one made in Germany on June 26, 1844. Under the terms of the new agreement Fisher and Miller were given $5,000 and the promise of 250,000 acres (one sixth of the maximum amount of land that the Society could acquire from the state by colonizing the Fisher-Miller Grant). In return for these concessions Fisher and Miller transferred to the Society all of their rights in the Grant. The Verein was to pay $14,000 to Fisher and Miller if it failed to carry out its agreement to colonize the Grant. These terms gave rise to still further complications, which would add to the troubles of the Verein.

Fisher agreed to bring into the colony five hundred to one thousand people from North America, mainly the "Pennsylvania Dutch." Meusebach felt that benefits would come from the introduction of these people, German in origin, for they knew the practice of self-help better than the immigrants directly from Germany. The innate characteristics of the German, accustomed to supervisions and protection, were exemplified in the Society's immigrants; they expected their supervision to be continued by the Verein and they so relied upon its credit system that many made no effort to repay debts.

The Commissioner-General made a tabulation, which showed seventy-eight per cent of the immigrants had paid the cost of their voyage, but had paid for nothing else.[1] This meant that twenty-two per cent were supported by the Verein—actually, were depleting its capital. Only half of the first five hundred immigrants had paid for their transportation; the Verein had paid for the transportation of the others. Fisher was the only person in the first administration who knew business well, but he paid no attention to costs, since the money did not come out of his pocket.[2] Some disgruntled immigrants declared that they would not pay their accounts until they were taken to the Grant. One of the immigrants approached Meusebach in San Antonio and openly declared that the Verein was a cheat—that the Verein wanted to abscond with his money—and that he had asked the Prince in vain for the cash. Meusebach, in a burst of emotion, pulled his pistol to shoot the man on the spot. A quick second thought, however, told Meusebach that the man was alone and unarmed and that he deserved an explanation.[3]

Some of the colonists actually had made sufficient deposits to have money in the Verein treasury in Texas. Had they asked for their savings and had the cash not been forthcoming panic would have resulted. Many had made deposits in Europe in the fall of 1845 with the Society acting as the bank, but the list did not reach Texas until the spring of the following year.[4] When the depositors asked for their money in Carlshafen and the Society's agent had no lists or, for that matter, no money, the

[1] Meusebach, Galveston, January 20, 1846, to Castell. Solms-Braunfels Archives, LII. 100.
[2] *Ibid.*, p. 72.
[3] *Ibid.*, p. 89.
[4] John O. Meusebach, *Answer to Interrogatories*, p. 18.

colonists threatened to blow up the magazine. The depositors came on to New Braunfels, where they again found an empty treasury. All Meusebach could give them was assurances. The immigrants' just claims had to go unpaid. This led to deep resentment against the man representing the Society.

Meusebach wrote again and again that unless the credit system was lifted entirely the Verein would go bankrupt, even if it doubled its capital.[5] He urged further that every point in the contract with an emigrant be signed before the emigrant left Germany. The colonists brought the Commissioner-General what they considered broken promises and they showed ingratitude, when in reality they owed the opportunity of a new life to the Verein.

The thought of the budget he was to send to headquarters made Meusebach state that the "expenditures must be based on income so that the two are in harmony; included in all of this is the holding in readiness the correct means or resources that may be called for."[6] He refuted Prince Solms's report of February 12, 1845, which stated that $7,000 stood as credit, because facts revealed that there was an $8,000 debit and no credit.

Without knowledge of the many variable facets of the situation, neither estimates nor budgets could be made accurately. Meusebach, however, dispatched a tentative budget on December 3. Since the Executive Committee in Germany determined how many emigrants were to come budget making began there. Money paid in for transportation in Texas and as savings deposits could not justly be counted as funds belonging to the Verein treasury. These funds should have been at the disposition of the Commissioner-General in advance of the immigrants' arrival.[7] Such was not the case!

Six days after the receipt of the $24,000, on November 2, 1845, Meusebach had written that the sum covered only debts. He had stated that at least an additional $60,000 was needed to care for the several thousand prospective immigrants. Since Castell's letter of November 29 had stated that credit was to be enlarged according to need,[8] Meusebach had sent a messenger, F. H. Schladoer, to New Orleans with a draft on Lanfear, the Society's banker. The draft was rejected. This rebuff put the Commissioner-General in an unbelievably embarrassing position. He said that

[5] Meusebach, Galveston, January 20, 1846, to Castell. SB Archives, LII, 89.
[6] *Ibid.*, p. 91.
[7] Meusebach, *Answer to Interrogatories*, p. 18.
[8] Meusebach, Galveston, January 20, 1846, to Castell. SB Archives, LII, 43.

the Verein was a commercial firm in many aspects and that the rejection reflected upon its honor and ruined its credit. Writing on January 20, 1846, he stated that up to the present no funds beyond the $24,000 had arrived. Three to four thousand immigrants, however, *had* arrived despite his having advised that no more than two thousand be sent at that time. "It is no joke," he wrote, "suddenly to be on the rocks."[9] Making only partial payments to creditors for supplies, as he had done before, was not possible, for he had no funds whatsoever. Meusebach had used all his personal funds brought from home;[10] and he had not drawn any of his salary checks.

Not having money available prevented his concluding advantageous contracts. For example, he had arranged to buy 500,000 pounds of meat at three cents a pound, but an advance payment of $500 was required. Since he did not have that amount, the price rose to five cents a pound, whereby the Verein lost $10,000.[11] Making provision for corn was certainly essential. The Verein wagons were in constant use hauling corn from the farms where Meusebach had arranged to purchase it. On the return trip the wagons brought the immigrants up from the coast. With so much baggage allowed, a wagon for each family was usually needed. If $20,000 had been at his disposal, Meusebach could have bought one hundred wagons and dispatched the people as they arrived instead of allowing them to be concentrated in Carlshafen at Indian Point.

The number of immigrants arriving at the ports exceeded the entire population of western Texas.[12] Meusebach went to Galveston to make further decisions about the distribution of the people. The trip by horseback took three weeks because of flooded roads. Conditions in that port city were distressing; there was a mass, a huddle of human beings who needed and were expecting succor. Who was to give help? Who but Meusebach? He wanted desperately to save the situation. It was a matter of honor to him—his position was a post of honor.[13] From there Meusebach's letter of protest was one of his few examples of written sarcasm: "One could certainly not expect to bring 4237 people suddenly to the open prairie in the wilderness and then let them sit there. Sufficient provisions cost money, as does their transportation—even *here.*"[14]

Beyond the strain, by day and by night, of keeping the Verein out of

[9] *Ibid.*, p. 45.
[10] *Ibid.*, p. 50.
[11] *Ibid.*, p. 48.
[12] *Ibid.*
[13] *Ibid.*, p. 56.
[14] Meusebach, Nassau [Farm], May 2, 1846, to Castell. SB Archives, LII, 184.

large and small predicaments was the constant threat of bankruptcy. With particular emphasis Meusebach wrote, "I regard this whole undertaking as a desperate one and its continuance as uncertain."[15] The Verein was so deeply in debt that, in truth, insolvency should have been declared. Meusebach would have gained personally by insolvency because he had claim to considerable indemnification. In fact, his contract stipulated that he would receive a sum of $5,000 if the Society dissolved within five years. Meusebach did not question the honor of the men making up the Society. What perturbed him was their lack of business perception. He knew that they would underwrite, personally if need be, a promise they had made to him, Meusebach, one of their own number.

In the meantime he would write yet again to Count Castell, setting forth the whole picture. In aggregate figures, five thousand people needed provision. At the lowest possible estimate, ten cents per day per person, $500 per day must be available for subsistence for three months. The figure set for transporting people did not cover the cost, but even more discouraging was the unavailability of means of transportation. A sparsely settled land needed everything of a vehicular nature for use of its own population. Anything mounted on wheels was needed to traverse the long distances.

Examining only one item in the list for which funds were needed in Texas, Meusebach reasoned that providing shelter, within a few months, for four thousand persons would have been a mammoth undertaking even in Germany. He reasoned further:

The poorest calculator could have foreseen, in Europe, that it needed in Texas, in the fall of 1845, at or before the arrival of the emigrants—

1. $24,000 for the payment of the floating debt.

2. $45,000 for goods and provisions, to entertain 5000 persons, or less, for three months only.

3. $33,161 60–100 for land transportation of 4304 emigrants.

4. $12,000 for houses to be built in colony.

5. $26,067 to pay drafts or orders for deposits of emigrants. Total, $140,228 60–100.

Of all the amounts needed at the arrival of the emigrants, only the trifling item for the payment of the old debt had arrived.[16]

Relief must come, thought Meusebach, distraught to the point of desperation. Combing every possibility, he determined to appeal in person to Lanfear. Meusebach asked for a loan, giving as security Nassau Farm, the

[15] Meusebach, Galveston, January 20, 1846, to Castell. SB Archives, LII, 87.
[16] Meusebach, *Answer to Interrogatories*, p. 18.

property of the Society in Texas. Lanfear recognized the crisis and was moved by the appeal. He requested time to consider the question for a few hours. That night, with the ray of hope shining, was the first time of relaxation for Meusebach in many months. The next morning Lanfear reported that he had studied his instructions from headquarters about financial matters and that everywhere he read, "Construe strictly."[17] The banker was left with no alternative but to refuse the loan.

Deeply dejected, Meusebach hurried back to Galveston, hoping yet again that Castell had sent money. This was February, 1846. Castell had been despatching immigrants by the shipload since October of 1845, but money to care for them, to transport them, and to house them he had not despatched. Meusebach conferred with D. H. Klaener, the Society's agent in Galveston, and found him so desperate about supplies for the immigrants that he had mortgaged his own property.[18] Klaener's position was not an easy one to fill, but he did not falter in doing all in his power to help.

Only one remedy seemed to be left: the public press in Germany. In his capacity as trustee of the Society, Meusebach could not issue a statement, but Klaener, as agent, could, and he agreed to do so. Meusebach instructed him to make a correct statement about the sufferings of the immigrants caused by the Society's failure to fulfill its promises and to give that statement to the press.[19] Simultaneously a deputation from the immigrants themselves was sent to appeal for help directly to the Verein. Not until after the newspaper releases were extraordinary efforts made to raise money on a large scale.

The unfavorable publicity was very displeasing to Count Castell, who wrote under the date of July 10, 1846 [to Meusebach]:

"The letter of Mr. Klaener, addressed to the Mayor of Bremen, Mr. Schmidt (published in the papers), has made the worst impression. It has been communicated to the governments who now call for an explanation. It states that sickness and death prevail in Indianola and New Braunfels, and that the Company does not come up to its promise to remove immigrants upwards. We would have risked everything if we could not say we have acted immediately as soon as we heard how matters stood."[20]

A letter to Meusebach from Castell dated March 24, 1846, had put the whole situation in the right perspective: " 'The leading committee did

[17] Meusebach, Galveston, January 20, 1846, to Castell. SB Archives, LII, 85.

[18] Meusebach, *Answer to Interrogatories*, p. 20.

[19] *Ibid.*

[20] Castell's letter [to Meusebach] is quoted in Meusebach, *Answer to Interrogatories*, p. 20.

make the fault to send the immigrants and not the money for transportation'."[21]

The crucial situation at Carlshafen, however, had not been felt by the
members of the Verein; they could hardly conceive of a life other than
their own orderly existence. Furthermore, the members resting in the belief that the small sums that they had sent from time to time somehow
could have accomplished the care and transportation of the people, had
relied on their executive secretary, Castell, to keep things in order. Only
when their honor or standing was affected did they give the situation their
attention. After the newspapers revealed the calamitous conditions at Carlshafen a general meeting of the Verein was called; only seven of the forty
members answered. An emergency decision was reached to send funds
immediatedly by a special messenger and to subscribe to a loan of $80,000,
for which the Duke of Nassau gave security.

Relief thus came in the form of a credit of $60,000, which was brought
over by Philip Cappes, a special messenger. The banker's letter announc-
ing the credit was dated July 14, 1846; the notice from New Orleans
came August 17; the money reached New Braunfels on September 7,
1846. Meusebach succinctly stated the cause for the tragic situation: "If
the same amount had been sent one year before, in September, 1845,
when the money was due or overdue, probably the most, if not all, of the
inconveniences, troubles and misfortunes would have been avoided."[22]
Says Tiling, "Nothing could arraign the Adelsverein more severely than
this statement."[23]

---

[21] Castell is quoted, *ibid.*, p. 17.

[22] Meusebach, *Answer to Interrogatories*, p. 21.

[23] Moritz Tiling, *History of the German Element in Texas from 1820–1850, and
Historical Sketches of the German Texas Singers' League and Houston Turnverein
from 1853–1913*, p. 90.

The Face of Tragedy

CHAPTER 13

Financial problems were but the beginning of the troubles that plagued the immigrants. Meusebach tried to evaluate the situation at Carlshafen, which seemed like a chain reaction of tragic circumstances:

1) Indebtedness and lack of money to meet the needs,
2) Arrival of too many immigrants within too short a span of time and without means of transporting them,
3) Outbreak of war with Mexico in the area of the disembarkation of the immigrants,
4) Unexpectedly severe winter weather,
5) Disease of epidemic proportions.

Why, asked the Commissioner-General, was his task attended with so much heartbreak, so much tragedy? Despite his constant efforts, the crisis at Carlshafen became acute.

After his unsuccessful trip to borrow money in New Orleans in February, 1846, Meusebach had gone to Houston, where he persuaded the teamsters, Torrey Brothers, who were well disposed toward him personally, to accept $10,000 in drafts on the Society in Europe as payment for a train of one hundred wagoners to transport the immigrants. An agreement was reached and Meusebach's hopes were raised, only to be extinguished. Torrey Brothers were obliged to answer the call of the United States government to transport troops and equipment to the army of General Zachary Taylor, which had been stationed, since mid-June, 1845, at Corpus Christi, a small Mexican village inside the disputed strip of land between the Nueces River and the Rio Grande. Taylor's army had been ordered to that location by President Polk a month before Texas ratified annexation and six months before Texas became a state. By the end of July, 1845, Taylor had his forces in Corpus Christi, where they had remained until March 8, 1846. On that date, acting on further orders from the United States War Department, General Taylor began moving his army from the Nueces to a location on the Rio Grande opposite Matamoros.

When the Mexican General Pedro Ampudia, with his forces, reached Matamoros early in April he sent a formal demand to General Taylor to withdraw from the soil of the "Department of Tamaulipas" within twenty-four hours. "Rough and Ready" Taylor did not withdraw; a battle near Brownsville ensued, in which the Americans were victorious. Four days later, on May 12, 1846, the United States Congress declared war and voted men and money for an invasion of Mexico.

The duration of the war, which ended with a peace treaty signed February 2, 1848, coincided almost exactly with the period during which most of the German emigrants were arriving in Carlshafen at Indian Point, that remote Texas shore not far from the army movements. This proximity multiplied the difficulties for the colonists and, of course, for their leader.

Another leader in the same area of Texas, Lieutenant Colonel Ethan Allen Hitchcock, had somewhat similar difficulties in maintaining supplies, health and morale. Colonel Hitchcock commanded the Third Infantry and the encampment at Corpus Christi. The conditions of the military men are described by DeVoto: "They drank bad water and sickened; they drank bad whiskey and brawled. Their rations gave them scurvy; the food they bought from sutlers and Mexicans gave them dysentery."[1] With the United States Army backing him, however, Colonel Hitchcock, the "executive brain" of General Taylor,[2] was able to pay prices that secured the needed supplies. A case in point was the Torrey Brothers breaking of the transportation contract with Meusebach. They had succumbed to the higher offers of the government at Lavaca. Had money been available to Meusebach earlier, he could have bought wagons with equipment and made use of them immediately, in advance of the complexities that the war brought.

Colonel Hitchcock had written that Polk's election meant " 'a step towards the annexation of Texas first and then, in due time, the separation of the Union'."[3] The Colonel's prophecy proved correct, but Meusebach certainly could not agree with Emerson's statement that " 'The annexation

[1] Bernard De Voto, *The Year of Decision: 1846*, p. 15.
[2] *Ibid.*
[3] Hitchcock is quoted in De Voto, *Year of Decision*, p. 15.

of Texas looks like one of those events which retard or retrograde the civilization of ages'."[4]

Meusebach would have liked to discuss Emerson's idea through correspondence with him; however, at this point, Meusebach had to use all his energy to provide the daily necessities of life for his people. His every conversation dealt with material matters—with money or how to obtain it. Meusebach felt as if his mind were literally starved for intellectual food.

Emerson's view about the annexation of Texas was not shared likewise by those in a position to direct events. While President of the United States, John Tyler had written to his Secretary of State, Daniel Webster: "I gave you a hint as to the probability of acquiring Texas by treaty. I verily believe it could be done. Could the North be reconciled to it, could anything throw so bright a lustre around us?"[5] Since the Congress had not seen fit to bring the lustre by means of treaty, the President had succeeded in accomplishing the annexation by a joint resolution of the two houses of Congress. Speaking to the lawmakers about the resolution President Tyler had said, " 'I have regarded it as not a little fortunate that the question involved was in no way sectional or local, but addressed itself to the interests of every part of the country and made its appeal to the Glory of the American name'."[6] Tyler manifestly had not seen eye to eye with Emerson that the annexation of Texas was a crime against civilization.

The events connected with Texas' relinquishment of her independence to become one of the United States were of transcendent importance to Meusebach. His study of law had sharpened his desire to be present where history was unfolding. He knew protocol and desired to present himself to the President of the Republic, Anson Jones, but he could not take the time, because the immediacy of life and death, like the legendary albatross, hung about his neck. An unfounded report rumored that President Jones had desired the defeat of annexation. A wave of sympathy went from Meusebach to President Jones when the story was told that the members of Congress voted down a resolution of thanks to the President for his labors in behalf of annexation.

While Anson Jones was still President of the Republic no military movements against Mexico were permitted. Meusebach heard that Jones was doing all in his power to keep Texas at peace with its neighbor. If

[4] Emerson is quoted in Peter Molyneaux, *The Romantic Story of Texas*, p. 462.
[5] John Tyler, Washington, D.C., October 11, 1841, to Daniel Webster, *Tyler's Quarterly and Genealogical Magazine*, VIII (July, 1926), 18–19.
[6] Tyler is quoted in Molyneaux, *Romantic Story of Texas*, p. 435.

that condition had continued and if war had been averted, untold suffering would have been spared the combatants, as well as the immigrants stranded not too distant from the military encampment. President Polk, however, apparently let nothing deter him from seeing that the United States Congress declared war against Mexico. This was accomplished on May 12, 1846.

As could have been expected, the excitement of war stirred through the immigrants, sitting idle at Carlshafen. Eighty-eight of them enlisted in a company which Augustus Buchel, one of their number, had organized on May 1, 1846.[7] Although the evidence of patriotism was commendable, the colony was deprived of the energy and optimism of its younger men.

The quality of hopefulness was utterly lacking at Carlshafen. Disillusionment stared from vacant eyes. Day after day, night after night, wore on without relief. The Verein's agent for the area, Theodore Miller, could hardly withstand the pressure of the immigrants' demands to move inland. Journeying out of the Indian Point area was not possible. The immigrants were immobilized by circumstances seemingly beyond their control.

The mass of humanity at Indian Point reveled in a liberty to which it had not been accustomed in Germany. The people indulged their freedom to the point of running wild, in unbridled licentiousness. Just at this time three ships bearing immigrants were wrecked on the coast near Carlshafen. The people themselves were saved, but the provisions that the ships carried—supplied by the Verein to provide for the immigrants after they landed—were spoiled. All semblance of order among the immigrants on shore was lost; regulations were forgotten. Riffraff moved in from all sides to live off the Verein; the people indulged in excessive eating and drinking. A wave of illness spread that often resulted in complete demoralization or even death.

Then a prolonged siege of rainy weather set in; the oldest residents of Texas could remember nothing like it. Roads became bottomless quagmires; streams and rivers spread for miles beyond their banks; communication with the interior was severed.[8]

During this time Meusebach had sought means of transportation from the Colorado and Brazos River areas. But the floods cut off access to Carl-

---

[7] Rudolph Leopold Biesele, *The History of the German Settlements in Texas 1831–1861*, p. 193.

[8] The details of the colonists' situation on the coast are recorded in Minutes of Verein, Mainz, n.d. (Solms-Braunfels Archives, XXVIII, 67–68).

shafen, and the immigrants were left to their own resources. Since the transportation to the land on which they were to be settled could not be furnished, they now demanded refund of their deposit money. Meusebach felt the justice of their claim since the Verein had obligated itself to get them to the colony. Difficulties multiplied: food supplies were insufficient; immigrants not sponsored by the Verein attached themselves to the group. All provisions for the four thousand people now had to be brought in from a distance, even from as far away as New Orleans. The costs eroded the the funds until they were exhausted. Since everything had to be bought without delay, the spirit of speculation drove prices to new heights. In the midst of these difficulties word came that the ship *Nahaud* had been wrecked off the coast of England, and that the emigrants had barely escaped with their lives. The compassionate inhabitants of the seaside village of Zorbay cared for the passengers until the Verein sent a rescue ship. This expenditure further cut into the Society's resources.

In this sea-level location of Carlshafen, with wholly inadequate living facilities, disease spread rapidly and soon became epidemic. The most devastating illness of all was diagnosed later by Dr. William Hermes, Sr., as petechial fever, known also as spinal meningitis. Dr. Hermes, not a physician until some years later, came as an immigrant in 1846 and had the dread disease himself.

Disease raged; the unduly severe weather in the winter of 1846 increased the illness and the death toll was heavy. When the immigrants finally were moved from the coast, the contagion spread to New Braunfels and on to Fredericksburg. Although physicians were in attendance, diagnoses were sometimes in error, and treatment was often unavailing. One estimate places the total number of deaths between 800 and 850. All burial ceremony had to be dispensed with. The emotional strain on the survivors was so great, reports say, that some lost their reason and some threw themselves into revelry of all kinds. Such was the effect upon those who, having come to seek a new life, met desolation instead.

What Meusebach had foreseen as a march to the place of hopeful beginnings now became the slow, measured tread of disheartened pilgrims. Instead of welcoming them with acclamation, all he could do was to extend sympathy and to feel compassion. He saw to it that provision was made for the orphans. As evidence of his sorrow and concern, he gave the last of his chests, brought from Germany, to be used in making caskets.[9] The tragedy of it all struck deep within him.

[9] Meusebach, Galveston, January 20, 1846, to Castell. SB Archives, LII, 110.

A Search for Solace

CHAPTER 14

When the thirty-three-year-old Meusebach accepted the position of commissioner-general he recognized that the task of receiving and settling people who arrived from a foreign land and spoke a foreign language had many complications. He lost no time in becoming a citizen of his adopted country. Thus he could welcome the Germans to this new land, though he had preceded them by only a few months. He looked forward to helping them become oriented. German customs of course, were to be observed, but Meusebach introduced American practices as well. Furthermore he welcomed American people into the colony. Close contact with the people—the folk—did not have first appeal for Meusebach. His inherent interest lay in bringing the land to its fullest fruition. But men deserved his consideration, and at present they were his prime repsonsibility. His current aim was to give these fellow Germans, now Americans, the chance to develop their potential.

Goethe's lines were the foundation stone of his concept of democracy:

> To stand on free soil among a people free.

For him this meant that all people, of whatever class, would be able to exercise free choice of their officials, of their religion, and of their associates. He was in complete accord with the American principle of the separation of church and state.[1] Somewhat in the same line of thinking, he wanted each individual to be free to make his own decisions, to be responsible personally to his God, and to worship as he saw fit. For himself, he was a freethinker, not bound by any formality, yet accountable to his own conscience for his actions. He bound himself by strict principles wherein he was true to himself while recognizing a duty to his fellow man. In the midst of all

[1] Meusebach, Galveston, January 20, 1846, to Castell. Solms-Braunfels Archives, LII, 108.

the turmoil about him Meusebach found a measure of surcease in the flight of his thoughts; no limitations, except those within himself, held him earthbound.

Far-flung thoughts did give him respite for a time, relief from his tension. But after months of endurance the devastating events closed in on him. Though he was considered the architect of the colonization project, he no longer could sustain the stress and strain of the task. Life and death were too poignantly focused on him. He had demonstrated to the utmost the art of consolation, of sympathy; he came at last to the point of bending or breaking.[2]

He had to relax his standards of work for a time or he could not bear his burden. The experiences had taken their toll. He was physically ill, and his very soul was sickened by the realization that this pilgrimage had brought such disaster, in spite of every possible human effort to prevent the tragedy. He decided to seek rest at Nassau Farm.

When a solution to a problem presented itself, Meusebach grasped it. The new colony at Fredericksburg needed a doctor and a director. With the appearance of an individual who supplied both requirements, Meusebach felt that one problem was solved. This man was Dr. Schubbert. Writing Castell from Houston on March 6, 1846, Meusebach had stated that he was taking Dr. Schubbert—no given name was reported—to Nassau in the hope of persuading him to join the colonization project. After Dr. Schubbert's name Meusebach wrote in parentheses "Baron Sch. v. Brückenau??"[3] A person's name being followed by two question marks no doubt indicated that questions were in Meusebach's mind. The uncertainty about this title was never cleared.

Schubbert had been in charge of the German colony at St. Gabriel (Milam County) and was associated there with Henry Francis Fisher. The fact that these two men were natives of Kassel, Germany, no doubt had brought them together. With the dispersal of the immigrants of the St. Gabriel colony, it can be taken for granted that both Fisher and Schubbert were glad that a new situation was opening. Schubbert accompanied Meusebach in April to Nassau Farm, where they remained for some time.

Nassau Farm provided a change of place for Meusebach, but not a change of pace, for at this time he had not yet received the money from

[2] Meusebach, Fredericksburg, January 19, 1847, to Castell. SB Archives, XXVIII, 188.

[3] Meusebach, Houston, March 6, 1846, to Castell. SB Archives, LII, 138.

the Verein. He was under continual harassment from creditors,[4] and his work for the colonists crowded in upon him, even at this spot removed from the vortex of activities. However Schubbert, a man of the world, conversed intelligently and thus brought some change of thought to the distracted mind of his host. At table, as a variation from the corn-bread-and-bacon menu, the host sometimes served sardines, potato salad with capers, or perhaps olives. Plans for growing olive trees and other oil-producing trees were discussed; in fact, the development of the colonies to become self-sustaining was of prime concern. Both men were highly imaginative, and they made plans that reached far into the future.

Schubbert, psychologically intuitive and six years the senior of Meusebach, did not appear eager for the position of director of the new colony at Fredericksburg. Since no other qualified person was available and because the need for the director was urgent Meusebach agreed to certain future commitments relative to Nassau Farm, a valuable piece of property. Schubbert overcame his hesitation and accepted the post when these possibilities opened up. In mid-June, 1846, Dr. Schubbert was helpful in arranging for the second expedition to Fredericksburg, consisting of about four hundred men, which he supervised.[5] Accompanying this expedition as a guide and protector was Julius Splittgerber, whom Dr. Schubbert had employed.[6]

While at Nassau Meusebach had planned to complete his accounts that were to be sent to the Verein headquarters. He was unable to carry out this plan because of interruptions. Castell desired a detailed accounting of funds as well as a definite picture of how the members of the Verein would be compensated for their investment.[7] He wanted to know also the status of the Grant: whether it was in the Verein's possession and whether land there could be sold. To get such a report, wrote Castell, is "more important than every operation you carry on where you are."[8] Meusebach was at fault in not supplying the information, but from his point of view nothing transcended the importance of providing for the actual existence of the immigrants. Until they were settled in the Grant, there was no possibility of claiming the land. With many of the immigrants still huddled at Indian Point, from whence there were few wagons to move

---

[4] John O. Meusebach, *Answer to Interrogatories*, p. 25.

[5] Meusebach, Nassau [Farm], April 17, 1846, to Castell. SB Archives, LII, 169.

[6] Robert Penniger (ed., comp.), *Fest-Ausgabe zum fünfzigjährigen Jubiläum der Deutschen Kolonie Friedrichsburg*, p. 65.

[7] Castell, Wiesbaden, June 23, 1846, to Meusebach, SB Archives, LII, 173, 189–191.

[8] Castell, Wiesbaden, December 27, 1846, to Meusebach. SB Archives, LII, 239.

them, Meusebach could not comprehend why the question of claiming the land should be considered.

He recognized that he was responsible for the accounts, although a competent bookkeeper should have been at hand to assist him. At Nassau, when Meusebach settled to work, the most distressing interruptions were the requests of the immigrants who wanted the refund of their deposit. Meusebach had no funds with which to meet their demands. Even his personal money had been used for the colonists. One persistent individual wishing his deposit was Leopold von Iwonski, who remained on Meusebach's doorstep fourteen days.[9] A teamster, one of the creditors, came demanding payment for services rendered, while brandishing a pistol. Meusebach suggested to the teamster that they both try to hit a target on a tree. Meusebach's first shot hit the bull's eye. Thereupon the teamster accepted Meusebach's invitation to breakfast. Presently he was willing to extend the credit.[10]

The conditions at Indian Point gave Meusebach deep concern. He sent medicine there costing $80 or more.[11] Earlier, details about three boats stranded in Lavaca Bay had come to him. While the captain of the schooner *New Braunfels* was climbing the mast to put up the S O S flag the eighty-nine passengers became excited and threw all their possessions overboard. Under the leadership of Baron von Donop, they were rescued and taken by steamboat to Corpus Christi and then Indian Point.[12] At Nassau, Meusebach again sought means of restoring their losses.

Writing to Castell from Nassau in mid-June, Meusebach explained that bankruptcy would have become a reality long before had not word gone out from Nassau that significant sums of money were on the way from Germany. Meusebach, to strengthen the tottering financial structure, had allowed the report to spread. One of his reasons for remaining at Nassau had been to give some basis to such a report.[13] After a time, however, people lost confidence in such reports, and Meusebach added: "I can hold the situation at the most four weeks longer. Unless money comes, all of us will have to flee as von Coll in New Braunfels and [Theodore] Miller in Indian Point mean to do."[14] Meusebach related also that he had

---

[9] Cappes, Galveston, July 31, 1846, to Castell. SB Archives, XLI, 20.
[10] Lucy Meusebach Marschall, Notes and Memoranda. MSS. Meusebach Family Files.
[11] Meusebach, Nassau, April 17, 1846, to Castell. SB Archives, LII, 171.
[12] Meusebach, Galveston, December 24, 1845, to Verein, SB Archives, LII, 12–13.
[13] Meusebach, Nassau, June 14, 1846, to Castell. SB Archives, LII, 200.
[14] *Ibid.*

papers served on him, both in Galveston and Houston, for debts of the Verein.[15]

Such experiences, pressing upon the Commissioner-General even at Nassau, left his spirits at a low ebb. An opportunity to use his mind in some intellectual pursuit was always the best means of lifting Meusebach out of depression. The exchange of ideas with men who could project their thoughts beyond the immediate moment gave him true satisfaction. Two such men were Ferdinand Lindheimer, a botanist, and Ferdinand Roemer, a geologist, about whom Meusebach had written, "I hope similarly minded people will come here [to New Braunfels] so that we can make a permanent place for German knowledge at the side of American freedom."[16]

The spirit of this naturalist seemed to revive as he stated his intention to work up a scholarly booklet in collaboration with Lindheimer and Roemer. In this pamphlet he would tell about the settlements and then portray in detail the west-central part of Texas, where a great primordial cataclysm had lifted up the hills. Meusebach's friendship with Lindheimer, a trained naturalist, was stimulating. Lindheimer, who had come to Texas in 1836 and was now at home in New Braunfels, was making botanical collections for Professor Asa Gray of Harvard College. Like Meusebach he had attended the University of Bonn before coming to America. Meusebach sent his own specimens of flora and fauna to the University of Halle, and to the Berlin Zoo he sent two live panthers and six partridges, with the plan of later establishing a Texas menagerie in Berlin. He requested that the Universities of Berlin and Munich send meteorological instruments to Lindheimer, whom he named director of a botanical garden in New Braunfels. Together the friends made plans to set up a pilot school to grow fruits which might prove valuable commercially to the colonists.

The second young scientist, Roemer, was in the New Braunfels area during 1846–47. Prince Solms, on his return to Germany from New Braunfels had recommended that a geological survey of Texas be made, with particular attention given to the area within the Fisher-Miller Grant, where he hoped there were rich mineral deposits. He appealed to the Berlin Academy of Sciences, whose members chose Roemer as the person competent to make the survey. This geologist, a graduate of the University of Berlin, had come to Texas with a letter of introduction from Alexander

[15] Meusebach, New Braunfels, August 12, 1846, to Castell. SB Archives, LII, 222.
[16] Meusebach, Galveston, January 20, 1846, to Castell. SB Archives, LII, 125.

Humboldt, who said that "Dr. Roemer, like a book, needs but to be opened to yield good answers to all questions."[17]

Roemer was the guest of Meusebach during his stay in Texas, and he used his host's extensive library to advantage. These two scientists shared many experiences. The geologist wrote an account of his experiences in the state in his book *Texas*, first published in Bonn, Germany, in 1849. In the Foreword to the book he expressed appreciation for Meusebach's interest in his work. Meusebach wrote about this association: "Professor Dr. Roemer, on his arrival in Texas, consulted me and with him I made in 1846 and 1847 the first geological exploration in the State, the results of which have been published. . . .[18] I first discovered the real Coal Measures . . . at the mouth of Brady's Creek into the San Saba. . . ."[19] Roemer's accurate, early geological observations are the basis for his being called "Father of the Geology of Texas."

Excursions, such as the one to the lower Brazos River, where he found the bones of prehistoric animals, and the explorations with Roemer were rewarding, but the exercise of his mental faculties, even more important to Meusebach, took precedence over everything. Knowledge and freedom were the forces that motivated him; they bespoke his inmost being.

Meusebach was a person whose mind, with few exceptions, controlled his actions. This characteristic made him appear authoritative, a quality that sometimes irritated his associates. When one of them, von Coll, once threatened to put a bullet through Meusebach's head rather than take a further word of correction, he was disarmed by Meusebach's calmness. Meusebach later wrote: "If he threatens me personally, I am ready to meet him. I have stood in the line of fire before. I never shunned a student's duel. The matter is different in official relationships. I recognize neither enmities nor friendships. Only accomplishments determine my evaluation."[20] Striving for perfection was a part of Meusebach's thinking. A Verein official reported that Meusebach had to descend from a "world of ideals" to approach the practical. The official did not intend this evaluation as a compliment, but the essence of a compliment was in the phrase, for this "idealist" counted the ideal essential as a goal.

To Meusebach growth without learning was hollow. A school had been

[17] Samuel Wood Geiser, *Naturalists of the Frontier*, p. 184.

[18] Ferdinand von Roemer, *Die Kreidebildungen von Texas und ihre organischen Einschluesse* [*The Cretaceous Formations of Texas and Their Organic Inclusions*] (Bonn: Adolphus Marcus, 1852).

[19] Meusebach, n.pl., January 19, 1858, to Governor Runnels. MSS. Governors' Correspondence.

[20] Meusebach, Galveston, January 20, 1846, to Castell. SB Archives, LII, 76.

estabished in New Braunfels on August 11, 1845. An elm tree served as the meeting place until the next year, when the school moved into the block church. In Fredericksburg the first school was held in the octagonal church, *die Vereins Kirche*, even before it was finished. The Verein, said Meusebach, should do all it could to support schools and to undergird learning, for "sensible persons are generally also good people."[21]

Meusebach soon observed typical American characteristics. He was impressed by the fact that the Americans were innately business people and therefore could evaluate the importance of the undertaking by the Verein. He also sensed their basic values; "Names mean nothing to Americans," said Meusebach, "Gold and votes carry importance."[22] He recognized that both values are witnesses to ownership. Gold predicates ownership of something tangible; the vote is an intangible possession, yet one that the owner may utilize as he sees fit. With the vote, as it could be exercised in Texas, Meusebach felt the possibility of attaining something far beyond the material. Only when he was able to exclude the material did he feel that life had come into fruition. With Goethe, he felt that life is great and meaningful as one fills it with beautiful things to remember.

[21] *Ibid.*, p. 108.
[22] *Ibid.*, pp. 55–56.

The Special Commissioner

Meusebach's stay at Nassau Farm had been successful in holding off bankruptcy for the time being. Postponement no longer availed. He determined to face matters as they presented themselves; shrinking from duty was foreign to him. Although he was only partially recovered from illness, he returned to New Braunfels in July, 1846. There he took up the reins of responsibility, which had been held somewhat lightly by the officials and agents of the Verein, who were referred to in one newspaper account as "speculating leaders."[1] This unfavorable publicity gave Meusebach great concern and he hoped the matter would end with the newspaper reports. But as if in fear of a panic, the colonists rushed to Meusebach for payment of their deposits. He had asked himself, "Does the Verein want to stand before the world bankrupt, with promises broken?"[2]

Although this was a rhetorical question, it held the essence of reality for Meusebach. He wondered often whether Castell realized the full extent of the colonization project. On many counts the Executive Secretary was a theorist, so Meusebach had advanced the idea that Castell should come to Texas in person. He would certainly have found a gruesome situation unless he had brought sufficient money along to meet all commitments.[3]

The testimony of persons actually in Texas revealed what could have been observed there by Castell. Ottomar von Behr, a visitor in the colony, said, "It went so far that the notes of the depositors against the Verein were sold at one-fourth face value." Von Behr stated that the Commissioner-General was left without funds for three-fourths of the year. "This lack of money could have caused the downfall of the whole undertaking,"

[1] Meusebach, New Braunfels, July 28, 1846, to Castell. Solms-Braunfels Archives, LII, 215–216.

[2] Meusebach, Galveston, January 20, 1846, to Castell. SB Archives, LII, 89.

[3] Meusebach, Nassau [Farm], June 14, 1846, to Castell. SB Archives, LII, 201.

said von Behr, "and the worst was warded off only by Meusebach's energy."[4]

Another observer of the scene in New Braunfels, Victor Bracht, recognized the financial straits when he wrote, "For more than a year the Verein has not sent any money." Bracht continued, "Through negotiations and the raising of small sums of money, Herr Meusebach has once more retrieved the cause of the Verein, which seemed already lost."[5]

One observer commented that the Commissioner-General was expected to extricate a wheelbarrow stuck in a mire made by others. His solution was for the Verein to furnish $100,000 cash immediately and to present a new program.[6]

Meusebach met the situation as it stood; he regarded the deposits as a "holy heritage." The sum total of deposits for the year 1845, as given by Friedrich Kapp, who was not officially connected with the Verein, was $84,516.41.[7] Those deposits had been counted as part of the sums that the Verein had sent to be used for the work in general. This practice had added intricacies to the accounts.

Had Castell come to Texas, as suggested, he would have been pulled in every direction to answer the daily needs of the settlements and to direct operations. He quickly would have found that bricks cannot be made without straw—least of all the golden bricks he expected. The Secretary would have learned that no precious minerals had been discovered in the Grant and that no land had been sold there, for the quite sufficient reason that the Grant was in the firm possession of hostile Indians. However, he would have ascertained that the Commissioner-General was making definite efforts to approach the Indians in the hope of reaching an accord with them so that the colonists could receive the land promised them. The discontent caused by unfulfilled promises certainly would have made an impression on Castell.

If the Executive Secretary had been obliged to deal with the immigrants themselves, he would have selected them with greater care. Complaints were voiced that officials on Verein ships did not require certificates of good character.[8] Hence, disreputable immigrants were included. Castell referred to a portion of the colonists as *Halunken,* that is, rascals.

---

[4] Ottomar von Behr, *Guter Rath fuer Auswanderer nach den Vereinigten Staaten von Nordamerika mit besonderer Beruecksichtigung von Texas,* p. 101.
[5] Viktor Bracht, *Texas im Jahre 1848,* p. 201.
[6] Alwin H. Sörgel, *Für auswanderungslustige: Briefe eines unter dem schutze des Mainzer vereins nach Texas ausgewanderten,* p. 50.
[7] Friedrich Kapp, *Aus und ueber Amerika. Thatsachen und Erlebnisse,* I, 266.
[8] Sörgel, *Für auswanderungslustige,* p. 22.

Men to serve on the staff of the Commissioner-General were chosen not because they were qualified for work but because a Verein member wished to reward an individual or because he had to seek aslyum. In the latter classification was C. Herber. He was reputed to be a counterfeiter, but, as Castell said, "Herber is popular with people."[9] A mutual dislike developed between Herber and Meusebach.

Nearer at hand Castell would have seen disease so devastating that deaths were numbered by hundreds. Unfortunately the disease germs were brought from Indian Point to New Braunfels and on to Fredericksburg. While physicians were in attendance, Castell would have recognized that doctors in both settlements made glaring errors. According to Dr. William Hermes, Dr. Schubbert in Fredericksburg diagnosed spinal meningitis as scurvy, an error that probably caused many fatalities.[10] In New Braunfels the sick were cared for under a long shed, which was erected to serve as a kind of hospital. An orphanage was established to care for children who had lost their parents during the epidemic. Castell's compassion would have extended to such situations, but he could not have lingered, because plans for the future had to be projected.

Such plans, of course, were the work of the Verein, but Castell also took time to write frequently to Philip Cappes and to determine procedure with him. Cappes was the special commissioner, who was sent with the funds to relieve the desperate state of the colony after the members of the Verein had been awakened to their responsibilities in Texas by the newspaper disclosures. The Verein had voted that his assignment was to stand "helpfully by the side" of Meusebach.[11]

Count Castell had chosen Philip Cappes as the envoy. Although Count Leiningen questioned the choice, Cappes' unbounded loyalty to Castell seemed to be the important factor in the decision. Castell had recognized Cappes as a member of the Verein in January, 1846, without requiring that he buy shares in the organization. The two men had a friendly as well as an official relationship, for Castell had asked Cappes to seek out "an establishment in Texas, bought inexpensively, but well situated." He continued, "We might even be neighbors."[12]

Cappes likewise had been interested in Texas, for he had mentioned the idea of going there as early as October, 1845. That journey was delayed

---

[9] Castell, Mainz, March 16, 1845, to Meusebach. SB Archives, LI, 32.

[10] Wilhelm Hermes, "Erlebnisse eines deutschen Einwanderers in Texas," *Kalender der Neu-Braunfelser Zeitung feur 1922*, p. 23.

[11] Minutes of Verein, Wiesbaden, June 13, 1847, SB Archives, XXVIII, 72.

[12] Castell, Hanover, March 4, [no year], to Cappes. SB Archives, XLII, 249.

nearly a year. During the interim much had transpired. Castell had dispatched several thousand immigrants to one point in Texas. At ease in his Mainz office, pleased with his accomplishment, he wrote, "We certainly have fulfilled our contract about sending the people, even at the risk of getting, for the moment, into a predicament about money."[13]

To extricate his friend Castell from this predicament was part of Cappes' assignment. He wrote back on July 31, 1846, from Galveston, "I could not explain to Klaener, the Galveston agent of the Verein, the connection of sending immigrants but no money; moreover I had to give a plausible turn to the complicated purpose of my coming."[14]

A part of the "complicated purpose" seems to have been to gather material for a report on Meusebach. Castell had been grievously hurt by the scathing criticism that had resulted from the newspaper publicity regarding the plight of the immigrants at Indian Point. His bright dream of wealth and glory had turned to ashes. Then, too, Castell was accountable to the members of the Verein. They expected gain, not shame; to find a person on whom to put the blame would relieve Castell's burden. Meusebach would be that person.

Castell wished to throw off the responsibility for the faltering situation when he wrote to Meusebach, "You will say it was madness to send people and not money." In the same letter he admitted, "it would have been much better if $50,000 had come in December, 1845."[15] A sufficient answer from Meusebach to both confessions might have been, "How true!"

Instead, Meusebach wrote lengthy letters calling Castell to task for his inhumanity in heaping the immigrants on the bleak Texas coast without transmitting means to care for them. To this reprimand Castell replied, "How nice it would be to hear something pleasant; it is hard to digest only Job's news."[16]

Cappes perhaps fulfilled Castell's desires, for he sent in page after page about Meusebach, even a list of food ordered, which included sardines, capers, and olives. A member of an investigating commission appointed by the Verein at a later time asked, "Shall Cappes ride Castell's stick horse and hunt up personal qualities?"[17]

Philip Cappes recognized the weak spot in the administration of the affairs in the colony, the lack of adequate, official reports to the head-

---

[13] Castell, Wiesbaden, April 24, 1846, to Meusebach. SB Archives, LII, 152.

[14] Cappes, Galveston, July 31, 1846, to Castell. SB Archives, XLI, 19.

[15] Castell, Wiesbaden, July 9, 1846, to Meusebach. SB Archives, LII, 191–194.

[16] *Ibid.*, p. 196.

[17] Becker, Galveston, July 9, 1848, to Reuscher. SB Archives, LVI, 143.

quarters office. Meusebach realized the need for reports, but the requirements enveloping him took every moment: first, daily necessities; second,
efforts to cover the lack of money and thus to avoid declaration of bankruptcy. Because he was bringing money, Cappes saw only obvious errors
in management. However, before his departure from the colony in March,
1847, he agreed with Meusebach's urgent pleas for additional money and
recommend that $200,000 be advanced.[18] Coupled with this request was
the expressed belief that the capital sum would be recouped. Also at that
time Cappes made the statement that only Meusebach could cut the Gor-
dian knot of the Verein's complicated affairs.

The Commissioner-General appreciated the apparent competency of
the Special Commissioner, especially his excellence in clerical work, which
lightened Meusebach's load. Cappes wrote voluminous letters to Castell
and reported that "since my arrival new courage is evident everywhere."[19]
On his return from a trip to Houston, he wrote, "During my absence nothing was accomplished."[20] While in Houston he came to know Fisher,
a man adept in cultivating the friendship of a person who could in any way
benefit him. Cappes possessed the same ability and ingratiated himself
with the bickering officials. He listened to ideas of intrigue and soon
showed that he had had some lessons in entanglement.

Castell knew about the entanglement when he wrote to his envoy
Cappes, "This is between us and us alone."[21] In a letter to Castell, Cappes
asked, "What shall I do on a horse that has no feet, even if I have my foot
in the stirrups?"[22] Exactly what such cryptic statements relate to can
only be conjectured, but that there must have been something to be kept
under cover is revealed by a letter from Castell to Cappes saying, "Tear
up my letters."[23]

A member of a Verein commission, L. Becker, wrote about Castell,
"What disillusionment in a person."[24] A committee of the Society sitting
in Wiesbaden, Germany, on September 14, 1849, asked Becker pointedly,
"What does Cappes do in Texas?" The reply was: "He goes pleasure riding and lives with his mistress. He has done nothing for the Society and is

[18] Cappes, New Braunfels, February 20, 1847, to Castell. SB Archives, XLI, 142,
161.
[19] Cappes, Indian Point, January 2, 1847, to Castell. SB Archives, XLI, 84.
[20] *Ibid.*, p. 86.
[21] Castell, Biebrich, May 8, 1848, to Cappes. SB Archives, XLII, 255.
[22] Cappes, New York, March 30, 1848, to Castell. SB Archives, XLI, 263.
[23] Castell, Wiesbaden, March 22, no year, to Cappes. SB Archives, XLII, 250.
[24] Becker, Galveston, July 9, 1848, to Reuscher. SB Archives, LVI, 143.

doing nothing for it at the present. He corresponds with Count Castell."[25]

On November 22, 1849, the Verein was instructed by Kroeber, the attorney, to have all the letters of Castell and Cappes copied.

[25] Committee of Verein, Wiesbaden, September 14, 1849, to Becker. SB Archives, XLII, 42.

The Hanging Mob

CHAPTER 16

P hilip Cappes capitalized on the unhappiness of the colonists to set up the framework of a plot. The colonists had reason for their discontent; they had come to Texas picturing themselves as land-owners, but here they waited in New Braunfels, many miles from those acres. The time limit for claiming the land was closing in—August, 1847. The Verein had failed in its promises, and the resultant ill feelings were vented on the man who stood for the Verein—Meusebach.

Although Cappes was not in New Braunfels on the last day of the year, 1846, he helped to set the stage for a revolt against the Commissioner-General. Contrary to Meusebach's advice, Cappes invited Fisher to New Braunfels. After having done so, however, Cappes wondered to himself, "Is Fisher likely to change horses?"[1]

Meusebach was Fisher's host at breakfast on December 31, when a group of colonists led by disgruntled Rudolph Iwonski began vociferously making its demands. These demands had been listed with the obvious assistance of Fisher:

1) All immigrants shall receive land in the Grant without preference; Mr. Fisher shall look after the interests of the immigrants.

2) The survey of the lands shall be carried out without any preference; Mr. Fisher shall safeguard the interests of the colonists in seeing to an early survey.

3) The immigrants who did not receive town lots in New Braunfels, though they were in Prince Solms's original group, shall now receive those lots.

4) The disposition of the wooded area claimed by the colonists as a city park, the title of which is still held by the Verein, shall be cleared by testimony of Prince Solms.

5) Mr. von Meusebach shall demand discharge from his present duties from

[1] Cappes, Galveston, October 29, 1846, to Castell. Solms-Braunfels Archives, XLI, 46.

the directors of the Verein. He will continue to direct its affairs until the arrival of his successor.[2]

Fisher was ostensibly placating the rioters, when in reality he was inciting them to action.[3]

The mob, spurred on by Iwonski's shouts, pressed into the room; Herber brandished a large whip that he found there. Meusebach stood quietly and talked with them in measured tones. This cool composure so heated the mob that some called out, "Hang him!" Meusebach remained unruffled, and presently the crowd of about 120 men dispersed, but not until a full box of cigars was entirely emptied. As the proceedings of the morning came to a climax Fisher was noticeably absent.[4]

On the afternoon of this mob action a deputation of Americans living in New Braunfels came spontaneously to Meusebach to express their indignation over the event and their willingness to stand by him to their "last drop of blood." On the following day, January 1, 1847, a group of Americans as well as a number of German colonists assembled and passed resolutions condemning the action of the mob and declaring it a slander to the wishes of the community.[5] The assembly authorized publication of the resolutions in the *New Era Houston Democrat*.[6]

This action on the part of responsible citizens gave satisfaction to Meusebach, but he decided to go ahead with the resignation he had determined months earlier to make. After only a few weeks in New Braunfels, he had recognized that the Verein did not actually know what its business was and he had wanted to resign immediately so that he could return to Germany and inform the members of the Society of the conditions of their undertaking in Texas. He had remained at his post, however, to guide the project through its perilous times. Now before laying down his work he decided to carry out his plan of long standing, to make a peace treaty with the Indians. Since a representative of the Verein, Philip Cappes, was at hand, Meusebach decided to turn his office over to him, at least for the time being.

Meusebach knew, to an extent, the duplicity of Cappes, for in his letter

[2] Meusebach, Fredericksburg, January 19, 1847, to Verein. SB Archives, XXVIII, 20–23.

[3] *Ibid.*, p. 165.

[4] Oswald Mueller (trans.), *Roemer's Texas*, p. 217.

[5] Alwin H. Sörgel, Indian Point, January 1, 1847, to Cappes. SB Archives, XXVIII, 23–25. Sörgel was in New Braunfels on December 31, 1846, but was sent to Indian Point the next day by Meusebach.

[6] Meusebach, Fredericksburg, January 19, 1847, to Verein. SB Archives, XXVIII, 163–165.

asking Cappes to handle matters while he was absent on the expedition to the Indians, he said that it was Cappes' invitation to Fisher—which Meusebach had advised against—that had provided Fisher with the opening he wanted to gain control of the land grant. Fisher included provisos for that purpose in the demands voiced by the mob, which he helped incite.

One of the grievances listed by the rioters related to the ownership of a certain park area. During the single month of April, 1845, in which Prince Solms was actually in New Braunfels with the colonists, he had designated a wooded area as a park for them, but he did not give a title making it a community property. Now the colonists wanted the Prince in Germany to decide whether the area belonged to the Society or to the colony-community. When this question arose at a meeting of the Society in Germany in March, 1847, Castell remarked: "Why should we be so foolish as to give a forest to a city whose future citizens we do not know? These *Halunken* make a thousand demands but want to do nothing."[7]

The uprising against Meusebach hurt him deeply. The colonists were justified in wanting the land which had been promised to them; in that he concurred with them wholeheartedly. But their manner of demanding their rights—mob action—distressed him. He, however, found some balm in thinking that he was taking the blame for the Society and that his own integrity had not been assailed.

He would let nothing deter him from securing the titles to the lands. The Grant should have been ready for occupancy before the Verein sent one person to Texas. In reality the immigrants were the donors, for it was only by their presence in the land that the Society had claim to it, although the Society wished to appear as the donor to those immigrating. Meusebach made a point of letting the colonists know that they were under obligation to the Republic of Texas for the grant of land.

Surveying the land now occupied by Indians was the first step to securing a title. An American courier who had been employed by the colony vanished when he learned that Meusebach intended to go into the heart of the Grant.[8] Surveyors refused to go unless Meusebach settled the Indian question.[9] In early December he had organized his expedition, with plans to go as far as "the San Saba Fort."[10]

[7] Castell, Wiesbaden, March, 1847, to Cappes. SB Archives, XLI, 274.

[8] Meusebach, Fredericksburg, January 19, 1847, to Verein. SB Archives, XXVIII, 182.

[9] John O. Meusebach, *Answer to Interrogatories*, p. 23.

[10] *Ibid.*, p. 24.

Meusebach's determination to get into the Grant was strengthened when he heard that Dr. Schubbert had enlisted a number of the Fredericks-burg colonists and, armed with a cannon, had set forth to be the first white man inside the limits of the Grant. When the expedition reached the vicinity of the Llano River scouts were sent out to find a place to ford the river. The scouts brought back the news that a large body of Indians— 40,000 to 60,000—was encamped on the other side of the river. That night the guards left their horses saddled. The next morning, without a shot having been fired, Dr. Schubbert ordered an immediate return home. Julius Splittgerber, who reported this incident, said that he and Lieutenant Bene experienced the feelings of Moses, who saw the Promised Land, but got no farther.[11]

This expedition had not been authorized by Meusebach. The Fredericks-burg director had made the decision himself, without any consultation. When the time came to report to Meusebach, Schubbert could not include any self-glorification. He stated that it was impossible to get into the Grant because it was full of hostile Indians. Meusebach realized immediately that "that report could not be allowed to go abroad unrebuked. It would have created despondency amongst the emigrants and the company."[12] Rumors were current that Texas state officials felt that this was an un-propitious time to go into the Indian lands, because a conflict with the Comanches would be unavoidable. Meusebach did not let this report deter him; he did, however, take every precaution possible, including supplying his company with side arms.

As he meditated about an approach to the Indians he discarded en-tirely Prince Solms's plan of a military attack. In fact, Meusebach had never entertained such an idea. A small expedition, he decided, should advance into the Comanche territory peacefully. William Penn, he knew, had made a treaty with the Indians in Pennsylvania using that approach, and a lasting peace was the result. Meusebach determined to use Penn's peaceful method with the warlike Comanches.

Meusebach set out from New Branufels to travel through Fredericks-burg in early January, 1847, soon after the uprising against him. It was obvious that the uprising had been engineered through intrigue.[13] Meuse-bach, aware that similar machinations were going on among the officials

---

[11] Robert Penniger (ed., comp.), *Fest-Ausgabe zum fünfzigjährigen Jubiläum der Deutschen Kolonie Friedrichsburg*, p. 71.

[12] Meusebach, *Answer to Interrogatories*, p. 23.

[13] Meusebach, Fredericksburg, January 19, 1847, to Verein. SB Archives, XXVIII, 180.

in the Fredericksburg colony, was prepared for any unpleasant reception at the new settlement. Yet he expected his friendship with Schubbert to be lasting and free of deception. He was to be disappointed.

Apparently, Schubbert felt so frustrated and perhaps humiliated over his abortive plan of being first in the Grant that he looked awry at the man who was going straight ahead with plans to face the Indians in the Grant and even to explore for minerals in the San Saba area. Schubbert knew of the "revolution" against Meusebach in New Braunfels and wanted to instigate a similar revolt in Fredericksburg. Just the opposite took place—the entire colony came out to meet the Commissioner-General and saluted him by firing the cannon. They presented him with a written resolution urging him, for the good of the colony, not to resign. The resolution was signed by ninety-five citizens and heads of families:

Fredericksburg, January 17, 1847

Bene	Heinrich Leifeste
Georg Fritze	Jacob Hart
Conrad Wittneben	Peter Honis
Lehrer J. Leydendecker	Christoph Voges
Schlickgerber	Albert Meinhardt
Johannes Schmidt	Christian Ebers
Heinrich August Heimann	Ludwig Wahrmund
H. Wittke II	Gottfried Triebs
Ernst Dannhilm	Paul Cost
Johann Klein	Michel Thomas
Christofel Brinckrolf	H. G. Hasserodt
Andreas Möllering	Jakob Treibs
Friedrich Lochte	Adam Muter
Adam Schüssler	Christoph Feuge
Martin Helmuth	Wendel Mittel
Braun	Leonard Welyn
Phillipp Simon	Conrad Ernst
Ludwig Mayer	Herrmann Hitzfeldt
Philipp Klärner	Aug. Spilker
Gottfried Bader	Johann Metzger
Friedrich Kiehne	Johann Görg Görg
Johann Philipp Mahr	Carl Meier
Martin Mahr	Christian August Hase
Joh. Ad. Keller	J. Herber
Joh. Keller	Johann Leyndecker I
Anton Menges.	August Schüler
Friedrich Siegmann	C. Wissemann

Nickolaus Mosel	Peter Burg
Jos. Bape	Wilhelm Kraile
C. Althaus	Quintel
Cunst	Conrad Nückel
F S Kutscher	Heinrich v. d. Brelje
George Crusmann	Jo. Mugling
Wilh. Stieren	Grün
Jakob Arhelger	Budde
Daniel Arhelger	Heinrich Wittnebe
Heinrich Kussenberger	Friedrich Suchart
Peter Kurzenaker	Adolph Hermann.
Johannes Peter Keller III	F L Rudolph
Jakob Röder	Peter Lerens
Conrad Plunneke	Wilhelm Krämer
Heinrich Bierschwalle	A. Nitte
Heinrich Schmidt	Schuh
Friedrig Schmidt	Anton Maier
Daniel Weinershausen	Dr. jur Roemer
Frierich Winkel	Friedrich Schmidt
Heinrich Taltoor	Bickel[14]
Friedrich Leifeste	

Meusebach was pleased that despite Schubbert's attempt to arouse the colonists in protest they had taken it upon themselves to make a spontaneous jubilation to honor him. The attempt at rebellion brought to mind Fisher's alienation of colonists in February, 1845, which caused them to break their commitment to the Verein and go to Schubbert's St. Gabriel colony.[15] The double-dealing of Fisher apparently was practiced by his one-time associate, Schubbert. This man seemed to heap favors on his circle of friends; the people whom he disliked he dealt with summarily, even to the point of sending them out of the community, making it indelibly clear that they were never to return. He used this method with the individual who revealed that the name "Schubbert" was an alias for Frederic Armand Strubberg.[16]

Despite the high-handed methods of their director, or perhaps because of them, the colonists at Fredericksburg had developed a quality of resourcefulness. They were thrown back on their own ingenuity, and looked nowhere else for answers. One of their number remarked, "This much was

[14] Petition of citizens of Fredericksburg, January 17, 1847. SB Archives, XXVIII, 197–198.

[15] Certificates arranged by Henry Francis Fisher, Galveston, February 12, 1845. SB Archives, XL, 110.

[16] Penniger (ed., comp.), *Fest-Ausgabe*, pp. 79–81.

certain, there was no way around the fact: we had much work before us."[17]

These newcomers to the Fredericksburg area early had made friends with nature and within a short time had the good earth ready to provide food. With the native grass, almost half the height of a man, they had built the first huts.[18] When covered with this grass, the roofs were rain proof. Already in 1847 there was evidence that the colonists would build more permanent structures. From the rock-ribbed hills they were bringing limestone—the stone, about which Meusebach had written the previous year, that "hardens in the air and would be excellent for houses,"[19] Artisans, using that stone and the sand and gravel at hand, would soon bring an indigenous style of building to the colony. They used also hewn logs for building. The log framework filled in with mortar, reeds, and sage grass formed the distinctive *Fachwerk* construction.

Much of the lumber that they used came from the sawmill on the Pedernales in the Mormon community of Zodiac, four miles southeast of Fredericksburg. Meusebach had welcomed the Mormons when they established a settlement in 1847. Their technical skill in the building and operation of a sawmill, as well as of a gristmill, was a useful addition to this pioneer region.

Meusebach was pleased that the colonists were taking the initiative in making a living. He was relieved that health conditions were improving; illness and death had taken a fearful toll. Dr. Schubbert had certainly exerted himself in establishing a working colony, but the reports of his attention to "wine and women" persisted. His reputation suffered further when it was learned that he was using an assumed name and when it was rumored that he had had no professional medical training. Only one conclusion could be reached: "Doctor" Schubbert would have to be replaced.

Meusebach's realization that he could not rely on Dr. Schubbert was a great disappointment. Now the association of Schubbert and Cappes raised questions in Meusebach's mind about each of them. The Commissioner-General came to the conclusion that it would be unwise to turn his office over to Cappes.

Meusebach shoved to the background, as far as that was possible, the disturbing situation near at hand. He gave his full attention to the requirements of his expedition, soon to start for the Grant. The state could provide no escort. One report was that the Mexicans had incited the Indians

[17] *Ibid.*, p. 67.
[18] *Ibid.*
[19] Meusebach, New Braunfels, July 28, 1846, to Castell. SB Archives, LII, 219.

against the whites. Meusebach tried to remain composed in his thinking, for he needed to call up all the skill and resourcefulness he possessed. He desired that every possible precaution be taken. Life or death being precariously in the balance for his troop and for himself when dealing with the Indians. After preparations were complete he gave the go-ahead signal. The men's farewell to their families made him poignantly aware of his responsibility.

The expedition, under Meusebach's orders, started two days ahead of him. He remained to write a lengthy report to Castell, in which he related the current conditions of the two colonies and his plans for work. He emphasized his plan of determining the site of the settlement of Castell,[20] which was to be on the north bank of the Llano. The settlement would at last put the Verein within the bounds of the Grant. He planned further to have several log houses erected at the proposed site of Castell. The work was to be done by the men in the wagons accompanying his expedition to the Indians. These men were not to go to Fort San Saba, but were to return to Fredericksburg immediately after the Indian parley. The road from New Braunfels to Fredericksburg was to be improved; it was already one of the best roads in Texas. After that work was completed, he planned to have the road from Fredericksburg to Castell improved also.

Because the surveyors would not agree to go into that region unless some form of protection was arranged, Cappes had been instructed to form a small civilian company. Payment for the surveyors needed to be provided. Though payments could be made in monthly installments, the sum total would come to $80,000, the amount of capital with which the Verein had started.

Meusebach pointed out that seven hundred immigrants still remained at Indian Point, although at least 180 hired wagons had been in constant use for four months transporting people. Because the teamsters had broken their contracts, Meusebach had bought 78 wagons so that transportation would not be stopped. For supplies, he had ordered 24,000 bushels of corn at ninety cents a bushel, which were delivered to New Braunfels; 1,000 cows and calves at $10.00 each; and 1,400 sheep and goats at $1.25 to $1.50 each. Butchering, which went on daily in both settlements, was another expenditure.

Meusebach reiterated the request made four months earlier for $80,000. The cost of surveying would have to be paid as each survey was completed, because interest accrued on overdue bills. Meusebach pointed out the possi-

[20] Meusebach, New Braunfels, January 9, 1847, to Castell. SB Archives, XXVIII, 182.

bility of receiving 1,600,000 acres bonus from the Republic of Texas. If the Verein sold the land at $1 per acre, the original investment of $80,000 would be increased to $1,600,000. But unless funds came at the right time, everything would go progressively downward. Nothing would be left but the claims of the immigrants to their land and the obligations of the Verein to satisfy the claims.

Meusebach's ray of hope was the possibility of finding the silver mines believed to exist between the Llano and San Saba Rivers. But he added, "I do not really count the silver mines until we have them."[21]

The Commissioner-General stated that the entire financial report through December 31, 1846, was in preparation, but before it could be concluded reports had to come in from Fredericksburg, New Braunfels, Indian Point, Galveston, and New Orleans. He planned to send the complete report immediately on his return from the Indian expedition. The books stood open to Cappes or anyone authorized to inspect them.[22]

In conclusion Meusebach said that he wished to be relieved of his position; he expected to go to Germany, where he would report in person to the Verein. He felt that he would be discharging his last responsibility to the Verein in showing that the Grant could be visited, that surveying could be undertaken without government protection, and that colonies could be founded far beyond the line of the present settlements. Meusebach's final words were in the form of a plea: "From this point on, it will be necessary to march forward on the way that has been opened, to carry on what has been made ready, to improve and finish what has been begun."[23] With this appeal for cooperation he closed the letter.

Arising early the next morning, January 24, Meusebach rode out with the belated surveyors to join the expedition that had started two days earlier.

Hazards of known and unknown proportions awaited him.

[21] *Ibid.*, p. 189.
[22] *Ibid.*, p. 186.
[23] *Ibid.*, p. 187.

Land of the Comanche

CHAPTER 17

The Comanche tribe was notorious for its savagery and atrocity, Bernard De Voto, in *The Year of Decision: 1846*, states that "No one has ever exaggerated the Comanche tortures."[1] Furthermore, Rupert N. Richardson, an authority on Indians, gives this account of Comanche behavior:

The Comanches rather than the Spaniards had come to be aggressors. . . . During their century of contact with Spaniards and Mexicans, the Comanches acquired many bad habits. They learned to expect presents and regarded them as a reward for keeping the peace during those times when they found it expedient not to make war.[2]

In the face of these conditions Meusebach undertook an expedition with peace as its only objective.

On January 22, 1847, Meusebach had sent about forty men, including an interpreter, Lorenzo de Rozas, and three wagons out of Fredericksburg, headed north for Comanche territory. The Commissioner-General joined them two days later. Difficulties arose immediately. A member of the party, the best hunter, was severely wounded the first day out and had to return to Fredericksburg. A prairie fire raged at the second camp for thirty-six hours, destroying all forage for the horses for many miles.

Several Shawnees who could speak broken English came into the camp, and Meusebach engaged three of them as hunters. Indian scouts followed the troop secretly. Some miles beyond the crossing of the Llano at the mouth of Beaver Creek, the Indian Chief Ketemoczy came into the open. From that point, Meusebach's laconic recitation of this epochal expedition is quoted from his booklet, *Answer to Interrogatories*:

[1] Bernard De Voto, *The Year of Decision: 1846*, p. 245.
[2] Rupert Norval Richardson, *The Comanche Barrier to South Plains Settlement*, p. 75.

. . . [I] was met by the Comanche Chief Ketemoczy, at the place where now stands the town of Mason, and held the first council with him where now the store of Mr. Doole is located, I believe. Ketemoczy promised to gather, within a few days, the head chiefs at the San Saba [River] to hear my propositions for a treaty of peace, and showed us the nearest road to the river. When I had been in council for a number of days, with large bands of well-drilled and armed Comanches, and their chiefs, at the San Saba (at the place which is now known as the Camp Colorado crossing), Major [Robert S.] Neighbors came on as the bearer of a dispatch from Governor Henderson, dissuading from entering the colony, as the Indians were reported to be on the war path; at the same time recommending the Major as an expert in treatying with the Indians—if I would not return. The Major had been Indian agent for the Lipans under the Republic of Texas.

I engaged him for the remainder of the trip, dismissed most of my company with the wagons, keeping only about seven men, agreeing with the Indians that at the next full moon the peace council with all the head chiefs of the western bands of Comanches should be held at the lower San Saba, and use the time remaining untill full moon for an exploration of the lands on that fabulous San Saba River, Spanish Fort, Brady Creek, and surrounding places. At full moon we were at the agreed spot on the lower San Saba, about 25 miles above its mouth into Colorado River, made a treaty with the head chiefs. Buffalo Hump, Santa Anna, and Mopechucope, and their people, for all the western bands of Comanches, promised them $3000 worth of presents, for which consideration they on their part promised and agreed not to disturb our surveyors in their work, nor to do any harm to our colonists. Dr. Roemer, the geologist, whom I had invited to stay with us as our guest at New Braunfels during his sojourn in Texas, came along with Major Neighbors, when I was encamped with the Indians some days at the San Saba. I invited him to go along with me and my company on our further trip.[3]

Roemer related his experiences with the expedition in his book *Texas.* He mentions the "royal reception" accorded Meusebach when he reached the central camp of the Comanches: "About two hundred (of whom about eighty were warriirs) dressed in festive attire and arranged themselves on a hill in military formation. After Herr von Meusebach had ridden toward them and by discharing his rifle had given proof of his confidence in them, mutual greetings were exchanged." The scene was picturesque, even imposing. Roemer continues:

The three covered wagons which had been drawn into the center of the camp, were an arresting sight in this pathless wilderness, in which up till now no wagon very likely had entered. Around these the tents had been erected and

[3] John O. Meusebach, *Answer to Interrogatories,* p. 23–25.

in front of them whites and Indians mingled in a motley crowd. Even the whites were of diverse appearance and of mixed origin. In addition to a number of unaffected Germans with genuine peasant features, one noticed in the immediate vicinity a group of Mexican muleteers with the unmistakable southern facial expression; then there were a number of American surveyors, equally peculiar representatives of a third nationality, which von Meusebach carried with him in order to point out to them the land to be surveyed.[4]

Roemer mentions two young persons among the Indians who attracted his attention: One was a young man about eighteen years of age, easily recognized as an Anglo, but now "Indianized." Behind him rode an eight-year-old Mexican lad. When Roemer asked the Anglo-American how the Mexican lad had come there, he answered, " 'I caught him on the Rio Grande'." Roemer writes, "This was said in a tone of voice, as if he were speaking of some animal."[5] The second person to attract Roemer's attention was a twelve-year-old Indian boy who spoke English. Roemer found out that the lad had been captured by the whites during the 1840 Council House Fight in San Antonio. He was later returned to the Comanches. The marked respect with which the tribe treated this lad indicated the high rank of his father, who had been killed in the San Antonio fight.

In addition to Meusebach's and Roemer's accounts of the expedition, one of the six officer aides from Germany who accompanied Meusebach wrote an account of his experiences:

When Chief Ketemoczy approached Meusebach, he demanded to know whether the white men visited this land with friendly intentions or to do battle with the Indians, the latter of which Ketemoczy declared would be entirely agreeable to him.

Meusebach replied that his group had come to visit as neighbors; that the two towns which he represented intended to extend hospitality to the Indians. He now expected hospitality from them, his Indian hosts. Further, he demanded that they meet his group with integrity, that they practice no treachery, and steal no horses. Ketemoczy promised to notify the chiefs of the Comanches of the visitors' intentions and to summon them to a great gathering at the next full moon to conclude a solemn peace. The Comanche chief declared that he considered Meusebach "as great a chief as the sun."[6]

While Meusebach's primary purpose for going into the Fisher-Miller

---

[4] Oswald Mueller (trans.), *Roemer's Texas*, p. 242.

[5] *Ibid.*, p. 243.

[6] Anonymous, "Meusebach's Zug in das Gebiet der Comanche-Indianer in Januar 1847 (Aus einer alten Nummer des 'Magazin für die Literatur des Auslandes')," in Robert Penniger (ed., comp.), *Fest-Ausgabe*, p. 101.

Grant was to bring about peaceful relations with the Indians, he also wanted to visit the San Saba Mission, or Fort, and to discover whether the region of the Grant was suitable for the settlement of the colonists.

For the duration of the expedition, Jim Shaw, a Delaware Indian, had been engaged by Meusebach to act as interpreter. At a council meeting Shaw told the chiefs the following for Meusebach: " 'He has come with his people on the peace path to view the land and to greet you as friends. You will also be received as friends when visiting the cities of his people. He now desires to go up the river to see the old Spanish fort'."[7]

One of the chiefs replied with great dignity, as follows: " 'The hearts of my people were alarmed when they saw so many strange people, who had not previously announced their coming, and whose intention they did not know. But now, since we are assured that they have come as friends and have declared the purpose of their coming, all is well'."[8] Being thus reassured, the expedition set forth to visit the Spanish fort. This had been their intention from the beginning, since there was a "persistent rumor among the Texas settlers that the Spaniards had worked some silver mines in the vicinity of the fort."[9]

Because of the difficulty in moving wagons over the pathless hills, some of the men took them back to the settlement. The seventeen men remaining then traveled for seven days, and on February 18, 1847, they reached the old Spanish fort on the San Saba River. Roemer gives a minute description of the ruins. On the portals of the main entrance the visitors found the names of men who had been there during this century: Padillo, 1810; Cos, 1829; Bowie *(con su tropa)*, 1829; Moore, 1840. Various things made Roemer doubt whether a mission had ever been there. His conclusion suggests that the structure was primarily a fort erected to gain a foothold in the San Saba Valley. Roemer relates further that Texas legends say "the fort was supposed to have been starved into submission in the last quarter of the previous century by the Comanches; the Spanish garrison was put to death and the buildings destroyed."[10] According to other legends, the Spaniards "were supposed to have worked some rich silver mines here, and the old fort was supposedly erected to protect a mine nearby."[11]

Roemer and Meusebach studied the area on a geological basis. Roemer states his conclusion in these words: "One may make the claim without

[7] Mueller (trans.), *Roemer's Texas*, p. 246.
[8] *Ibid.*
[9] *Ibid.*, p. 247.
[10] *Ibid.*, p. 257.
[11] *Ibid.*, p. 258.

hesitation, that at least in the vicinity of the fort no deposits of precious metals are present."[12] But he did not rule out the possibility of ore in both the San Saba and Llano regions.

The second reason for investigating the land lying in the Fisher-Miller Grant was to find whether the soil was suitable for farming and whether the region itself was a desirable place for settlements. Only relatively small sections were found to be satisfactory for farming. On the subject of settlements, Dr. Roemer gives his opinion succinctly: "After careful deliberations I must declare, although with reluctance, since so many exertions have been put forth, that the land in question on the right bank of the Colorado and the region north of the Llano is not the proper place for a settlement by the Germans, at least not at the present time."[13]

At the full of the moon, according to agreement with Ketemoczy, the Meusebach-Roemer group returned from the San Saba excursion to the main Comanche camp. There on March 1–2, 1847, negotiations took place.

All the young warriors of the tribe, several hundred of them, dressed ready for a foray into Mexico, lined up on one side of their camping ground near the San Saba River, the squaws and children on the other. In the center of this array the three head chiefs, Buffalo Hump, Santa Anna, and Mopechucope, sat on buffalo robes.

Meusebach's first act was to ride down one side of the assembled warriors and up the other side. Then he emptied his firearms into the air. His aides did the same. The act of discharging their firearms has been interpreted in various ways. Some say it showed foolhardiness; others say it was a gesture to show confidence in the Indians. A credible interpretation has been recorded by one of the German aides, who actually discharged his gun at the parley. He wrote the following account after his return to Germany:

Although the fact that the Germans discharged their guns at the meeting with the Comanches was considered imprudent and seemed to show an entire lack of understanding of Indian character, it was the best policy or course of action which could have been followed. Several hundred warriors faced us and great numbers were behind us. Each one was well armed—many with guns, a number with spears, and all with bows and arrows. Had it been their purpose to kill us, it would have come to hand-to-hand combat. In this our guns would have been useless and only our pistols and knives (Bowie knives) would have served for our defense. So why should we not show confidence?[14]

[12] *Ibid.*, p. 259.
[13] *Ibid.*, p. 286.
[14] Anonymous, "Meusebach's Zug," in Penniger (ed., comp.) *Fest-Ausgabe*, p. 101.

With confidence established Meusebach advanced toward the chiefs. Buffalo robes were provided for Meusebach, his aides and interpreter, and negotiations began. Meusebach conducted the meeting with great skill. The Indians recognized the bravery of this young negotiator. As a mark of respect they called him "El Sol Colorado," The Red Sun. The giving of a special name signifies a unique honor among Indians. As soon as the terms of the treaty were agreed upon, the pipe of peace was passed. It was determined that the chiefs would come to Fredericksburg to sign the treaty after conferring with other Comanche chiefs not present. To celebrate the conclusion of the treaty the Germans in the camp invited the Indians to a feast of rice and venison. This invitation had some undesirable results, for thereafter the Indians often came to meals unbidden. The Comanches never provided food. In due time, on May 9, 1847, the Comanche chiefs came to Fredericksburg to sign the treaty and collect the $3,000 worth of presents promised them.

According to W. W. Newcomb, the Comanches were "the principal and most stubborn adversaries the Texans had." Put onto reservations by the federal government in 1875, they were the last Indians to surrender. "Until the last years of their independence," continues Newcomb, "they raided through much of the state, to say nothing of Mexico, and killed or captured men, women, and children, carried off what loot they could, and burned the rest."[15] In view of this statement, it is significant that, in the main, the treaty which Meusebach made with the Indians was observed. It established a friendly relationship between the two peoples. The terms provided for free and unmolested travel in each other's territory. The surveyors and colonists could go undisturbed into the Indians' land. Chief Santa Anna was a frequent visitor to the white settlements; he was a staunch friend of the Germans and he kept the Comanches in line. Fredericksburg and the outlying farms were exposed to Indian depredations. Some atrocities were committed, but it is believed that the number was insignificant compared to what might have been had Meusebach failed in his mission. The Indians remarked that the government seemed to use German settlements as outposts. Pioneers have stated that as long as the German settlers did not infringe on such things as hunting rights, peace with the Indians prevailed.

Major Neighbors, Governor Henderson's messenger to Meusebach, was appointed special Indian agent on March 20, 1847. He reported the peace-

[15] W. W. Newcomb, Jr., *The Indians of Texas: From Prehistoric to Modern Times,* p. 155.

making events to Colonel W. Medill, United States Commissioner of Indian Affairs, as follows:

For your information, I here state—That Gov. Henderson, apprehending serious difficulty with the Comanches about the 1st of Feb. last, from the introduction of setlers [*sic*], and the surveying of that section of Country granted to a German Company, by its late Replic [*sic*] of Texas in 1841–2, whilst at war with the Comanche Tribe (a part of said Grant being now inhabited by the Comanches). The said Company was compeled [*sic*] to complete their survey by 1st Sept. next or forfeit their claims, they were under the impression that a force would be necessary, and had commenced organizing the German Colonists into companies to force their Surveys—Gov. Henderson solicited my interference. I immediately met the Comanches, and succeeded in forming the preliminaries of a friendly arrangement which is to be carried into effect the 1st of May.[16]

"At least two accounts of this expedition disagree with Neighbors that he formed the preliminaries of a friendly arrangement with the Comanches,"[17] says R. L. Biesele. The two accounts referred to are those given by Meusebach and Roemer. Neighbors' report is at variance with Meusebach's in several respects. The German group, for example, had no intention of organizing "into companies to force their surveys." The Indian agent, claiming that he met with the Comanches "immediately," ignores the fact that Meusebach had been "in council for a number of days." And in assuming credit for the "friendly arrangement," he gives no indication that anyone else had a part in the negotiations. A mere statement of facts would have named Meusebach and his men responsible for arranging the meeting; the same holds for the implementation of the treaty on May 9, when the equivalent of $3,000, largely in presents, was paid to the Comanches by the Germans.

In his dissertation on the Major, Kenneth F. Neighbors takes cognizance of the variance in the accounts by saying: "It has been urged that Major Neighbors claimed too much in the last sentence of his report . . ." In answer to this criticism K. F. Neighbors remarks, "Had Neighbors wished to aggrandize himself, he would not have buried the episode in two cryptic sentences at the end of the report."[18]

Meusebach included the contribution of his companions as he said ". . .

---

[16] Rudolph Leopold Biesele, *The History of the German Settlements in Texas, 1831–1861*, p. 185.

[17] *Ibid.*

[18] Kenneth Franklin Neighbors, "Robert S. Neighbors in Texas, 1836–1856: A Quarter Century of Frontier Problems" (Ph.D. Dissertation, The University of Texas), p. 112.

we were at the agreed spot . . . [and] made a treaty with the head chiefs
. . . and their people." Major Neighbors was present and helpful during
the occasion, but it was Meusebach who negotiated the treaty of March
1–2, 1847, with the Comanches.

Neighbors' report appears to be the basis for statements regarding the
treaty made by Newcomb, who says that Neighbors was able to settle the
"dispute" by a treaty in which the Indians were given $3,000 worth of
presents.[19] Newcomb, by his failure to name the person or organization
who supplied the gifts, implies that it was Neighbors. The report also
appears to be the source on which Richardson[20] bases his statement that
Neighbors, aided by the tact and good sense of the Germans, settled the
immediate difficulty. The actual role of Neighbors in making the treaty,
however, appears to fall short of that which has been ascribed to him.

Both Newcomb and Richardson quote extensively from Roemer on
other matters; yet they seem to have ignored his statement which bears
most directly on this particular incident: "To Herr von Meusebach goes
the credit for having recognized the importance of this undertaking and
for carrying it out with determination and great circumspection."[21]

Meusebach's success with the red men may have been due in part to
his attitude toward the Indian race. We have, for example, the following
statement made by Meusebach when he was negotiating the terms of the
treaty: " 'When my people have lived with you for some time, and when
we know each other better, then it may happen that some wish to marry.
Soon our warriors will learn your language. If they then wish to wed a
girl of your tribe, I do not see any obstacle, and our people will be so
much better friends'." Further, in the same speech, he says, " 'My brother
speaks of a barrier between the red men and the palefaces. I do not disdain
my red brethren because their skin is darker, and I do not think more of
the white people because their complexion is lighter'."[22]

Certain innate characteristics cannot be changed by the signing of a
treaty. Meusebach's own experience demonstrated this fact. Shortly after
his resignation from the work of the Society in July, 1847, he was living
at Comanche Springs, twenty miles north of San Antonio. There the
Indians came to visit him. The farm overseer came running to warn
Meusebach to seek safety. Instead of doing that Meusebach said, "Prepare

[19] Newcomb, *The Indians of Texas*, p. 353.

[20] Richardson, *The Comanche Barrier to South Plains Settlement*, p. 147.

[21] Mueller (trans.), *Roemer's Texas*, p. 284.

[22] Anonymous, "Meusebach's Zug," in Penniger (ed., comp.), *Fest-Ausgabe*, p.
104.

food for the Indians,"[23] then he went out to meet them and invite them to dinner. He ate with them at his table, set with his best linen and silver. Soon they went peacefully on their way to Austin. On their return from Austin, where their demands did not receive favorable attention, they came again to Comanche Springs. This time they helped themselves to the horses on the farm.

Allowances for minor infringements must be made. The fact that the treaty, in the large, established a peace that was actually adhered to was confirmed some eleven years after it had been signed, when Colonel Jack Hays, the celebrated Indian fighter, was a visitor in the Meusebach home at Comanche Springs. The Colonel told Meusebach "that he was never molested nor lost any animals during his travel within the limits of our colony, but as soon as he had passed the line he had losses."[24]

Surveyors refused to go into the Grant before the treaty was made. Soon thereafter, however, they carried out their assignment without harm from the Indians. If the Society had not had its lands surveyed the contract with the government of Texas would have lapsed and the colonists would not have received their allotments of land. The records in the General Land Office show that the Republic of Texas granted 1,735,200 acres to the Verein's settlers. The treaty opened to civilization 3,878,000 acres of land, from which these counties, or parts thereof, have been formed: Concho, Kimble, Llano, Mason, McCulloch, Menard, San Saba, Schleicher, Sutton, and Tom Green.

Legends of the Indians and of the Old World, and a story created to meet the need of a moment in Texas are woven together to produce the fabric of the "Easter Fires" at Fredericksburg, a celebration that commemorates the making of the peace treaty and the safe return of the colonists and their leader.

During the absence of the white men on the expedition the Indians reportedly watched the settlement to see that no treachery was perpetrated there while the Indian chiefs were gathering on the San Saba River to hear Meusebach's proposals of peace. Messages were transmitted by smoke signals. When the honesty of the colonists was apparent to the Indian scouts the fires burned high on the hills surrounding Fredericksburg as a sign to the Indians that all was well.

In Germany for centuries the custom has been to set Easter Eve fires ablaze on the hills near the villages. Long in advance the young people

---

[23] Lucy Meusebach Marschall, Notes and Memoranda. MSS. Meusebach Family Files.
[24] Meusebach, *Answer to Interrogatories*, pp. 25–26.

collect firewood, and neighboring villages vie with each other to send up
the brightest blaze. The farmers believe that as far as the light from the
fires reaches, the fields will be fruitful, and that the soil over which ashes
or even the wind from the fires is blown will have increased fertility.[25]
They believe also that the houses on which the light shines will be safe
from sickness.

Why the fires burned on the Texas hills or how they peaceably came
to be on this particular Easter Eve during the expedition did not concern
the little children of one man who was away in the Indian country. The
fires frightened the children and the mother sought a way to still their
fears. She recalled the hilltop fires in Germany and the stories her mother
was wont to tell her of the Easter Rabbit. She knew that her own children
and those of the neighbors had been delighted when they once saw a bunny
rabbit in the Texas fields, and they had reported with especial pleasure
seeing a long-ear jack rabbit, several times as large as a bunny.

The mother ingeniously put the various ideas together and made up
her own story. She told her children that the Easter Rabbit placed eggs
in kettles that were boiling over the fires on the hilltops, then colored
them with flowers, and on Easter morning laid them in nests. Often the
color of the eggs matched the colors of the flowers in the nests. If the eggs
were extra large the jack rabbit provided them.

The Easter Rabbit story soothed the children into a happy sleep. Thus,
an incident of history developed into a colorful tradition. The ceremony of
burning the Easter Fires and of dramatizing the story of Meusebach's
treaty-making expedition to the Indians continues in Fredericksburg
today.[26]

At times the Indians made overtures of friendship, as was the case
with the colony of Bettina, the first settlement within the boundary of the
Grant. Dr. Ferdinand von Herff, a surgeon in the colony, successfully
removed a cataract from the eye of a chieftain. A great oak tree served
as an umbrella for the operation. The Indian chief was nonplused when
Dr. Herff would not accept a Mexican girl brought as a token of gratitude.
While the Indians were camping near Bettina some of the settlers' utensils
were stolen by the squaws; but the Indian men returned them the next
day. When the white men visited the Indian camp the Indians spread out
their deerskins and pressed their visitors to take their largest pecans. One

[25] James George Frazer, *The Golden Bough: A Study in Magic and Religion*, pp.
614–615.
[26] William Petmecky, *Legendary Tales—Easter Fires of Fredericksburg, passim.*

of the colonists, Louis Reinhardt, declared, "For everything we gave them, we were paid back three fold."[27]

The stimulus for the founding of Bettina was provided by Prince Solms and Hermann Spiess. During the year 1846 these two men, in speeches at the universities of Heidelberg and Giessen, described Texas so glowingly that it set the students on fire. The Prince pointed out that there was no call in Germany for the professional men whom the universities were turning out. They must find a new and developing country where their services would be in demand. These ideas found lodging in the minds of forty young professional men from the Darmstadt area. Sometimes called the "Society of Forty," they banded together using the watchwords "friendship, freedom, and equality." Dr. Ferdinand von Herff, a relative of Meusebach, and Hermann Spiess were the leaders of the "Society of Forty," who founded Bettina.

Before laying down his office, Meusebach had an opportunity to test the treaty he had recently made with the Indians. Together with Hermann Spiess and a few companions, the treaty-maker forded the Llano River at Catfish Crossing, near which he had chosen the site for Castell while on his expedition to the Indians. Now he selected a site three miles east of future Castell as a location where the forty young men from Darmstadt would soon establish Bettina.[28] The Indians did no harm whatsoever, although they easily could have overpowered the small group of men.

The site was named in honor of Bettina von Arnim, the German feminist who kept abreast of political movements. When Meusebach selected the location for this colony, he was pleased that Bettina, long a friend of his family, was honored in Texas. It was she who had often given stimulus to liberal ideas in Germany.

One of the members of the colony, Louis Reinhardt, called it the "Communistic Colony of Bettina." Henry Dielmann, writing on Dr. Herff, says, "The earliest communists were idealists who attempted to establish communities in which brotherly love and good will were to replace the police rule and in which the voluntary common effort was to take care of the material needs of the group."[29] Gerry C. Gunnin says, " . . . *communitive*

---

[27] Louis Reinhardt, "The Communistic Colony of Bettina, 1846-8," *The Quarterly of the Texas State Historical Association*, III, No. 1 (July, 1899), 39.

[28] Meusebach, New Braunfels, July 20, 1847, to Castell. Solms-Braunfels Archives, XL, 239.

[29] Henry B. Dielmann, "Dr. Ferdinand Herff, Pioneer Physician and Surgeon," *The Southwestern Historical Quarterly*, LVII, No. 3 (January, 1954), 269.

and *communitarian,* terms used as early as 1840, are free of the connotations possessed by *utopian* and *communistic.* Between 1846 and 1900 about seven *co-operative communities* were established in Texas."[30] Bettina and Zodiac were two of the seven.

The agreement that Castell made with the founders of Bettina was that they were to settle, besides themselves, two hundred families in the Grant. In return the group was to receive $12,000 or its equivalent in livestock, agricultural implements, and provisions for one year. The group was expected to support itself by communal efforts after the first year. These young men, called the "Darmstadters" as well as "The Forty," had a glorious experience until it came time to work. At the end of the year, when the community was left to shift for itself, the colony of Bettina dissolved.

The directors of the Society were keenly disappointed that this colony fell through, as they had hoped for others from the cultured classes to follow this group. One member of the Society had remarked, "What an elite group with capital and competence we have now instead of the earlier peasants!"[31]

One result of the establishment of Bettina was the marriage of Hermann Spiess to a young Mexican maiden brought by an Indian chief to live with one of the German families. When she reached the marriageable age, she and Spiess were wed. The couple moved to Missouri, where they lived happily.

Three miles west of Bettina, on the north side of the Llano River, Meusebach chose the site for the second settlement within the limits of the Fisher-Miller Grant. During the year 1847 Baron Emil von Kriewitz led a number of colonists from Fredericksburg to the location, which was given the name of Castell. Each settler received from the Society a log cabin covered with thatch and ten acres of land running back to the river. Although Count Castell's desire to have a county named for him did not materialize, the community bearing his name has the honor of being the first permanent settlement in Llano County. A third settlement, named Leiningen, was established in 1847 five miles east of Castell. It did not flourish long. All settlements originated on the north side of the Llano since that river was the southern boundary of the Fisher-Miller Grant. Two other settlements, Schoenburg, located a few miles down the river from Leiningen, and Meerholz, located north of Castell, were both founded

[30] Gerry C. Gunnin, "French Communitive Socialist Experiments in Texas, 1846–1868" (M.A. Thesis, Baylor University), p. iv.

[31] Grosse, Darmstadt, February 1, 1847, to Castell. SB Archives, LVII, 156.

in 1847. Each endured for only short periods, probably because the settlers preferred to live near Fredericksburg.

Thus, the year 1847 saw the opening to settlement of some 3.80 million acres of wilderness and the actual establishment of several small communities along the edge of the previously uninhabitable Fisher-Miller Grant. Moritz Tiling gives the following evaluation of Meusebach's negotiation of the treaty:

We cannot but admire the courage of von Meusebach, who, with a few followers, fearlessly penetrated into the unknown territory, but must also give due credit to the able and skilled manner in which he dealt with the ferocious and warlike Comanches, inducing them to sign a treaty, which opened the hitherto forbidden land to German settlements.

The opening of this vast territory of 3,000,000 acres [actually 3,878,000] to civilization and cultivation is without doubt the most important pioneer work of the Germans in Texas, and could only be accomplished through the absolute confidence the Indians placed in the Germans' promises and pledges. The Lone Star State owes a debt of gratitude to the early German settlers of the San Saba territory, and their courage and perseverance deserve proper mention in all Texas histories.[32]

---

[32] Moritz Tiling, *History of the German Element in Texas from 1820–1850, and Historical Sketches of the German Texas Singers' League and Houston Turnverein from 1853–1913*, p. 104.

Web of Intrigue

CHAPTER 18

Meusebach came back to New Braunfels after his expedition to the Indians and, with satisfaction, reported that the surveyors were at work in the Grant. As soon as they completed surveying a tract, a colonist could claim it. Except for an arrangement with the very first colonists, each colonist was required to pay the cost of the survey of his tract in advance of claiming it. The total cost of the survey of the entire Grant would be between $120,000 and $130,000 when the enormous expenses attached to the work were included, though Meusebach had first estimated the cost to be $80,000.

As soon as the Commissioner-General had attended to matters that pressed upon him, on April 1 he composed a report to be sent to a meeting of the entire membership of the Verein.[1] It was of primary importance that members know of the existing indebtedness and of expenditures which were forthcoming, particularly those connected with the surveying of the Grant. Five groups of surveyors had been sent to the Grant immediately after the conclusion of the treaty with the Indians. Some surveyors had already been recalled because of the lack of funds with which to pay them.

Retrenchment must be made in every area; in Fredericksburg alone the $8,000 monthly costs should be curtailed. The headquarters for the Verein, suggested Meusebach, should be moved to Fredericksburg and, as soon as possible, moved to Castell, the proposed new settlement. The reason for such a step was to bring all Verein activities within the boundary of its own land.

Meusebach proposed that a tract of six hundred to one thousand acres be opened and planted in corn, which could be harvested immediately if

[1] Meusebach, New Braunfels, April, 1847, to Verein. Solms-Braunfels Archives, XXXI, 61–70.

the fields were adequately cultivated. The work should be done by Americans, since they were acquainted with the land and weather conditions. He believed that the Mormons, who had already shown the Germans how to cultivate their land, would agree to the undertaking. The yield of corn was to be sold and the resulting funds to be used for the expenses of the Verein.

The Commissioner-General suggested that when it became apparent that such a development was thriving colonists from other settlements would come and claim their tracts in the Grant. The Verein would then receive its quota of land in the Grant, which could be sold. This proposal answered a vital question concerning the future of the Verein. Opening entirely new settlements, unless privately financed, was no solution. Unless the Verein consolidated and narrowed its operations bankruptcy was inevitable. In that event all land would be lost and panic would ensue.

As early as November, 1845, Meusebach had written to the Verein that he was ready to resign his post; nevertheless, he had carried on despite increasing difficulties. But in January, 1847, he had submitted his formal resignation. After his return from his expedition to the Indians he reported to the Verein that he had acquired a small farm at Comanche Springs, twenty miles north of San Antonio. He was willing to sell it for the use of the next commissioner-general. He felt, however, that the location was not convenient for an official, since it was some miles away from either Verein settlement. Part of Meusebach's contract with the Verein stated that he was to receive a grant of five hundred acres, just as Prince Solms had. In preference to living within the limits of either New Braunfels or Fredericksburg, Meusebach had chosen Comanche Springs, midway between the two. Here he had water springs and several hundred acres, which he could develop. A part of the land allowed him by the Verein, near New Braunfels, he sold to Count Ernst Coreth.

As Meusebach reflected on his suggestion to move the Verein headquarters to Fredericksburg he knew that decided steps had to be taken to improve the administration there. The stories about Dr. Schubert that were given to Meusebach as he had returned through Fredericksburg were even less favorable than when he was there en route to the Grant. Earlier the excellencies in Schubert had been observable; now an undesirable side came more and more to light. Schubert's instability may be accounted for by his many tragic experiences prior to his coming to Texas. These experiences included two duels—both connected with love affairs —the first one taking place in his native Germany. In the second duel, fought in New York, Schubbert killed his antagonist and "was obliged to leave New York in haste in order to escape legal prosecution."[2] His rightful name was Frederic Armand Strubberg but he "found it expedient to assir ne another name."[3] Thereafter Strubberg became Schubbert. After a short term taking a medical course in St. Louis, the adventurer arrived in Texas in 1844, using the name "Dr. F. Schubbert."

Among the factors contributing to Meusebach's reversal of opinion of the Colonial Director were the disclosure of his using an assumed name, his unauthorized venture to the Indians, his evidence of favoritism, and his extravagances. It is not surprising that Dr. Schubbert sought retaliation by writing accusing letters to the Commissioner-General. In the line of accusations, Schubbert refers sarcastically to Meusebach's acquiring advantageous farm land at Comanche Springs with a view to future development. Official records reveal that Meusebach paid $2,600 for approximately 2,577 acres.[4]

Armin O. Huber, German author, defending Strubberg on many counts, describes him as a "fanciful director" who "certainly loved wine and good-looking women . . . and wore always two pistols in his belt."[5] John O. Meusebach, writing in 1893, almost half a century after his experiences with Dr. Schubbert, says about him: ". . . he turned out . . . to be a great humbug and adventurer, and I had to dismiss him from office before I resigned myself in 1847."[6]

Meusebach appointed young William Keidel, just returned from the Mexican War, as the Verein physician in Fredericksburg. Dr. Keidel, a graduate of the University of Göttingen, called on Dr. Schubbert, expecting an official greeting. The reception was neither professional nor cordial. A little later, when Dr. Keidel presented a prescription to be filled, it was rejected on orders from Dr. Schubbert.[7]

In a letter dated April 20, 1847, Schubbert described his successor as having arrived on horseback with two small chests, presumably filled with medicine, hanging on either side of the horse. When the chests were opened, one was found to contain a large number of lanterns. The letter

---

[2] Preston Albert Barba, *The Life and Works of Friedrich Armand Strubberg*, p. 33.
[3] *Ibid.*
[4] Record supplied by Archivist Richard G. Santos, of Bexar County, June 3, 1966.
[5] Armin O. Huber, "Frederic Armand Strubberg, Alias Dr. Shubbert, Town-Builder, Physician and Adventurer, 1806–1899," *West Texas Historical Association Year Book*, XXXVIII (October, 1962), 55.
[6] John O. Meusebach, *Answer to Interrogatories*, p. 22.
[7] Keidel, Fredericksburg, April 26, 1847, to Meusebach. SB Archives, XL, 231–236.

continued, "Although it is well to have a light surround the physician, this lighting apparatus from the chest was something too overdone."[8]

On July 12, 1847, Meusebach wrote Dr. Schubbert that at the time he had accepted the position of director of Fredericksburg Schubbert had said, ". . . when an honorable man can no longer feel agreement with the principles of his superior, employment will cease." Meusebach's letter continued, "Since that is the condition now, you are relieved of your position as of this day."[9] Lieutenant J. Jean von Coll was appointed to succeed Schubbert as director.

Funds had never been sufficient in the colonies, yet Louis Becker, a member of a Verein commission, recorded the following: "F. Schurbart [*sic*] in Fredericksburg, dissipated over $100,000. He and Eickel [sometimes spelled Bickel], whom after all one should have known from Wiesbaden, carried on in an irresponsible manner."[10]

Philip Cappes likewise had a friend in Wiesbaden, with whom, according to Dr. Grosse, "he plays and deals in sums beyond his salary."[11] Cappes, who was in Fredericksburg during Meusebach's expedition, in contrast to Meusebach, was impressed in every way with Schubbert, on whom, Cappes declared, he "depended entirely."

Immediately after having heard Meusebach describe conditions in the Grant, Cappes had written Castell the following from Fredericksburg:

Dr. Schubbert, who has received the necessary instructions from me and who possesses competence, has given me his word of honor that he will hold the business until I send information out of Germany. . . . In fact, if I may speak frankly, my [return to] Texas will give new life to the situation and will lift the courage of everyone. . . . Also I will fully instruct von Coll, on whom one can depend, if one knows how to handle him, and I will acquaint him with the regulation of the finances.[12]

This letter implies that Cappes and Castell obviously had a plan in which Schubbert and von Coll were involved. This plan semed to be that immediately following Meusebach's resignation, Castell would have Cappes appointed as the next commissioner-general. In the same letter, dated March

[8] Schubbert, Fredericksburg, April 20, 1847, to Meusebach. SB Archives, XLI, 204.
[9] Meusebach, New Braunfels, July 12, 1847 to Schubbert. SB Archives, LIV, 124–125.
[10] Becker, Wiesbaden, November 27, 1848, to Verein. Archives, LVI, 129.
[11] Grosse, Koblenz, December 25, 1846, to Castell. SB Archives, LVII, 84.
[12] Cappes, Fredericksburg, March 9, 1847, to Castell. SB Archives, XLI, 174–176.

9, 1847, Cappes says further "Therefore, my dear Count, you now know what you are about."[13]

What Castell's next step was to be remained for him to determine. Cappes took as his responsibility the sending of a report on Meusebach to the Verein. In the belief that Meusebach would carry out his plan of going to Germany, Cappes hurried there to give his version of affairs to the Verein. This must have included a denunciation of Meusebach for the minutes of the Verein for July 23, 1847, report that Cappes retracted the derogatory remarks in an oral statement before a stockholders' meeting on June 15.[14]

Cappes took yet another step in his opposition to Meusebach by asking Castell to present a report to the Verein, meeting on July 21. In this document, Cappes justifies himself while he denounces Meusebach in the following manner. "He has the strange practice of keeping things secret that should have been disclosed to his associates, particularly to his treasurer. This gives ground for misinterpretations. In this manner he removes the incentive of his employees."[15] Meusebach had deliberately kept secret the imminence of bankruptcy lest his associates show their uneasiness to the colonists. Earlier in the same letter Cappes gives his evaluation of Meusebach, a resumé of which follows:

> He has learned much from books, has a fluency in speech and in writing which may deceive one at first acquaintance. He has the best qualities of a bookworm. His knowledge would have served him well, except that his education, unrestrained by practical knowledge, leads him into mistakes. Since he was accustomed to bureaucratic procedures in everything, he tried to institute that system in Texas. This procedure irritated the other officials, resulting in mistrust of him. He lacks tact in handling his agents: some he shuns; some he prizes. He does not forget an insult; he is often suspicious. Although he attaches great importance to decorum, he neglected even to call on Governor Henderson. He has no sensitivity to human relationships: what is one to think of a person who calls others "sheepsheads," even if only in fun?[16]

The Verein's reaction to this report was hardly what Cappes expected. On July 23, 1847, at Biebrich the Society passed a resolution stating their appreciation of Meusebach and their confidence in him. This memorial was signed by seventeen members of the Society, including Prince Friedrich and Count Castell.[17] The members of the Verein requested Meusebach

---

[13] *Ibid.*, p. 174.
[14] Minutes of Verein, Biebrich, July 23, 1847. SB Archives, XXXI, 75–76.
[15] Cappes, Biebrich, July 21, 1847, to Castell. SB Archives, XLI, 227.
[16] *Ibid.*
[17] Minutes of Verein, Biebrich, July 23, 1847. SB Archives, XXXI, 75–76.

to retain his post; if he could not accede to their request, the position was to be offered to his brother.

The document recites the fact that the sending of Special Commissioner Cappes in 1846 was caused not by a lack of confidence in Meusebach but by the nonarrival of information about the conditions of the Society's affairs in Texas and by the desire to promote its own interests by strengthening its administrative personnel in Texas. The document declares that the report made by Cappes did not create any mistrust in Meusebach and that the Society did not approve the conduct of the Special Commissioner.[18] Meusebach's resignation became effective July 20, 1847. Since Hermann Spiess, an official approved by the Verein, was in Texas it was logical that he should become the next commissioner-general. After Spiess was installed he received from Meusebach an itemized account of Meusebach's entire term of office.[19]

Although Castell and Cappes had schemed for Cappes to succeed Meusebach, the plan had not been successful. Cappes had brought Schubbert into the original scheme, but according to von Blücher, a gentleman who was well acquainted with the members of the Verein, Schubbert had actually worked against Cappes. "This you did not wish to believe," said von Blücher to Cappes, "but that Schubbert, or rather Struberg, certainly is a rascal."[20]

Despite Meusebach's report to the Verein on new methods to be used now that the Grant was opened, none of the ideas was applied; instead the Verein took steps toward liquidation. With Meusebach no longer at the helm the ship floundered and the Verein collapsed.

Behind the scenes of the Verein's collapse was intrigue between Castell and Cappes. Castell's position as executive secretary had been an extremely difficult one, for he had the responsibility of putting into execution a project for which there was no pattern and which involved the actual existence of thousands of people. He had carried on under the most harassing circumstances; when he had come to a difficult problem on which he needed advice, he had turned to his assistant in the headquarters office, Philip Cappes. As a result of the consultations, Cappes had become Castell's confidant. An example of this confidential cooperation was their expectation that the unfavorable report on Meusebach would result in the Verein's appointing Cappes to the position of leadership in the colonies.

Spiess, not Cappes, received the appointment, and Cappes was dis-

---

[18] *Ibid.*, p. 75.
[19] Spiess, New Braunfels, July 27, 1848, to Verein. SB Archives, LXV, 31.
[20] Blücher, New Braunfels, February 29, 1847, to Cappes. SB Archives, XLI, 236.

avowed by the Verein.[21] Members of the Executive Committee called attention to this repudiation when, in spite of it, Castell was able to bring about Cappes' appointment as a representative of the Verein at a later time.

Castell and Cappes continued to exchange letters frequently, particularly on the subject of a commission which had been sent to Texas to deal with the creditors of the Verein. Besides Spiess, the commission consisted of Gustav Dresel, an expert in business, and Louis Becker, a recognized secretarial accountant.

As events transpired, Castell proved untrue to Cappes. Following a brief illness, Dresel died, and in accordance with legal requirements his papers were opened. They revealed that Castell was conspiring against Cappes.[22] Thereupon Cappes remarked, "If I'm to be made the goat, I shall use my horns."[23] He threatened to reveal private correspondence between himself and Castell.

In a vain effort to revive the Verein, Castell began negotiations for the sale of holdings to Ludwig Martin, who proved, however, to be wholly unreliable. After the failure of this effort Fisher was instrumental in having the Verein reorganized under a new name, the German Emigration Company. Under Fisher's management various legal methods for sustaining the life of the German Emigration Company were attempted, all of which failed. In the end Fisher even became liable for the cost of a suit which had been a final effort on his part to secure some of the land in the Grant.

Count Castell, the man who found it advisable to " 'keep the threads of intrigue in my own hands, so as to know when to manipulate the threads',"[24] must have been caught in a web from which he could not extricate himself. An accusation written by Louis Becker directly to the Duke of Nassau declared that Castell, and he alone, was the cause of the failure of the Verein in Texas.[25] In a vain effort to justify himself, Castell appealed on June 15, 1849 to the Verein:

I request the general committee [of the Verein] to name a commission to examine my administration as an act of justice to answer the malicious slander and false charges brought against me. If the committee authorized earlier had

21 Minutes of Verein, Mainz, March 20, 1848. SB Archives, XXXI, 4.
22 Committee of Verein, n.pl., June, 1851, to Verein. SB Archives, XL, 145–149.
23 Cappes, Galveston, June 9, 1848, to Castell. SB Archives, XLI, 304.
24 Cappes, New Braunfels, October 4, 1848, to Castell. SB Archives, XLI, 341.
25 Castell, Mainz, December 27, 1848, to Reuscher. SB Archives, LVI, 161.

not left things in the lurch, in a state of confusion, then the disorder would not have developed and many things would not now have to be disentangled.[26]

In a ringing reproach to Castell, Cappes declared, "I defended you against every type of attack. How could you go so far from the path of truth? Or are perhaps truth and intrigue identical?"[27]

A statement made by an impartial observer was, "What a chaos of intrigue!"[28]

[26] Castell, Biebrich, June 15, 1849, to Verein. SB Archives, LIV, 183–184.
[27] Cappes, New Braunfels, October 4, 1848, to Castell. SB Archives, XLI, 341.
[28] Becker, Galveston, January 4, 1849, to Reuscher. SB Archives, LVI, 143.

The Verein Evaluated

CHAPTER 19

The question may be asked, Why did this organization with such splendid ideas and ideals fail to reach its goal?

Philip Cappes, knowing the internal workings, tried to find reasons for the failure of the organization when he wrote: "To find grounds for an *apologia* for this organization is difficult because it had entangled complications since its founding. All measures laid out were only taken halfway and topsy-turvy at that. This makes it difficult to come to any kind of a logical *apologia*."[1]

A second writer, Dr. E. Grosse, a publicist for the Verein, like Cappes, saw flaws in the Verein's construction. He said: "If a building lacks a secure foundation, it does not help to hang tapestries over the cracks in the walls which are not yet erected. It is just as curious to put varnish on a painted picture not yet executed, may the outline be ever so charming."[2]

Perhaps the most discerning evaluation comes from Dr. Friedrich Kapp, the German lecturer and writer, speaking at New York City just a decade after these once-credulous princes had declared themselves bankrupt:

The Society for the Protection of German Immigrants in Texas fancied that their high protection alone was sufficient to rectify everything. They had no idea of what was required for the success, or for the mere outfitting of such an enterprise, and they cared not to be enlightened on the subject. They did not know people and their necessities, nor had they the remotest idea of the toil and hardship of settling a new country.[3]

[1] Cappes, Wiesbaden, May 1, 1851, to Verein. Solms-Braunfels Archives, XL, 304.
[2] E. Grosse, Koblenz, December 12, 1846, to Castell. SB Archives, LVII, 48.
[3] Friedrich Kapp, "Lecture by Friedrich Kapp delivered at Clinton Hall in Astor Place," New York *Daily Tribune*, Saturday, January 20, 1855.

Treitschke, the historian of the nineteenth century, gives this evaluation:

Unfortunately the well meant undertaking was inaugurated with a superficiality characteristic of distinguished persons knowing nothing of business. The capital of $80,000 was quite inadequate. The political calculations upon which the scheme was based proved illusory for Texas joined the American union in the year 1845. Prince Charles of Solms Braunfels, a fanciful, good humored and boastful youth paid a visit to Texas, where he founded the town of New Braunfels and organised the district of Sophienburg, and named it after a German princess whom he delighted to honor. But he soon tired of the affair. Of the five thousand emigrants sent by the princely society to Texas during the years 1845 and 1846, more than two thousand perished miserably. The fifteen hundred survivors, vigorously led by Commissioner General von Meusebach, learned to fend for themselves; but in the end like all the other German immigrants who came into the American union, they became German-English Americans. The lamentable failure of this Society, which was dissolved in the year 1847, had an unfortunate reaction upon home politics, for the radicals, who beneath the surface were at work with growing success, were not slow to turn the unfortunate affair to account.[4]

John A. Hawgood says that Prince Carl Victor Leiningen apparently regarded the undertaking in Texas as an unwieldy monster and the association that had created it as constituting a sort of corporate Frankenstein.[5]

An arraignment made by Solon Loving is somewhat in the same line: "It is supposed the Society thought they were purchasing land, but they could hardly have thought they were getting the amount of land they thought they were getting for the price they were paying, even though land was ridiculously cheap in Texas at the time. Exen though the Society did think they were buying land, they cannot be excused for thinking so."[6]

Despite the severe pressures on Meusebach as commissioner-general, he was able to view the Verein and its accomplishments objectively. At a crucial time, June 26, 1846, he wrote: "Even if all is lost the Verein has done much; it gave German colonization a foothold, an influence that cannot be overlooked. Later, time will tell and recognize how much the Verein did. Here ten thousands more was done for the immigrants than anywhere in the world!"[7]

---

[4] Heinrich Gotthard von Treitschke, *History of Germany in the Nineteenth Century* (Eden and Cedar Paul, trans.), VII, 276.

[5] John A. Hawgood, *The Tragedy of German-America*, p. 175.

[6] Solon Ollie Loving, "A History of the Fisher-Miller Land Grant from 1848–1860" (M.A. Thesis, The University of Texas), p. 40.

[7] Meusebach, Nassau, June 26, 1846, to Verein. SB Archives, LII, 206–207.

That the Verein, though a failure on many counts was partially successful cannot be gainsaid, because its activities made possible for fellow
Germans who came to Texas the full realization of the value of democracy. Such an accomplishment was not the original intent of the founders.
One of the avowed purposes of the Verein was to enlarge the sphere and
certainly the influence of Germany; certain members expected that idea
to be attained by a feudal entity—a German state or a Germany colony.
The idea was never realized, except through the temporary colonies. A
more desirable result came ultimately in the formation of a German community, a community which has retained its unique quality through the
years.

Sacrifices to overcome what seemed to be insurmountable difficulties
drew the immigrants together. With similar backgrounds as a starting
point, the people were able to work out solutions for their problems as
well as to find comfort and strength from each other. That feeling has
induced the solidity of a community, which is felt by Texans of German
extraction to this day.

The people overcame untold hardships to win their soil and to make it
productive. The same situation held for whatever other means of liveli-
hood they chose. In facing and conquering challenges, the colonists re-
leased a reservoir of energy and of resourcefulness. Because they struggled
to overcome the hardships of this pioneer land they came to treasure their
attainments the more.

Certain personal qualities of independence were developed in these
people, who had been so long subservient to their German sovereigns.
These rulers had given their subjects protection. It was the idea of protection set forth in the official title of the Verein that drew many emigrants
to the organization. With the dissolution of the Verein and its arm of
protection, a quality of assertiveness in the individual came to the front.
The people lost their feeling of dependence; they were able to rise to the
needs of the situation. They became self-sufficient.

The adventurous spirit inherent in the German word *Wanderlust* por-
trays a national characteristic early in origin. Added to that spirit was
the feeling among many Germans in the nineteenth century that they were
tired of Europe (*Europamuede*). Thus the Verein opened a welcome door.
What the colonists were tired of is revealed in their letters to friends in
Germany, saying, "the taste of freedom is sweet"; "he who comes here
penniless is richer than a German nobleman"; "here no one is master—
there is no German yoke"; "here each one is what the other one is."

A European of this period wrote: "No one succeeds in America until he has lost his last European coin. Many experienced a tragical fate and almost all learned the truth of the proverb."[8] The colonists themselves recognized that the new world had given them something so valuable that they wished to share it. The following letter sets forth this idea:

Fredericksburg, Texas   January 15, 1850
Dear Brothers, sisters, and friends, leave Germany and come here where you can live happily, well, and contentedly. If you work only half as much as in Germany, you can live without troubles and "put by" for the future. In every sense of the word we are *free*, no soldier, no police . . . we ourselves vote for our magistrates . . . everyone is equal and the poorest amounts to as much as the rich one . . . The Indians do us no harm; on the contrary, bring us meat and horses to buy. We still live so remote from other people that we are lonely, but we have dances; churches and schools, we have also. Buy an old horse to hitch to your wagon, drive in it to Bremen, sell your horse, disassemble your wagon to take to America. For the boat trip, take a few bottles of syrup and vinegar. Mixed with water this is a refreshing drink. Each of you bring a rifle, the kind that uses very small bullets. Do not let anyone persuade you to go to any other place . . . than here: Fredericksburg.[9]

James Truslow Adams, in his *Epic of America*, states: "American political philosophy dealt with the *rights* of the citizens, not with the *duties* of the subject. Even if the people are sovereign it is evident that the individual is still subject."[10] John O. Meusebach would have asked, To what is he subject, or to whom? He would have been quick to answer: Man is subject to no one but himself, provided he does not interfere with the rights of others. Man can develop his own potential, his own stature. In America there are no man-made barriers to freedom. There are burdens, but they lighten when borne together.

What happened to the land of the Fisher-Miller Grant? When the bankrupt German Emigration Company ceased to function in September, 1853, it assigned all of its "rights" under its contract to its creditors. But how much actual land in the Grant did these "rights" include? Very little, evidently, for after litigations Fisher and Miller, the chief creditors, were refused title to any land in the Grant. The gist of the matter seems to be that the great body of the Fisher-Miller Grant never legally belonged to the Society, and therefore it could not be given by the Society to anyone, the creditors included. Most of the land in the Grant still belonged to the

---

[8] Treitschke, *History of Germany* (Eden and Cedar Paul, trans.), VI, 141.

[9] Peter Birk, Fredericksburg, January 15, 1850, to family in Brechlingen. SB Archives, LIV, 197.

[10] James Truslow Adams, *The Epic of America*, p. 207.

state. All ended well for the colonists, however, for the state, by a legislative act, later granted public land from the Grant to each of the colonists. Heads of families received 640 acres, single men, 320 acres.

What happened to the colonies that had been established by the Verein?
Moritz Tiling answers:

. . . it proved well for them [the colonists] that they were forced to remain
at these primitive settlements . . . and by hard and persistent labor in cultivating their ten acres, and living on the barest necessities of life for several
years, they not only succeeded in establishing a firm existence for themselves
and their families, but in course of time made New Braunfels and Fredericksburg the garden spot of Texas. These German settlers, toiling incessantly under
adverse conditions for civilization, performed a most noble pioneer work,
and are entitled to our highest admiration. Texas would not be what it is today,
if these brave men and women of the forties of the last century had not un-
flinchingly and fearlessly taken upon themselves the dangerous and onerous
task of clearing this West Texas wilderness.[11]

[11] Moritz Tiling, *History of the German Element in Texas from 1820–1850, and
Historical Sketches of the German Texas Singers' League and Houston Turnverein
from 1853–1913*, p. 110.

PART III

Private Life, 1847–1897

"Texas Forever"

CHAPTER 20

The years 1845 to 1847 were filled for Meusebach with the immediacy of life and death. He had no time to pursue his personal goals. The girl—the woman—was in his heart throughout those taxing years, though he found little time to write to her. Yet she waited patiently, frequently sending tokens of her love—a purse for coins, an exquisite bit of silk tapestry she had woven, and then a handmade booklet with her own sketches of life in Texas as she saw it from afar. Her depictions on the cover pointedly showed slaves under the lash; the doffing of hats to bags of money; the school, and aspects of nature's gifts; and waving over it all, the Lone Star flag with "Texas Forever" a part of it. In her symbolic discernment Meusebach could see that the two of them had a true meeting of minds.

After Meusebach's resignation from the responsibilities of the Society, with tension relaxed, he sat down to write his hopes and plans to Elizabeth. He had acquired some acres at Comanche Springs; there they would have the stone house reminiscent somewhat of the Old World, friends within reach, and time to study nature. Writing of these attractions, he planned to return to Germany for her; together they would tour the United States, through which he had made a hurried trip on his arrival in 1845. In Texas they would make their home.

He waited eagerly for her answer, which would name the date. When the mail came, his dream was shattered. The letter was from her family; it was bordered in black. There was no escaping its grim message. Elizabeth von Hardenberg had died of typhoid fever.

Time and living close to nature softened Meusebach's sorrow and healed his hurt as much as it ever could be healed; yet Elizabeth's image was with him always.

A second personal sorrow that came to this grief-stricken man the same year, 1847, was the death of his father. The son had planned for a reunion with his family when he returned for his bride. His sorrow struck deep, for his father's death was the first break in the closely knit family. Knowing that his brother and sister were with his mother in Germany gave Meusebach a measure of solace.

The world of nature spoke to his inner being. As he looked toward the horizon he saw that haze hung over the hills like violet veiling; the crags lost their sharp edges; the violet deepened into purple—the color of Good Friday. Gradually the mist cleared to reveal the distant mountains until they stood out in azure blue—the color of Easter morning. Light was penetrating, but only enough for him to say, "Now we see through a glass darkly." The language of beauty, however, he understood.

With his personal plans broken, Meusebach gave a good portion of time to the settlement. He continued his interest in the immediate and future well-being of the colonists. He was pleased that the opening of Fort Martin Scott near Fredericksburg, in November of 1848, brought the chance of employment to the settlers and provided a market where produce could be sold for cash. Victor Bracht, in his *Texas im Jahre 1848*, gives the following grocery prices: Meat sold at 4 cents a pound; butter at 37.5 cents per pound; chickens, from 37.5 to 50 cents each; flour from $15.00 to $20.00 a barrel; sugar, five to six pounds for $1.00; and corn at $1.25 to $1.75 a bushel.[1]

The wilderness had been tamed enough to provide sustenance and even a surplus. The innate thriftiness of the Germans was awakened and has continued active ever since. They learned early how to use everything advantageously. Each plot came to have a well-tended garden, always adorned with flowers. These people, hungry for land, loved it, and it prospered under their hands. In his *Naturalists of the Frontier,* Samuel Wood Geiser states:

These German gardeners were recognized as an asset in early Texas. The British Consul William Kennedy wrote in 1844 in a diplomatic dispatch to the Earl of Aberdeen: "Among the European settlers, the Germans have the reputation of being the most successful. They are generally laborious, persevering, and eager to accumulate—orderly for the most part—and they keep well together."[2]

Another evaluation is given by a man who was to become the nine-

---

[1] Viktor Bracht, *Texas im Jahre 1848*, p. 216.
[2] Samuel Wood Geiser, *Naturalists of the Frontier*, p. 116.

teenth President of the United States. Rutherford B. Hayes kept a diary while making a horseback trip through Texas in the winter of 1848–1849. About New Braunfels and its people Hayes wrote: "Those fair-headed Teutons have built in a short three years the most prosperous, singular, and interesting town in Texas. This is a German village of two or three thousand people at the junction of two of the most beautiful streams I ever saw, the Guadalupe and the Comal . . . The water is so transparent the fish seem hanging in the air."[3]

After Meusebach was absolved from daily responsibility for others, he sought the quietness and freedom that the small farm at Comanche Springs provided. There a life close to nature gave him refreshment of soul and body. Ferdinand Lindheimer, the botanist with whom Meusebach had worked in New Braunfels, was his guest at this farm, where the two nature lovers made botanical collections. Lindheimer's classification labels for 1849 bear the place tag of Comanche Springs. These two scientists found delight in giving appropriate names to their findings, such as *Lindheimera Texana*, a flower yellow in color, known more commonly as the "Texas Star." At his Comanche Springs farm Meusebach had made pets of two bear cubs, the mother of which he had killed earlier. One day while he and Lindheimer were admiring the cubs, one put both paws on Meusebach's shoulders. Seeing this, Lindheimer said, "From this point on there is danger for human beings."[4] The idea of danger from the cubs that appeared so warmly attentive made Meusebach shudder. On impulse he drew his pistol and with one shot for each bear he put an end to the danger. When he saw his pets lying prostrate, he recoiled. Lindheimer consoled him by saying, "You acted wisely. If you had waited to shoot, it would have been harder." The two friends walked away, with Lindheimer calling attention to the native larkspur and wondering whether it was as prolific in Germany.

The desire to see his family in Germany was with Meusebach constantly, but the report of political conditions there was so discouraging that it arrested his incentive to return. The years 1848 to 1849 were marked by retrogression rather than progress in gaining a constitution for Germany. The promise in that revolutionary movement toward a constitution, which ended in failure, caused many Germans to seek a place where promises of freedom could be realized. A country where the different states were

---

[3] Claude Michael Gruener, "Rutherford B. Hayes's Horseback Ride through Texas," *The Southwestern Historical Quarterly*, LXVIII, No. 3 (January, 1965), 357.
[4] Lucy Meusebach Marschall, Notes and Memoranda. MSS. Meusebach Family Files.

united, the United States of America, seemed to hold the answer to their desires. Some of the liberal leaders were imprisoned in Germany. Among them was Carl Schurz, who managed to escape to the United States, where later as senator from Missouri he contributed to the advance of democratic government.

Meusebach welcomed the newcomers to the Texas scene; they gave him direct touch with the currents of the world. The family of Wilhelm Marschall von Bieberstein he welcomed especially, because the family had lived in the duchy of Nassau, whose ruler, the Archduke Adolf, had been designated officially as "protector" of the Society for the Protection of German Immigrants in Texas. Furthermore, Ernst, the father of Wilhelm, was prime minister to the Archduke. As in the case of John O. Meusebach, the Marschall son had broken the pattern of accepted form. The family, on arrival in a democratic land, relinquished the titular part of their name when they became naturalized citizens. William von Marschall selected land and the site for his house within the range of Fredericksburg. He spoke both French and English, but he liked to be near the environs of things German.

In 1851 Meusebach journeyed to Germany for a reunion with his family. The family warmed his heart, but the political conditions chilled him, for the liberal, democratic tendencies had been thwarted, and the old order held sway. These political disturbances hindered the final efforts to restore the Verein to solvency; its financial situation was critical. The Verein negotiated the sale of all its property in Texas to Ludwig Martin, only to find him irresponsible.

When Meusebach saw that the financial affairs of the Society were becoming more and more involved, he felt that he must divest himself of all financial connection with the Society. His buying of the shares originally had not been entirely voluntary; he had done so at the behest of the executive secretary, Castell. He had never sat in on any deliberations of the Society; his advice sent from Texas had been given no attention; his requests for mony to sustain the colonists had gone unheeded until tragedy descended. In view of these facts he felt justified in asking that he be disassociated officially from the Society and that he be reimbursed for his investment. The request was finally acceded to after lengthy discussion. When the question of the accounts in Texas came up Meusebach referred the membership to the full and final report given to Commissioner-General Spiess on Meusebach's retirement. For this report of the financial accounts, Spiess had given a receipt which was part of the record.[5]

The perspective of Germany's political state that Meusebach surveyed in 1851, after six years' absence, was disheartening. The fateful years of 1848 and 1849 had seen political reformers make vigorous efforts at reform. Their success was brief, and by 1850 conservatism, practically absolutism, reigned. The Prussian Army by this time was the agent of repression. For the time being, democracy was held at bay.

Not so in Texas, thought Meusebach. As if to substantiate his opinion, word came that in his absence he had been elected to the Texas Senate. He was to represent the counties of Bexar, Comal, and Medina. For Meusebach it was a signal honor. In America he had found that gold and votes are sometimes the only certification of position. His personal gold was limited, but these votes cast for him represented something of greater value that money. They bespoke to him the confidence of the people. In Texas titles of nobility were discounted as a basis for leadership; it was the worth of the individual that was recognized.

Though Meusebach was welcomed in Germany on his return, he had no intention of remaining there; he was a citizen of the New World. This call to the Senate gave him reason to hasten back to Texas.

Leaving the family was a poignant experience for Meusebach, especially saying goodbye to his mother, who had been alone since his father's death. He had found delight in his young nieces and nephews, his sister's children, and nothing had strengthened Meusebach so much as did the visit with his brother. The relationship between the brothers was very close; the fact that the ocean lay between them did not seem to separate them. If Meusebach ever needed a defender, Carl, the younger brother, was always his advocate. The two discussed plans for the future. Meusebach unequivocally favored Texas; Carl, who had considered Texas at one time, now favored the offer of a diplomatic post in Bucharest. (At the completion of that appointment he became the Prussian minister plenipotentiary in Rio de Janeiro.)

Meusebach said farewell to the old Germany that he had known, cultured and cosmopolitan, the side of his native land that he hated to leave. The highly organized bureaucracy which made no concessions to democracy he was glad to turn his back on. By 1851 he was more at home in Texas than in the land of his nativity.

[5] Minutes of Verein, Wiesbaden, September 19, 1851. Solms-Braunfels Archives, LXV, 6.

He welcomed the opportunity to participate in the making of laws for his adopted state—now his own country. He had much to learn from that experience. Since Texas, the state, was only five years old, he was eager to see how the transition from an independent nation to statehood was being handled. He had ideas to advance, particularly those of making education available to all. He had felt himself a citizen of the Republic because he was naturalized in 1845—but it was no less an honor to be a citizen of the state. Only those recently come from a foreign land, thought Meusebach, could truly appreciate and value the democratic process in America.

Meusebach's desire to prove his interest in these matters made him hasten to Austin after his return from Germany. He stopped in New Braunfels to greet old friends, but he postponed real visits, because he would need ample time to tell all that had transpired in beautiful but harassed Germany.

Texas Senator

CHAPTER 21

W hen the Fourth Legislature of the state of Texas met for the session of 1851–1853, on November 7, 1851, Meusebach presented his credentials as senator. He represented the Twenty-Second Senatorial District, composed of Bexar, Medina, and Comal Counties.[1] Following the usual procedure, the Senate passed a resolution providing for the printing of the governor's inaugural address. Meusebach's first participation in the business of the Senate was to make a motion that the resolution be amended to provide that the address be printed in German and Spanish as well as in English.[2] Although he desired his German constituents to become American citizens without delay, five or six years' residence in their adopted country had not acquainted them with all the fine points of the language.

Governor P. Hansborough Bell recognized the many nationalities that made up this state, and his warm words gave them all a welcome. Those new Texans had the opportunity to read these words in Governor Bell's address:

From every land emigrants are flocking, in welcome crowds, to partake of our prosperity. From the vineclad hills of France and Germany, from Ireland's green shores and England's smiling fields, and from our own sister states, they swell the living tide until the solitary plains have been made to rejoice and the wilderness to blossom as the rose. A land more fair and happy never sun viewed in his wide career; salubrious, mild, its hills are green, its woods and prospects fair, prairies fertile; and to crown the whole, it is our home—the land of Liberty and all its sweets.[3]

[1] Texas State Legislature, *Journal of the Senate of the State of Texas, Fourth Legislature—Extra Session*, p. 15.
[2] *Ibid.*, p. 55.
[3] *Ibid.*, p. 27.

The gains in population bear out the Governor's flowery words. In 1847 the state census showed the population as 142,000. In 1850 the first federal census of Texas revealed a population of 212,592. Immigrants poured into the state in the next decade. In 1860 the census showed that the population had risen to 604,216, a gain of 184.2 per cent.

Meusebach was appointed a member of the Committee on State Affairs and of the Committee on Education. The Education Committee brought in a bill early in 1852 which provided for a system of common schools. The execution of the bill had to await the financial means provided by the State School Law of 1854. The Germans favored free schools removed from sectarian influences, with attendance made compulsory. They made their demands known to the state in a mass meeting held in New Braunfels in 1854. That same year Representative Gustav Schleicher introduced a bill to authorize New Braunfels to levy a tax for support of the free public school.

The Committee on State Affairs recommended a bill incorporating the city of Austin. This committee requested the Governor to obtain from a competent architect the plan of a building for a state capitol, "to be built of brick or stone, in a substantial manner but on as cheap a plan as practicable."[4] The amount authorized for the building, $100,000, came up for a vote several times. On February 13, 1852, the Senate and House, sitting together, passed the appropriation. The architect-engineer who submitted the plan for the building was F. Giraud of San Antonio. During the 1851 session he received $100, which sum covered only the work of the draftsmen. An additional $250 was deemed as necessary compensation for the services of the architect himself. This sum was approved when the committee of which Meusebach was chairman submitted the bill to the Legislature.[5]

Three years elapsed before the capitol building was actually constructed. In June, 1856, a "Report on the building and furniture of the Capitol of the State of Texas" revealed dissatisfaction with certain aspects of the structure and the handling of related funds as well. A second architect, John Brandon, was employed, and received a fee of $500. He testified that he drew the plans for the building, with the help of assistants, in three and one-half days.[6] When this building was destroyed by fire in 1881 plans were already underway for the construction of a more suitable

[4] *Ibid.*, p. 56.
[5] *Ibid.*, p. 209.
[6] Texas State Legislature, Adjourned session (July 7–September 1, 1856), *Report on the building and furniture of the Capitol of the State of Texas* p. 13.

statehouse, one worthy of the state of Texas. A company of Chicago capitalists agreed to finance the construction, which was completed in 1885, in exchange for 3,000,000 acres of the public domain of Texas. Meusebach was glad that the German sculptor Frank Teich, lately become a Texan, influenced the decision to use the native red granite for the capitol building. Teich was instrumental in getting the members of the Legislature to go in person to see Granite Mountain in Burnet County, a visit which convinced the legislators of the merits of the native granite as a building material.

Texas had a great resource in the form of land, which it owned as a public domain, estimated at 181,965,332 unappropriated acres. In addition to the land, which the state retained from the days of the Republic, the state was awarded $10,000,000 in a compromise settlement of the dispute with the United States over boundary claims extending into the New Mexico territory. Meusebach was pleased that the dispute was settled by the Compromise of 1850, for excitement over the dispute ran high while he was in the Senate. Even the appeal of Governor Bell to the United States government to acknowledge the claims of Texas had been without immediate avail.

The immigration companies made various appeals to the Legislature while Meusebach was senator. He made the motion of February 6, 1852, that the bill to perfect the land titles in Castro's colony be passed, and he gave approval to a similar bill relating to land in the Peters colony. He introduced a bill to extend the provisions of an act that would secure for the German Emigration Company and its colonists the land to which they were entitled, and to adjust the liabilities of said company.[7] Sympathy for the creditors of that company was shown by his endorsement of a bill for their relief. He endorsed a resolution requiring an investigation of the validity of certificates issued to Fisher and Miller.[8]

Significant allocations of state land and money were made to facilitate transportation and travel, to provide public buildings, and to promote education. In addition to public schools for all grades, provision was made to establish the university for which President Mirabeau B. Lamar had given instructions as early as 1839. It was not until 1883 that the doors of the state university in Austin were opened. The Germans, particularly the residents of Austin County, made definite plans for the establishment of a university just five years after Lamar's instructions to open a state university. Hermann's University was incorporated in 1844. The

[7] Texas State Legislature, *Journal of the Senate—Extra session*, p. 98.
[8] *Ibid.*, p. 219.

Congress of Texas donated a league of land to the school, and in the name of the Verein, Meusebach also donated a league. He was named a trustee of the proposed university, which to him was a great honor. Professors were to be proficient in English and German. But despite all these plans and arrangements, lack of available funds prevented the university from being established.

Governor Bell called a special session of the Fourth Legislature to meet on January 13, 1853, to authorize the Governor to muster men, who would be paid by the state, for patrol service. Patrol and ranger duty had been done by Texans since the time of Stephen F. Austin, but had been paid for by the federal government. Now that the state was to meet the bills this organization could henceforth be called the Texas Rangers with entire justice. As these men ranged the Rio Grande Valley the inhabitants declared themselves "comforted" by their presence. Governor E. M. Pease advanced the Ranger force as did Governor Hardin R. Runnels, who sent the force fighting over a thousand-mile frontier. Meusebach heartily approved the idea of recognizing the Rangers—he considered his friend Colonel Jack Hays as embodying the best tradition of that organization.

Before the session closed in February, Governor Bell recommended, for the second time, that a geological survey of the state be made, predicting that the results would repay the cost a thousandfold. Meusebach the geologist endorsed the recommendation to the fullest.

Active participation as a member of the Legislature was a rewarding experience to Meusebach. He followed the legislative process with interest the rest of his life, but in the final analysis, the field of politics was not his calling.

During Meusebach's term as senator a committee member of the Verein sent a message as representing the consensus of the organization. This message was sent to Commissioner-General Bene with the instruction that it be transmitted to Meusebach: ". . . in view of the fact that Meusebach had reason to feel aggrieved at the treatment accorded him at times by the Verein, the fact that he worked persistently and consistently on the side of the Verein in the Legislature deserves double recognition from us."[9] In addition, the following words were addressed to Meusebach directly: "Your service to us springs from your noble spirit."[10]

[9] Committee of Verein, Neuwied, March 4, 1852, to Commissioner-General Bene, Solms-Braunfels Archives, XLV, 294.
[10] Committee of Verein, Mainz, March 4, 1852, to Meusebach, SB Archives, XLV, 285.

The Hearth

CHAPTER 22

After he had discharged his duties as senator during the long session Meusebach returned to New Braunfels, where his friends were eager to hear about the legislative process in Austin and of course about the state of affairs in Germany. His firsthand report gave pleasure to several friends. One was Ferdinand Lindheimer, who heard with sorrow that liberal ideas fared little better at mid-century in Germany than when he had left there in the thirties. Lindheimer's attention at the moment was given to beginning a newspaper. The first edition of his *Die Neu Braunfelser Zeitung* came off the press in 1852 and continued under his editorship for twenty years. These two friends carried on their mutual interest in botany through the years, although Meusebach's interest took on a practical turn, that of a horticulturist.

Another friend was Ernst Coreth. In 1846 he had brought his family, independently of the Verein, to New Braunfels, where he had bought from Meusebach the tract of land close to the settlement. When Coreth and his wife had realized the uncertainty of the political future in Austria they had decided that their young sons should not be at call to fight every war the Austrian overlords decreed. The Coreths had come to Texas because here the citizens had a voice. Ernst Coreth's own father, the Tyrolean Count Coreth zu Coredo Frei und Edler Herr zu Starkenberg, had died under the attack of Napoleon on the field of Austerlitz in 1805. Although the Austrian emperor had given personal attention to the upbringing of the children of the fallen officer, this fact did not hold Ernst Coreth in Austria indefinitely.

Coreth married Agnes Erler in 1834. Several years elapsed before the young couple finally decided to leave Austria. Their first child was a daughter, Agnes, born September 18, 1835, in the city of Innsbruck, picturesquely located in the Tyrolean Alps. No one in the family mentioned Innsbruck without speaking of the *Goldne Dachl,* the "golden roof," on the balcony of the castle. As Agnes grew in years, she delighted in showing her young brothers the gilded copper roof glittering in the sunlight. Often she would take them to the fast-flowing stream, into which she would throw pebbles that rounded into marbles in the whirling eddies of the Tyrolean mountain brook.

When Agnes was eleven years old her parents decided to carry out their latent desire to go to a country not ruled by autocratic decrees. If decrees were necessary, the citizens should have a voice in making them. At their destination, Texas, they found the liberty they sought.

The father trained his children to walk with firm steps and erect carriage. When he assigned duties to the children he expected full compliance. Agnes was her father's companion and, in some matters, his confidante. He told her his disillusionments as well as his triumphs. One report said Count Coreth was the kind of man that the Texans idolized,[1] although the compliment meant little to the man. When it was known that the Coreths were to attend a ball in the area a feeling of expectancy prevailed, for many felt it an honor to have a count and countess as guests. Agnes who gave the impression of being at ease in any situation, was pleased with the attention.

After Meusebach's return from Germany in 1851 he saw Agnes in a new light. She was no longer merely Ernst Coreth's little daughter; she was a person in her own right—and at sixteen, how lovely! When Meusebach and her father talked of what was going on in the world Agnes listened with interest, but said little. Her sparkling brown eyes and dark curly hair contrasted with Meusebach's Nordic coloring; she had a definite appeal for him. Presently, he suggested that they walk in the garden, where he and this girl, her beauty breaking in on him, had opportunity to talk. They soon found mutual interests. He helped her gather a bouquet, for which she always chose yellow flowers. When he realized how she enjoyed growing flowers and plants he ordered as his first gift for her a subscription to the German magazine *Die Garten Laube* (*The Garden Arbour*).

Meusebach's responsibilities as senator kept him in Austin much of the year 1851. On holidays he came to New Braunfels to visit. At Easter of 1852 Agnes had a basket of strawberries which she had grown ready to present to him. His gift for her was a glowing topaz encrusted in gold.

[1] Cappes, Galveston, March 7, 1848, to Castell. Solms-Braunfels Archives, XLI, 321.

Since Agnes preferred yellow, he hoped this jewel would appeal to her. The brooch was a piece of family jewelry that his mother had given him as she said farewell in Germany. Her unspoken hope was that he would find someone to fill the void left by the death of Elizabeth von Hardenberg.

In the summer time Meusebach and Agnes took horseback rides and walks together in the woods. One evening they sat under the stars together, each thinking "thoughts too deep for words." Meusebach broke the silence to tell Agnes about Elizabeth. Then while he listened, she told him about her friend, a young, upstanding man, near to her in age, who lived not too far away. She and he were congenial—close to love, she revealed.

Meusebach started to rise. Agnes tugged at his sleeve until he sat again. After a long silence she told him that her father advised against her marriage to the young man, and she agreed that his reasons were justifiable. Her strong resolution shone through when she concluded her story, "I would never be content if I went against my father."[2] They sat quietly for a long while. Before they parted they said, "We have shown each other what is in our hearts. Honesty is something to build on."

Time passed and they made their plans. Their wedding date would be ten days after her seventeenth birthday—September 28, 1852. Meusebach was forty years of age: old enough to value youth, young enough to value maturity.

When the wedding day came, a tinge of autumn was in the air. The crispness of the weather made them welcome the sweaters that Agnes had knitted for them to wear on their horseback wedding trip. The rooms of the Coreth home were brightened with flowers that Agnes had grown. The morning ceremony was simple—only the family and close friends were present. Agnes' mother had prepared a wedding breakfast that would have delighted an epicure; it was served on china, a gift from the Emperor Francis Joseph, that the family had brought from Austria. As the bride's father watched the couple mount their horses, his mind dwelt on the changes wrought by the New World. How different this occasion would have been had all the participants remained in Europe! But Coreth and Meusebach had chosen Texas, and both had taken root. Texas was rewarding each according to his need.

Count Ernst von Coreth zu Coredo turned to reminisce with his wife. They stood long, watching the departing couple—two people transplanted from life in a formal, fixed pattern to a life in which the individual rises

---

[2] Lucy Meusebach Marschall, Notes and Memoranda. MSS. Meusebach Family Files.

to the heights within himself. The horses started in a walk but soon moved
into a canter. As the young couple rode through the country, she brimful
of life, he a bit grave, the promise of autumnal glory was all about them.
Sufficient for them was the present moment: it was their wedding day.

Meusebach took his bride to Comanche Springs to begin their life together in the house in which he was already established. The family silver,
linen, china, and Venetian glass, Meusebach's favorite, which he had
brought back from his 1851 trip to Germany, had added some niceties,
which were in contrast to the crude furnishings. Agnes also added a few
items that gave distinction to the pioneer home.

The natural water supply at Comanche Springs made possible the
excellent growth of vegetables and flowers. The spring proved advantageous in keeping cool the butter and cream, which Agnes often used in
preparing dishes that her Austrian mother had taught her. Meusebach
liked the butter especially, for, he was wont to say, "Bread is made only
to hold butter."[3] The couple enjoyed the wheat flour ground at the
Mormon mill, where the first wheat flour of the entire region was made.
Corn meal, however, seemed foreign to the Meusebachs, even after they
had used it for a number of years. Agnes varied her cooking between
American and German; she would prepare fried chicken, American style,
but for dessert she would serve a strawberry *Torte*, Austrian style.

When Governor Bell called the special session of the Fourth Legislature
to meet on January 13, 1853, Meusebach left his bride with her parents
in New Braunfels while he journeyed to Austin. Upon his return Agnes
and her parents enjoyed hearing about his experiences; they had a good
laugh over what a Lipan Indian was reported to have said about Colonel
Jack Hays: "Me and Red Wing not afraid to go to hell together. Captain
Jack heap brave; not afraid to go to hell by himself."

Agnes enjoyed visits in New Braunfels, but a trip with her husband
to the "Latin Settlement" at Sisterdale was a stimulating experience. The
men and women constituting the settlement were cultured and intelligent;
so conversation was on an intellectual level. Merriment prevailed, too, and
they enjoyed waltzing, and singing, and concert music on a fine piano.
These Sisterdale settlers, self-constituted exiles from Germany, were not
so successful in agriculture as in intellectual pursuits, but they had found
their Arcadia in Texas and were content. Social and political freedom
enabled them to make the most of life.

[3] *Ibid.*

Sisterdale was called the "Queen City of the Guadalupe" because of the quality of graciousness that emanated from her people. Visitors came to the community while it flowered during the 1850's; among them was Prince Paul of Württemberg, a botanist of note. Another visitor was Frederick Law Olmsted, who recorded his impressions in his book, *Journey through Texas*. He passed, as he says, "a rarely pleasant day" with Otto von Behr, who, like Meusebach, had been a friend of Humboldt and of Goethe's Bettina. Olmsted gives this picture of the day in the backwoods of Texas: "The dinner was Texan, of cornbread and frijoles, with coffee served in tin cups, but the salt was Attic, and the talk was worthy of golden goblets."[4]

A dozen miles from the Latin Settlement another group of unusual persons made their homes for a short period. These five individuals had been members of the Bettina colony on the Llano River, which lasted only as long as supplies were provided—one year. The colony then went to "pieces like a bubble" and "scattered to the four winds."[5] After two years in the Sisterdale area, the five colonists moved a little farther west and, in time, founded the town of Boerne, south of Sisterdale. In that settlement the Meusebachs found congenial friends. The same held for the settlement of Comfort, which was founded in 1854 by Ernst Altgelt. The Altgelt family and the Meusebachs were closely associated all their lives. These friendships filled a need in the lives of the young couple, but soon their children had first call on their attention.

Their first child, a son, was born to the Meusebachs on July 26, 1853. His name, Ernst Otfried, was given in honor of his maternal grandfather and of his own father. The parents thought the baby was fascinating and wrote long letters about him to Meusebach's mother and sister in Germany. To their second son, born in 1855, they gave the name Otto; and to their third son, born in 1857, the name Max Rudolf. The father took great pride in these sons and wrote of their development in detail to relatives. No more sons came, but little daughters did, eight in number, and each seemed more welcome than the previous one. The names chosen for the daughters honored both sides of the family: Antonie, born in 1859; Elizabeth, 1862; Johanne and Francisca, 1864, twins who died as young children; Lucy, 1865; the twins Emmy and Lilly, 1868, of whom the

---

[4] Frederick Law Olmsted, *A Journey Through Texas: or a Saddle-Trip on the Southwestern Frontier*, p. 93.

[5] Louis Reinhart, "The Communistic Colony of Bettina, 1846–8," *The Quarterly of the Texas State Historical Association*, III, No. 1 (July, 1899), 39.

latter died in infancy. The last child was also named Lilly; she was born in 1872 and died two years later. Pilgrimages to the graves of the four little girls in New Braunfels were made by the family for many years.

The children of this family were shown attention and affection—more evident perhaps on the part of the father than the mother, who was the disciplinarian. The children were all born in New Braunfels, where the maternal grandparents lavished love on them.

In 1854 Governor Pease appointed Meusebach commissioner for the colony of the German Emigration Company. He served in this capacity for a year, issuing land certificates to his colonists, the titles to the land promised them by the Society. In fact, the amount of land promised by the Society was doubled. The colonists were now alloted the full 640 acres if married, 320 if single. The Republic of Texas granted every settler 640 or 320 acres and stipulated premium amounts to the contractor. At first the contractor, in this case the original Society, would promise each immigrant only one half of what the Republic granted each settler and the Society would retain the other half. Now, since the Society had disbanded, the colonists received the full allotment of land.

The bringing to final fruition of the promises of the Verein gave Meusebach deep satisfaction.

Meusebach personally issued certificates to 729 colonists for a total of 324,160 acres. Three other commissioners from the Land Office issued certificates, bringing the total amount of land granted the colonists to 1,735,200 acres. The land could be selected anywhere in the Grant where unclaimed land lay. Very few of the colonists moved to these tracts; those who retained the land found that it later became quite valuable. Some immediately sold the land certificates for a song.

In 1858 Colonel Jack Hays stopped at Comanche Springs. As he and Meusebach sat looking out over the valley, now so peaceful, they reminisced, one experience recalling another. The Colonel pointed to his rifle, saying that he had regarded it as a prized possession ever since Meusebach had presented it to him in the name of the Verein in the summer of 1845. The Colonel recalled how impressed he had been by Prince Solms. To see a prince in person was not an everyday occurrence. Prince Solms was a fine and tender-hearted gentleman, said the Colonel, as he thought back to the occasion when Henry Castro's colonists, looking in vain for their leader, were ill and destitute. The Colonel and his helper Johann Rahm assisted the Alsatians, and the Prince seemed to appreciate what they did.

Prince Solms, Meusebach recalled, recommended that the Verein present a rifle to the Colonel for his unselfish aid to the colonists. When it arrived from Germany, the gun was not of suitable quality, so Meusebach substituted his own rifle for presentation.[6] As Meusebach related these details the Colonel remarked that the initials on the gun had at first puzzled him, so he soon asked officials what "O. H. Freiherr v. M." stood for. They had explained that *Freiherr* could be translated *free gentleman* or *free man*, a definition that arose from medieval times when the lord, or baron, was *free*, with vassals subject to him. The Colonel added that plain "John O. Meusebach" appealed to Texans. Meusebach replied that to him it was a privilege to be a *free man* in Texas.

At ease with this German Texan who had the reputation of seeing the foibles and the strengths of both nationalities, Colonel Hays mentioned that the Prince's uniforms had been the marvel of the pioneer Texans. The men, ranging the frontier with their captain, had wondered what would happen to the Prince's plumes and medals if he rode through the thickets of the western frontier. The suggestion had not been put to the test, for the Prince had never gone far beyond the New Braunfels area. Yet, said the Colonel, the Prince had made several engagements with him to go to the land of the Grant itself on the condition that Fisher go along. Hays recalled with a chuckle that Fisher had always become occupied with other pursuits when such an excursion was proposed.

These two friends presently began recalling details about the treaty-making expedition. Colonel Hays said that he sometimes wondered whether Meusebach had felt during the parley that he and his party might suddenly be overpowered by the Indians, who were known for their treachery. Meusebach's answer was that at certain points he had had that fear, but that his own best weapon was straightforwardness, which he had used in dealing with them.

The Colonel asked the same thing that many Texans wondered: Did not Meusebach and his party feel uneasy after they had discharged their guns? Meusebach's answer was that seventeen men holding guns, loaded or empty, could not have survived long had several hundred warriors decided to attack. He continued by saying that the emptying of his gun had apparently given the Indians confidence in him.

After a pause Meusebach recalled that the point at which he had felt confidence in the Indians was when they called him "El Sol Colorado." The title had given him a sense of security, Meusebach said, because "I

---

[6] Meusebach, New Braunfels, September 15, 1846, to Verein. SB Archives, LI, 141.

felt that after I had been given a special name that then I had been taken into their inner circle."[7] Meusebach then told his guest the details of how the special name had been chosen. There was some basis for the designation in the reddish color of his beard, but the chieftain Santa Anna personally had given Meusebach this explanation: "When my warriors saw you walking among them unarmed, they felt you were a man to be looked up to, like the sun above us. So we wanted you to have that name, *The Red Sun.*"[8]

Meusebach made apologies for what might be interpreted as boastfulness, but he felt that the Colonel saw the story in the true light. Meusebach then asked Colonel Hays to recall his fight in 1841 when he had stood alone, separated from his company, against the Indians on Enchanted Rock. The Colonel, who had been a captain at the time, said he knew that he had to make every shot count, so he aimed more carefully than he had ever done before. In the end he overcame the Indians but several times he had thought it would be his last battle. The redoubtable fighter was apparent in both men as the two friends parted, for each knew that every passing day battles had to be fought—though luckily, not with Comanches.

The faithfulness of the Indians to the treaty of 1847 held throughout the lives of the chiefs with whom Meusebach had negotiated the treaty. In other sections the federal government attempted to solve the problem by establishing reservations for the Indians. This policy brought about a semblance of peace, which continued through the Civil War. During that strife the white Texans had not time to pursue the red men when they plundered. With the advent of the Civil War, troubles of a nature undreamed of came to pass.

[7] Lucy Meusebach Marschall, Notes and Memoranda. MSS. Meusebach Family Files.

[8] Emmy Meusebach Marschall, Notes and Memoranda. MSS. In possession of Mrs. Homer T. Love, San Antonio, Texas.

A House Divided

CHAPTER 23

D
uring the War years Meusebach lived in Gillespie County. Feeling the need of additional income for a growing family, he sold his Comanche Springs farm and established a mercantile business in Fredericksburg. The period of the Civil War was a time of emotional struggle for the Texas Germans living in the New Braunfels-Fredericksburg area. Many felt that loyalty to the Union precluded the right of the state to secede, and seriously questioned the institution of slavery. Prince Solms had said, "Out of a full heart I assure you that the business of slavery is in every way an unworthy affair, a genuine shame of humanity."[1] Olmsted, an impartial observer of American Germans, wrote, "The German was happy in the possession of freedom undebilitated by mastership or slaveship."[2]

When the vote on secession came, a majority of Germans were loyal to the Union. In the summer of 1862 an attempt was made to conscript the Germans of the western settlements into the rebel army. In objection to this effort some sixty young Germans from the Gillespie County region and beyond determined to proceed to Mexico and, if possible, to join the Union Army. While bivouacking near the Nueces River on the night of July 2, 1862, they were surprised by a detachment of one hundred Confederates. Though they twice repulsed their attackers, a large number of the Germans were killed, and the remainder suffered sad fates.

In 1865 the bones of the victims of the Battle of the Nueces (sometimes called the Massacre of the Nueces) were gathered and buried in the town of Comfort. A monument with the inscription *"Treue der Union"* marks

[1] "Berichte des Prinzen Karl zu Solms-Braunfels an den Mainzer Adelsverein," *Kalender der Neu-Braunfelser Zeitung fuer 1916*, p. 48.
[2] Frederick Law Olmsted, *A Journey through Texas: or A Saddle-Trip on the Southwestern Frontier*, p. 187.

the resting place of those martyred for their conviction of loyalty. The inscription, on the east side, stands as an epitaph for the men whose names are inscribed on the three other sides. The west side records the names of the nineteen men killed in the Battle at Nueces, *"Gefallen am 10 August, 1862"*; the south side records the names of the seven men killed at the Rio Grande, *"Gefallen am 18 Oct. 1862"*; the north side records those of the nine men "Captured, taken prisoners and murdered," *"Gefangen, genommen und ermordet."*

Harper's Weekly of January 20, 1866, makes this evaluation of their martyrdom:

"The little remote spot where they rest must be to the nation as sacred as those places where thousands of her fallen defenders are deposited. Small in number, far away from the patriotic heart and the strong arm of the loyal north, surrounded by fierce enemies of the Union, those brave and devoted Germans offered their lives as a holy protest against the treason of the recreant rebels."[3]

In his *German Pioneers in Texas*, Don H. Biggers says that the crime was unjustified even by the rules of savage warfare.[4] The atrocity of murdering prisoners of war was a horror so vivid to the people that a citizen of Fredericksburg. J. Weinheimer, Sr., writing thirty years later on "Remembrances of War Times,"[5] brands the murderers as "those monsters," who, following the Battle, shot the wounded and took the others to White Oak Creek in Gillespie County, where they either shot or hanged them.

Weinheimer relates earlier in his article that when the people of the Fredericksurg area recognized that war was inevitable a company of volunteers was mustered under Captain Frank van der Stucken. It was thought that this company would remain stationed in Fredericksburg as a protection against the Indians, who were more likely to attack when they knew the men were not at home. Gradually the young men of the region west of Fredericksburg were regarded as "Unionists." The Americans in the region, almost all on the side of the South, resented them. Ill-will already existing between the Germans and Americans increased to the point that some individuals took matters into their own hands without regard to law or justice. The narrator gives an example of this injustice

---

[3] *Harper's Weekly* is quoted in Guido E. Ransleben, *A Hundred Years of Comfort in Texas*, p. 125.

[4] Don H. Biggers, *German Pioneers in Texas: A Brief History of Their Hardships, Struggles and Achievements*, p. 60.

[5] J. Weinheimer, Sr., "Erinnerungen aus den Kriegszeiten," in Robert Penniger (ed., comp.), *Fest-Ausgabe*, p. 120.

in which four farmers, on the basis of false charges, were forcibly evicted from their homes. The next morning the four men were found hanging on trees not far from their houses.

Mob law was enforced by a group of renegades calling themselves the *Hängebund,* or "Hanging Band." The Germans reacted in various ways to the outrages committed by this band. Some kept themselves hidden near home, and to these the derisive term of "Bushwhackers" was given. When appeal was made for them to enlist voluntarily, most joined Kampmann's Regiment and served there to the end of the War. Still another group was requisitioned to transport supplies.

The Germans who stayed at home and worked secretly for the Union paid dearly for their convictions. Many were distrusted; the renegades often inflicted atrocities. The mob law which prevailed was resented by the Germans and as well by the non-Germans who were partisan to the Confederacy. Much of the injustice could be traced to individuals not native to the area. Under the cloak of patriotism, the mob violence, once started, swept like a fire. In its wake it left ashes that only time could blow away. With the abolition of slavery and the close of the Civil War, the causes of friction were removed, and gradually harmony was restored to the communities.

During the Civil War period, guns and pistols were of the cap type. In Fredericksburg, Engelbert Krauskopf, an immigrant of 1846 and a trained gunsmith, used his inventive skill to design the necessary machinery to make the percussion caps. Krauskopf was assisted in executing this work by his friend Adolph Lungkwitz, a silversmith. They brought the necessary saltpeter from the bat caves in the mountains around Fredericksburg and the quicksilver from Galveston. The two young Krauskopf daughters aided the operation by carefully filling the caps with the mixture. The final step in the process was imprinting a Texas star on the cap, which identified it as being the product of the Krauskopf factory. A considerable market for the caps soon developed and they saved the ammunition situation in Gillespie County and throughout the area.[6]

Meusebach had a special interest in this family which contributed to the war effort and to the protection of the area. Krauskopf had served as his hunter during Meusebach's residence at Comanche Springs, and an abiding friendship developed between the two men. Krauskopf's wife, the former Rosa Herbst, who had been made an orphan by the death of her immigrant parents during the epidemic of the 1840's, had been employed by Meusebach at his Comanche Springs farm.

[6] Biggers, *German Pioneers in Texas,* p. 99.

Meusebach thought long about the effects of the Civil War. His sympathy was with the brave young men who were willing to risk their lives for the sake of their convictions. He condemned the outrages of mob violence. In his own family a feeling of tolerance prevailed because three of his wife's brothers served on the Confederate side, two of them giving their lives for the Southern cause.

The years spent in Fredericksburg during the War engraved in Meusebach's thinking more deeply than ever the utter waste inflicted by war. In this settlement, detached from the center of activities, there was little desecration of the material, but the harm to human relationships could not be easily mended. The disruption of harmony between two nationalities was detrimental to each. If only each side of the wider conflict could leave the immediacy of the situation, thought Meusebach, they could weigh matters and they would stretch out hands to each other.

As Meusebach turned his thoughts to Germany, this Texan knew that there, too, men were at odds with each other. War would never settle the conflict of ideas in Europe. He believed that the one visible result of the War in America—the freeing of the slaves—would benefit both sides. The lifting of the bondage of another human being gave Meusebach peace of mind. Therein lay a blessing, which he hoped was recognized all over the land.

As an expression of his deep feelings concerning the conflict that divided nation and community, Meusebach gave the name of "Loyal" to the valley in which he came to dwell.

Loyal Valley

CHAPTER 24

I n 1867 Meusebach sold his Fredericksburg store and bought a small holding at Waco Springs, three miles above New Braunfels, on the Guadalupe. An abundance of water for vegetation had always attracted Meusebach, and no doubt the river influenced his investment in this farm. The location was accessible from his home in New Braunfels, where his family was living to be near the schools. The children enjoyed living in New Braunfels—the small lake on the grandparents' farm at the edge of town was a great attraction for the three boys, and Grandmother Coreth was there to pamper the little girls. In New Braunfels Meusebach's young wife had an opportunity to enjoy the companionship of other young women. Her reputation as a superior housekeeper was widespread. In her energetic nature was a fine orderliness. Of her children and her household servants she required adherence to high standards. She often taught morals to her children by repeating proverbs, such as *Wer das Kleine nicht ehrt ist das Grosse nicht wert* ("He who fails to honor the small, the unimportant, is not worthy of the great or important.") The little daughter Emmy at a later time recorded one hundred of the proverbs she had learned from her mother and father.[1] An example of the exactitude in the household was shown by the orderly wardrobes. The linen from Germany was embroidered with consecutive numbers. If ever these numbers were out of order, the entire stack came down. The maid did not make such an error twice.

Meusebach and his wife shared many interests. They made a beautiful couple as they danced together. She liked best to waltz to the "Blue Danube," because then she could tease her husband about the superiority of Austrian dance music. Sometimes a group of friends gathered to sing.

[1] Emmy Meusebach Marschall, Notes and Memoranda. MSS. In possession of Mrs. Homer T. Love, San Antonio, Texas.

Time out for conversation came often, particularly with Lindheimer, with whom Meusebach exchanged botanical specimens for idenification. When newspapers arrived from Germany friends came to discuss the contents. All agreed that autocratic Germany could learn much from democratic Texas. Their attitude concurred with Victor Bracht's earlier description of the state: "Texas . . . this flower of political freedom and social independence."[2]

At the season of the equinox, September 12, 1869, a tornado tore through the city of New Braunfels. The Meusebach residence was one of the houses in the path of the storm. The house and contents were demolished and "made even with the ground."[3] All of the family escaped injury except Meusebach himself, whose foot was pinned between heavy beams. It took the hard labor of two strong men to extricate him. Effects of the injury to his foot were with him the remainder of his life.

The Meusebachs made a point of employing persons who had been orphaned by the illness that ravaged the early colonists. Sometimes a helper was a representative of second-generation immigrants. One such employee, a sixteen-year-old nurse girl, proved providential. The Comal River flash flooded in New Braunfels on June 9, 1872. Just as the nurse finished decorating a small tree with candy as a surprise for the children, she saw a wall of water rushing down the narrow river. The girl was barely able to warn the family in time for them to escape; much of the house was swept down the torrent. With it went all the treasured German china and Venetian glass, which had been saved from the tornado.

The loss of material possessions was discouraging, but the help shown by friends at such a time was heart-warming. Meusebach wanted his children and his wife to enjoy social pleasures in a community with opportunities for cultural development. For himself, he was interested in a location where he could live quietly, without the press of so many activities. He therefore first put down his stakes in 1869 at a location midway between Fredericksburg and Mason. Definite prospects that a railroad would be built between these two towns, and the fact that the location was on the stage route to El Paso enhanced its value. He gave the sparse and scattered settlement the name of Loyal Valley to indicate his own loyalty to the Union, which he had sustained through the years.

The pull toward Loyal Valley was strong, but Meusebach and his wife waited until a propitious time in their children's schooling before they

---

[2] Viktor Bracht, *Texas im Jahre 1848*, p. 71.
[3] Lucy Meusebach Marschall, Notes and Memoranda. MSS. Meusebach Family Files.

moved. By 1875 all of the children, even the youngest, had had the benefits of the excellent New Braunfels schools. That was the year, therefore, that the move to Loyal Valley was made.

Low-lying hills encircled this valley. To the east, in the distance, stood majestic House Mountain, whose rose-red boulders indicated its granite foundation; to the south the chalky outcropping on the knolls showed a limestone foundation. Between was this valley, not as picturesque as some areas nearby, but promising great fertility because of its Archean geological formation. Soon after acquiring this valley land in 1869, Meusebach had begun planting an orchard, ornamental shrubs, and a rose garden. With care given them, they had grown well and seemed to speak a welcome when the family came to live there in 1875.

The site had attraction for Meusebach, who wanted to sow and reap the good earth. In his first letter to the Verein he had written, "I should like to obtain a large enough property to be the basis of nature study and the furtherance thereof in those rich fields."[4] He believed he had found such a place in those seven hundred acres just beyond the center of activity, yet not entirely removed from the hum of progress. Here was the eddy in the current of civilization. The associations were not to be broken: it was a half day's travel to Fredericksburg; two days, or less, to New Braunfels.

For these trips, particularly the semiannual visits to New Braunfels, Meusebach drove a hack with an excellent team of horses. One well-matched pair of grey horses he named Greeley and Pilgrim. In his valley, he kept horses to compete in the races which were held on the open prairies nearby. Meusebach's horses, however, seldom won against the wilder horses belonging to the local ranch people.

The region called for a mercantile establishment, which Meusebach set up in a building constructed of native stone. This store soon became a community center, the more so when Meusebach was appointed postmaster and notary public. The native stone was used in building several dwellings in the area, including the residence to which Meusebach brought his family. Frau Meusebach liked the house. The children were delighted to be able to pick peaches from their own trees and to gather great bouquets of the flowering crape myrtle. The family made a point of having a little celebration for almost every occasion. That first evening in their Loyal Valley home the father gathered his family outside under the grape arbor and had his sons slice the watermelons which he had grown. No restraint was put on the children since they were eating outside. Their joy was unbounded.

[4] Meusebach, Berlin, October 24, 1844, to Verein. Solms-Braunfels Archives, LI, 1.

Because schools were not yet developed in the region the Meusebachs employed tutors to teach their children. The tutors also used part of their time to help in the store. The children acquired a knowledge of Spanish from one of the tutors, who had been a professor at the University of Mexico. When he noticed that the Meusebachs celebrated the Fourth of July and the Second of March, he requested that they add Cinco de Mayo (the Fifth of May) to their celebrations, since that was Mexican Independence Day. After hearing an explanation of the significance of the day Meusebach told of the declaration of the independence of Texas on March 2, 1836, and of the importance of that day. He continued the story of historical events by telling of the ten years of the existence of the Republic. Texas was still a Republic when Meusebach, in 1845, first set foot on the soil of this "free land," but before the year was out, the inhabitants had voted to become one of the United States—the twenty-eighth state. Those were themes about which Meusebach never tired talking.

He associated the Second of March with his garden, for that day English pea seeds should be put into the ground. Frau Meusebach therefore said, "Let us observe the Fifth of May by gathering wild grapes—that is the day the grapes are usually just the right size for making preserves." "If the grapes are no larger than a currant, maybe," looking at her husband, "I can make you think you have your special French preserves, *bar-le-duc*."[5] In answer to her suggestion Meusebach proposed that they all go to House Mountain to gather mustang grapes. Ever after that the family made a point of observing Cinco de Mayo as a festive occasion and of gathering green grapes on that day, if they were the right size.

The Meusebachs admired the beauty and function of the native vegetation. The man of the household was fond of the agarita, a native shrub which resembled Christmas holly, and wanted it used as a decoration. Frau Meusebach made delicious jellies from the berries of the agarita, an eyewash and a yellow dye from the roots. The ratama and the bird-of-paradise shrub also provided that favorite color, yellow. The yucca, likewise, had its twofold use. Meusebach saw its beauty, while his wife used the roots for a shampoo which gave her curls a beautiful sheen.

Innovation and the use of available materials were necessities in this pioneer land. Meusebach made provision for bathing by building a small trellis-shaded structure between the well and an elevated stone reservoir, from which a windmill pumped the water. Under the trellis he had a bathtub constructed with steps leading into it, Roman style. The tub was well

---

[5] Lucy Meusebach Marschall, Notes and Memoranda. MSS. Meusebach Family Files.

shaped, made of the native stone properly cemented to hold water. A heavy coating of whitewash, applied carefully, gave the tub a finished appearance. When Meusebach would emerge from his frequent baths in this retreat, wearing a white shirt as was his custom, he would recite verses in Latin. "Why in Latin?" he was asked. His answer was, "I speak gratitude to the Romans in their language for instituting a bath of this style, entered by steps."[6] He planted white and purple wisteria to cover the bathhouse; the trellis over the terrace was sometimes a bower of pink roses. If Meusebach was absent from business unduly long, he could always be found reading on this terrace.

The appreciation of beauty was deep within this thinker, Meusebach; beauty was truth to him, and the outward manifestation of nature's truths was essential to his happiness. Bringing a plant, a shrub, a tree to its highest state of fruition gave Meusebach true satisfaction. He cultivated and fertilized carefully, and was a pioneer in plowing under green growth to enrich the soil. Meusebach spoke nature's language. Nature was the benefactor, he thought, and man needed to work in accord with her. Results came in direct proportion to care and attention.

The avenue of crape-myrtle shrubs leading to the family residence had a gradation of color that would have pleased an artist. The path to the cow pen had rows of lilacs on either side, and Vitex (American lavender) surrounded the outhouses. Bamboo plants grew near the pond, and jujube plums, or Texas dates, with their thick, thorny growth served as fences. Meusebach tended carefully a small-leafed boxwood, so that his wife could use the miniature leaves to decorate cakes for special celebrations. Trumpet vines flourished to attract hummingbirds. Bachelor buttons were made into dried bouquets for the winters; a pot of Parma violets usually stood in a sunny window to give fragrance to the winter air. The flowering willows provided thimbles for the children. Meusebach trained ivy to cover the stone walls, but grapes—the wild, mustang variety— he let nature's bounty in Texas provide. As he looked at those native grapevines, there came often to his mind the description of them that he had read to his father in Germany from Sealsfield's book about Texas, a book that had greatly influenced Meusebach's decisions as a young man.

Dr. Friedrich Kapp, writing in 1876, says that if Meusebach had remained in Germany "he would have risen to a high and influential position." He says further that "he had the qualities that would rank him as a diplomat of the first order." But he saw that certain qualities were lacking in Meusebach: he had "no appeal to the popular vein and no gift of

[6] *Ibid.*

awakening enthusiasm." Dr. Kapp observed that Meusebach was *"zu vornehm aufgeknöpft,"* "buttoned up too aristocratically."[7] The aristocratic caste into which Meusebach was born and in which he spent his formative years had put its trammels about him, and he could never throw them off. Despite his convictions regarding freedom in its truest sense and his desire that all individuals have equal rights under the law, he felt no compulsion to be on equal social footing with those around him. To live justly with others, yes, and to be true to himself—these concepts were part of his way of life. Goethe had said it well: "Only he deserves freedom who conquers it anew each day."

Texas as described to Europeans was romantic; truly the Texas of reality had never lost its fascination for Meusebach. There was space here where each man could rise to the stature he chose for himself. The determining values were not position, nor gold, nor even acres. The criterion for greatness was self-imposed. A name took on an aura only for accomplishment. Inheritance was important, but a man had to prove himself. And here in Texas lay the opportunity.

Another writer, N. A. Taylor, visited Meusebach in 1877 and discerned his innermost spirit as it found expression, not in "midstream," but in a quiet recess. Taylor wrote:

Loyal Valley is indeed a garden in a wilderness; a garden in which one can linger and be happy. Here is a nursery in which sixty varieties of roses grow, and hundreds of the finest flora of three continents; sixty varieties of pear, forty of peach, and an array of apples, plums, and grapes—all cultivated and arranged with taste and skill that cannot be excelled. It is curious to see such an industry in so isolated and remote a region; and nothing could possibly indicate so well the higher civilization of the people of the valley, as the fact stated to me by the proprietor [of the store] that he had liberal and profitable customers. "I am sure," said John O. Meusebach, "that our valley will soon have as fine vineyards, orchards and gardens as any country in the world, and I feel some little pride in the thought that it is I that am doing it." John O. Meusebach held that people could not be happy and really blessed until they had vineyards and orchards . . . in which view I heartily concurred. The proprietor is a German gentleman of high educational attainments and he is a blessing to Loyal Valley, and to remote regions beyond it. His light shines afar off."[8]

Meusebach felt the Texas climate to be beneficial to his way of life.

---

[7] Friedrich Kapp, *Aus und ueber Amerika. Thatsachen und Erlebnisse*, p. 263.

[8] H. F. McDanield, and Nathaniel Alston Taylor, *The Coming Empire; or Two Thousand Miles in Texas on Horseback*, p. 194.

The winter sunshine was comforting, especially in contrast to the icy blasts of the Baltic Coast. Even the hot Texas summer was tempered within the thick stone walls of his dwelling. In the early morning he directed his helper in tending the growth of his orchard. Then he gathered the fruit for daily use and some to be preserved for winter as well. Special celebrations, like family gatherings, gave this "house father" great delight and for them he provided extra decorations.

The Christmas season capped all the celebrations. The Christmas tree from the woods was selected weeks in advance, and at intervals a bit of cedar was burned to indicate the approach of Christmas. The family searched the pastures for bird's nests, for berries, and for winter ferns to be used as decorations. They hung on the tree gilded walnuts as well as decorated cookies shaped to represent the initials of each member of the family. Christmas was a never-to-be-forgotten festivity. When the wedding date of his daughter Lucy was set for December 28, Meusebach and the bride were pleased that a blossoming orange tree laden with golden fruit was ready, in full beauty, for the Christmastide occasion.

Working with nature was a healing remedy for Meusebach; some of the vitality that had been lost in those early stressful years was restored. And he learned much from his work outdoors. Passing that knowledge on was his pleasure. A Scottish lady came regularly, always asking "the bar-ron" to repeat the Latin names of his plants, while he drilled her on ways to improve plant growth. A certain colonist of the year 1846 reminisced so often and so long at a time with his "Herr von," as he called Meusebach, that the colonist's wife taught the forty-sixer to knit socks so he would have something to show for the hours consumed. Meusebach's shrubs were sent in many directions. He planted an evergreen in a great tub to be sent to Fredericksburg for the town's Christmas tree. (The offspring of that first tree ornaments a garden there today.) Again, he sent aborvitae (tree of life) to beautify Fort Concho, the distant and desolate outpost of the Fisher-Miller Grant, then occupied by federal troops.

The elemental forces did not spare the Meusebach family. Twice they had lost their houses and possessions through cyclone and flood; a fire caused a third catastrophe. On a wintry night of 1886 their residence was completely burned. When the father of the family found that all were safe, he said, "We overcame two other terrible losses; we'll manage the third—this new house is to be entirely of rock."[9]

[9] Lucy Meusebach Marschall, Notes and Memoranda. MSS. Meusebach Family Files.

Work on this residence began without delay. Native stones were laid with exactitude in ashlar fashion. Within a short time vines covered the walls—English ivy was the favorite. Pomegranates, bearing white and variegated flowers, outlined the limits of the walled-in terrace, and a laurel tree shaded the stone steps. The section of the house facing east had French doors leading to a broad gallery that overlooked the rose garden. When the garden was at its prime the actual count of rose bushes was 250, so large a number that one granddaughter described the garden as "phenomenal."

A feature of the new house very pleasing to Frau Meusebach was the cellar. Here she was able to show her aptitude in growing mushrooms, which pleased her husband. He in turn delighted his wife by cultivating artichokes, which were always reserved for her. A grandson reported that each time he and his sister and three brothers asked for artichokes they were told to wait until "next time."

For social and cultural contacts, Meusebach sought out friends with a background similar to his. He had known previously that the von Marschall family had settled in this area, at Cherry Springs, which was just seven miles from Loyal Valley. In that family were five young sons and one daughter. Carl, the eldest son of William von Marschall, had been a trusted employee in Meusebach's Fredericksburg store. Carl's death at the age of nineteen was a great loss to all concerned for he seemed at an early age to show great promise. In the course of time three von Marschall sons would marry Meusebach daughters.

The von Marschall and Meusebach fathers had a meeting of minds on European and German matters. Members of the two families were loyal Texans. Though representatives of each family held high diplomatic posts in Europe, the two men, now naturalized citizens of the United States, felt that the position of postmaster (which each held) was a mark of honor. Meusebach and von Marschall sometimes exchanged a few words in French. When the neighbors heard the foreign words, they spoke somewhat disdainfully of the "French airs" being shown by these two gentlemen. No overtures on the part of von Marschall and Meusebach broke down the feeling. The young people of the second generation, however, seemed to forget any differences.

The post office in Loyal Valley was a meeting place for the entire community. The neighboring frontiersmen gathered regularly for an exchange of ideas. One pioneer said, "I'd be an educated man if I knew half as much as Mr. Meusebach has forgotten."[10] At these sessions the

[10] *Ibid.*

neighbors often wondered what "Mr. Meusebach" would ever do with the rocks and fossils he was gathering and carefully labeling.

The tranquility and friendliness of this place was shattered in 1877 with the outbreak of what was to become known as the Mason County War. Conflicts arose between the American settlers and their German neighbors. Groups of armed Americans began to raid the German settlements with the idea of terrorizing the Germans. One such group stormed into Meusebach's store and found him standing quietly by a counter. He drew himself erect as they approached. Suddenly shots crashed into the floor, grazing Meusebach's legs. He did not move a muscle but with a withering gaze looked directly into the faces of the attackers. After a moment his molesters dropped their eyes, turned sheepishly, and rode away. Meusebach had earned his right to be an American. He had faced the group as he had faced the Comanche war chiefs on the San Saba River so many years before, armed only with iron will.

The post office also was the stopping place where the overland stage changed horses en route from San Antonio to El Paso. Except for the tutors for his children Meusebach had only a few links with the outside world—the post office, the mercantile and notary-public businesses, and the stage station. Correspondence with his family in Germany, which he carefully attended to, and newspapers and magazines kept him abreast with current happenings. He received the *Congressional Record* regularly. His library, though not as complete as his father's in Berlin, was rich in books. Darwin, with his bold pronouncements, appealed to Meusebach and books on travel and maps surrounded him. Goethe's volumes were always within reach, with certain pages worn from reading. A line that he quoted often to his daughters was "Oh lovely moment, linger on, thou art so fair."[11] The thoughts in these books took Meusebach far afield, but journeys per se he seldom took. New Braunfels or San Antonio was the extent of his travels.

Gradually Meusebach lost all interest in leaving home, but friends came to him. From Fredericksburg Charles Henry Nimitz came and told him how much comment was made about the hotel he had built to resemble a steamboat, its prow on a line with the main street of Fredericksburg. These two friends, who knew the sea, chuckled a bit at what the second and third generations in Texas said about this boat chugging along the broad, dry street. Nimitz congratulated Meusebach on his making provision for that broad thoroughfare in Fredericksburg. Nimitz laughed a bit as he asked, "Meusebach, where does that wide street lead to?"

11 J. Wolfgang von Goethe, *Faust* (George Madison Priest, trans.), p. 340.

Quick came the reply: "To freedom!" Then Meusebach added, "Or maybe just to Loyal Valley! But it suits the grandeur of the state."[12]

Meusebach inquired whether the park he had laid out in the center of the town was being enjoyed. Nimitz answered that it was a gathering place where people took time to talk things over. Friends coming out of the *Vereins Kirche* in the center of the park, or *Platz*, lingered there. Plans were in the making to have band concerts in the Park. Children enjoyed playing there, Nimitz reported, and mothers often designated it as a place to meet their children. All of this pleased Meusebach, for he felt that the colonists deserved everything which added to their pleasure. One can believe that he hoped this area surrounding the *Vereins Kirche* would be kept as a place which invites communication and private reflection and that commercial use would not intrude upon its quiet beauty.

Meusebach took his guest for a walk in his rose garden and then through the shrubbery to the orchard. There he filled a basket with choice fruits, such as nectarines, and to round out the basket he included artichokes and colossal asparagus. Nimitz used the word "colossal" when he gave a report to the Fredericksburg newspaper, *Das Wochenblatt*, which described his visit to the naturalist of Loyal Valley. The account names such a variety of stock in the nursery that it reads like a catalogue.

As time went on, Meusebach withdrew from the world; not, however, from his family. He called his loved ones by pet names: his wife was "Die kleine Minne" ("The little love"); his children, girls as well as boys, were "Ha Kerlchen" ("Hail, little fellow"). The oldest grandchild was "Beste, Allerbeste" ("Best of the best"); the youngest, crawling on all fours, was "Das kleine Kaninchen" ("The little rabbit"). The brown-eyed grandchildren were especially dear to Meusebach because their coloring came from their grandmother.

As he enjoyed the warmth of family love and the solitude of the Loyal Valley home Meusebach often visualized the circle of loved ones in their sheltered residence in Germany with their prized possessions about them. Their way of life, within its own environs, was gracious, but the shadow of the government was ever present; self-definition was not possible.

To be a Texan, for Meusebach, had meant bridging the Old World to the New, where liberty was at home. The locale was limited, but the final boundary was limitless. Now that he was free from dominance, he asked himself, for what was he free? That question he pondered often. Did he

12 Lucy Meusebach Marschall, Notes and Memoranda. MSS. Meusebach Family Files.

fulfill his destiny? he wondered as he let his thoughts, his imagination, encircle the world. He thought sometimes that history was like a river which carries men toward their destiny. The current holds some in midstream; others are moved to the side, into calm waters. He had chosen the calm, a cove it might be called. He did not need personal power; to have given a sense of purpose to the group around him was sufficient satisfaction to him.

"Still Forward Press"

CHAPTER 25

For the fiftieth anniversary of the founding of New Braunfels, in 1895, Meusebach was invited to be an honored guest. Because of his failing health he was forced to decline. The following year, 1896, Fredericksburg celebrated the fiftieth year of its founding. A book, *Fest-Ausgabe zum fünfzigjährigen Jubiläum der Deutschen Kolonie Friedrichsburg*, marking this anniversary gave the founder of Fredericksburg, John O. Meusebach, significant honor.[1]

Accompanying her parents to the Fredericksburg celebration, a little three-year-old granddaughter of Meusebach found exquisite delight in the bright lights all about. Her father held her high as she exclaimed, *"Mehr Licht! Mehr Licht!"* When her grandfather was told about the incident, he said: "Those were Goethe's last words. 'I shall want more light till the setting of my sun'."[2]

One of Meusebach's grandsons felt that the man who had handled land almost like merchandise should have acquired more for himself. Such was not the thinking of this argonaut, who sought not gold but something gold cannot buy—freedom of mind and spirit.

In his letter to Castell written from Galveston on January 20, 1846,[3] Meusebach had seen no lifting of the curtain of despair that was settling more heavily each day on the Galveston and Indianola areas. He realized that the destiny of hundreds of lives hung on his efforts. Despondency bowed him low at times, yet an inner source lifted him from hopelessness.

[1] Robert Penniger (ed., comp.), *Fest-Ausgabe zum Fünfzigjährigen Jubiläum der Deutschen Kolonie Friedrichsburg*, p. 58.

[2] Lucy Meusebach Marschall, Notes and Memoranda. MSS. Meusebach Family Files.

[3] Meusebach, Galveston, January 20, 1846, to Castell. Solms-Braunfels Archives, LII, 125.

To close the long letter that ranged almost the entire arc of the colonization project, Meusebach made a specific recommendation from which he seemingly took courage—to create a condition for German knowledge to blossom beside American freedom. He found something as tangible as the clasp of a friend's hand when he concluded with the poetic lines,

> *Dann hemme ferner keine Schranken des Denkens*
> *Flug, als die Bedingung endlicher Naturen.*
> Then let no barrier hamper the flight of thought
> But the limitations of finite nature.

The idea expressed in the lines sustained Meusebach throughout his life. A daughter, very close to her father, recognized how integral the projection of thought was to her father's very life. She wished, a few times, that her father's golden rain tree (*koelreuteria paniculata*) could somehow bring him tangible gold. But she knew he had chosen the better part when he could say with Keats,

> Much have I travell'd in the realms of gold.

Meusebach's thoughts probed deeply; his search for truth never ended. "Must one always be thinking?" he was asked. "Even so," was the answer.[4] Thus Meusebach, with Faust, perceived the whole truth:

> Night presses round me, deep and deeper still,
> And yet within me beams a radiant light;
> What I have planned, I hasten to fulfill.
> Only the master's word has weight and might.
> Up from your couches, vassals, every man!
> Bring happily to sight my daring plan,
> Seize shovel, spade! With all your tools lay on!
> The work staked out must with all speed be done.
> Strict order and swift diligence
> Result in fairest recompense.
> To consummate the greatest enterprises
> *One* spirit for a thousand hands suffices.[5]

Meusebach could ask and answer what one of the immigrants of 1846 wrote:

---

[4] Lucy Meusebach Marschall, Notes and Memoranda. MSS. Meusebach Family Files.

[5] J. Wolfgang von Goethe, *Faust* (George Madison Priest, trans.), Part II, ll. 11499–11510.

What is freedom?
What is light, air, water, bread?
Freedom is life—without freedom is death—
only death.[6]

John O. Meusebach's strength declined gradually during his last years. His life slowly ebbed away; death came on May 27, 1897—the previous day he had reached his eighty-fifth birthday. He is buried in the small, rock-walled Marschall-Meusebach cemetery, one mile east of Cherry Springs. His tombstone carries the inscriptions that were the strongest forces in the life of this democratic aristocrat:

Tenax Propositi

Texas Forever

[6] Alwin H. Sörgel, *Für auswanderungslustige: Briefe eines unter dem schutze des Mainzer vereins nach Texas ausgewanderten*, p. 37.

Appendix

THE TREATY[1]
BETWEEN THE COMMISSARY GENERAL OF THE
GERMAN EMIGRATION-COMPANY

John O. Meusebach

For himself, his successors and constituents, for the benefit and in behalf of the German people living here and settling the country between the waters of the Llano and the San Saba of the one part and the Chiefs of the Comanche Nation
hereunto named and subscribed for themselves and their people of the other part, the following private treaty of peace and friendship has been entered into and agreed upon:

I, The German people and colonists for the Grant between the waters of the Llano and San Saba shall be allowed to visit any part of said country and be protected by the Comanche Nation and the Chiefs thereof, in consideration of which agreement the Comanches may likewise come to the German colonies, towns and settlements and shall have no cause to fear, but shall go wherever they please—if not counselled otherwise by the especial agent of our great father—and have protection, as long as they walk in the white path.

II, In regard to the settlement on the Llano the Comanches promise not to disturb or in any way molest the German colonists, on the contrary to assist them, also to give notice, if they see bad Indians about the settlement who come to steal horses from or in any way molest the Germans— the Germans likewise promising to aid the Comanches against their enemies, should they be in danger of having their horses stolen or in any way to be injured. And both parties agree, that if there be any difficulties

[1] Text of English version. Original in Fürst zu Solms-Braunfels'sches Archiv in Braunfels, Lahn, Germany.

or any wrong done by single bad men, to bring the same before the chiefs to be finally settled and decided by the agent of our great father.

III, The Comanches and their Chiefs grant to Mr. Meusebach, his successors and constituents the privilege of surveying the country as far as the Concho, and even higher up, if he thinks proper to the Colorado and agree not to disturb or molest any men, who may have already gone up or yet to be sent up for that purpose. In consideration of which agreement the Commissary General Mr Meusebach will give them presents to the amount of One Thousand Dollars, which with the necessary provisions to be given to the Comanches during their stay at Fredericksburgh will amount to about Two Thousand Dollars worth or more.

IV, And finally both parties agree mutually to use every exertion to keep up and even enforce peace and friendship between both the German and the Comanche people and all other colonists and to walk in the white path allways and for ever.

In witness whereof we have hereunto set our hands, marks and seals.

Done at Fredericksburgh on the waters of the Rio Pierdenales this the ninth day of May AD 1847.

J. O. Meusebach	War Chiefs of	War Chiefs of the Comanches	
R. T. Neighbors,	the Delaware's	Santa Anna's	X mark
Spec. agt. U.S.	Jim Shaw's X mark	Poch-An-Sanoch-Go's	X "
F. Shubbert	John Connor's X "	Moora-quitop	X "
v. Coll		Matasane	X "
John F. Torrey		To-shaw-wheneschke	X "
Felix A. von Blücher		Nokahwhek	X "

Bibliography

UNPUBLISHED

Private and Public Documents

Marschall, Emmy Meusebach. Notes and Memoranda. MSS. In possession of Mrs. Homer T. Love, San Antonio, Texas.

Marschall, Lucy Meusebach. Notes and Memoranda. MSS. Meusebach Family Files. In possession of Irene Marschall King, Llano, Texas.

Maverick, Sam. Reminiscences. TS. Maverick Papers, University of Texas Archives, Austin.

Meusebach, von, von Witzleben, and von Polenz. Familien-Album. Drawings. Meusebach Family Files. MSS. In possession of Irene Marschall King, Llano, Texas.

Runnels, Hardin R. MSS. Governors' Correspondence, Texas State Archives, Austin.

Solms-Braunfels Archives. Transcripts (Originals in Fürst zu Solms-Braunfels'-sches Archiv in Braunfels, Lahn, Germany). 70 vols. University of Texas Archives, Austin (Cited as SB Archives).

Witzleben, C. M. von (comp). Geschichte der Freiherren von Meusebach. Bound MS with printed title page (Wittenberg, 1860). Meusebach Family Files in possession of Irene Marschall King, Llano, Texas.

Theses and Dissertations

Finch, Arthur L., Jr. "The Regulated Emigration of the German Proletariat with Special Reference to Texas Being also a Guide for German Emigrants by Dr. Ferdinand Charles von Herff, member of the Darmstaedter Colony of Llano and at New Braunfels." M.A. Thesis, The University of Texas, Austin, 1949.

Gunnin, Gerry C. "French Communitive Socialist Experiments in Texas, 1846–1868." M.A. Thesis, Baylor University, Waco, Texas, 1964.

Loving, Solon Ollie. "A History of the Fisher-Miller Land Grant from 1848–1860." M.A. Thesis, The University of Texas, Austin, 1934.

Neighbors, Alice Atkinson. "Life and Public Work of Robert S. Neighbors." M.A. Thesis, The University of Texas, Austin, 1936.

Neighbors, Kenneth Franklin. "Robert S. Neighbors in Texas, 1836–1856: A Quarter Century of Frontier Problems." Ph.D. Dissertation, The University of Texas, Austin, 1955.

PUBLISHED

Books and Pamphlets

Adams, James Truslow. *The Epic of America.* Boston: Little, Brown and Company, 1931.

Anonymous. "Meusebach's Zug in das Gebiet der Comanche-Indianer in Januar 1847 (Aus einer alten Nummer des 'Magazin für die Literature des Auslandes')," *Fest-Ausgabe zum fünzigjährigen Jubiläum der Deutschen Kolonie Friedrichsburg,* ed. and comp. Robert Penniger (Fredericksburg, Texas: Robert Penniger, 1896.)

Atkinson, Mary Jourdan. *The Texas Indians.* San Antonio: The Naylor Company, 1936.

Barba, Preston Albert. *The Life and Works of Friedrich Armand Strubberg.* Philadelphia: University of Pennsylvania, 1913.

Behr, Ottomar von. *Guter Rath fuer Auswanderer nach den Vereinigten Staaten von Nordamerika mit besonderer Beruecksichtigung von Texas.* Leipzig: R. Friese, 1847. Barker Texas History Center, The University of Texas, Austin.

Benjamin, G. G. *The Germans in Texas; A Study in Immigration.* Philadelphia: Publications of the University of Pennsylvania. New York: D. Appleton and Company, 1909.

Biesele, Rudolph Leopold. *The History of the German Settlements in Texas 1831–1861.* Austin: Von Boeckmann-Jones Co., 1930.

Bigelow, Poultney. *History of the German Struggle for Liberty, 1815–1848.* 3 vols. New York: Harper and Brothers, 1902.

Biggers, Don H. *German Pioneers in Texas: A Brief History of Their Hardships, Struggles and Achievements.* Fredericksburg, Texas: Fredericksburg Publishing Co., 1925.

Bolton, Herbert E. *Texas in the middle eighteenth century; studies in Spanish colonial history and administration.* Berkeley: University of California Press, 1915.

Bracht, Viktor. *Texas im Jahre 1848.* Elberfeld u. Iserlohn: J. Bädeker, 1849.

Bromme, Traugott. *Hand-und Reisebuch für Auswanderer nach den Vereinigten Staaten von Nord-Amerika.* Bayreuth: Buckner, 1848. Barker Texas History Center, The University of Texas, Austin.

Chabot, Frederick C. *With the Makers of San Antonio.* San Antonio: Privately published; printing by the Artes Graficas, 1937.

Constant, L. *Texas. Das Verderben deutscher Auswanderer in Texas unter dem Schutze des Mainzer Vereins.* Berlin: G. Reimer, 1847. Barker Texas History Center, The University of Texas, Austin.

De Voto, Bernard. *The Year of Decision: 1846.* Boston: Little, Brown and Company, 1943.

Dill, Marshall, Jr. *Germany: A Modern History.* Ann Arbor:: The University of Michigan Press, 1961.

Dohmen, Franz J. (trans.) *Life and Memoirs of Emil Frederick Wurzbach, to which is appended some papers of John Meusebach* (Yanaguana Society Publications, III). San Antonio: Yanaguana Society; printed by the Artes Graficas, 1937.

Eby, Frederick. *The Development of Education in Texas.* New York: Macmillan and Co., 1925.

Frazer, Sir James George. *The Golden Bough: A Study in Magic and Religion.* Abridged ed., 1 vol. New York: The Macmillan Company, 1930.

Gambrell, Herbert P., and Lewis W. Newton. *A Social and Political History of Texas.* Dallas: Southwest Press, 1932.

Garrison, George P. *Texas; a contest of civilizations.* Boston and New York: Houghton, Mifflin and Co., 1903.

Geiser, Samuel Wood. *Naturalists of the Frontier.* Dallas: Southern Methodist University Press, 1937.

Gillespie County Historical Society. *Pioneers in God's Hills.* Austin: Von Boeckmann-Jones, 1960.

Goethe, J. Wolfgang von. *Faust* (Parts I and II, translated from the German by George Madison Priest). New York: Covici, Friede Publishers, 1932.

Gooch, George Peabody. *Germany and the French Revolution.* New York: Longmans, Green, and Co., 1920.

Hawgood, John A. *The Tragedy of German-America.* New York and London: Putnam Sons, 1940.

Hoebel, E. Adamson and Ernest Wallace. *The Comanches: Lords of the South Plains.* Norman: University of Oklahoma Press, 1952.

Jones, Anson. *Memoranda and official correspondence relating to the republic of Texas, its history, and annexation.* New York: D. Appleton and Company, 1859.

Kapp, Friedrich. *Aus und ueber Amerika. Thatsachen und Erlebnisse.* 2 vols. Berlin: J. Springer, 1876.

Kennedy, William. *Texas: its geography, natural history and topography.* Boston: Benjamin and Young, 1844. Barker Texas History Center, The University of Texas, Austin.

———. *Texas: the rise, progress, and prospects of the republic of Texas.* London: R. Hastings, 1841. Barker Texas History Center, The University of Texas, Austin.

Kneschke, Ernest Heinrich. "Freiherren Meusebach," in Vol. 6, pp. 271–274, of *Neues allgemeines deutsches adels-lexicon,* 9 vols. Leipzig: F. Voight, 1859–1870. Library of Congress, Washington, D.C.

Kohn, Hans. *Nationalism, its meaning and history.* Princeton, New Jersey: Van Nostrand, 1955.

———. *The Mind of Germany: The Education of a Nation.* New York: Charles Scribner's Sons, 1960.

Krieger, Leonard. *The German Idea of Freedom.* Boston: Beacon, 1957.

Lotto, F. *Fayette county, her history and her people.* Schulenberg, Texas: Published for the author, 1902.

McDanield, H. F., and Nathaniel Alston Taylor. *The Coming Empire; or Two Thousand Miles in Texas on Horseback.* New York, Chicago, and New Orleans: A. S. Barnes and Co., 1877.

Meusebach, John O. *Answer to Interrogatories.* In Case No. 396, Mary C. Paschal, *et al.,* vs. Theodore Evans, District Court of McCulloch County, Texas, November Term, 1893. Austin: Eugene Von Boeckmann, Printer, 1894. Texas State Archives, Austin.

Molyneaux, Peter. *The Romantic Story of Texas.* Dallas and New York: Cordova Press, 1936.

Mueller, Oswald (trans.). *Roemer's Texas.* San Antonio: Standard Printing Company, 1935.

Newcomb, W. W., Jr. *The Indians of Texas: From Prehistoric to Modern Times.* Austin: University of Texas Press, 1961.

Newton, Lewis W. See Gambrell, Herbert P., and Lewis W. Newton. *A Social and Political History of Texas.*

Olmsted, Frederick Law. *A Journey through Texas: or A Saddle-Trip on the Southwestern Frontier.* With a statistical appendix. New York: Dix, Edwards and Co., 1857.

Penniger, Robert (ed., comp.). *Fest-Ausgabe zum fünfzigjährigen Jubiläum der Deutschen Kolonie Friedrichsburg.* Fredericksburg, Texas: Robert Penniger, 1896. In possession of Irene Marschall King, Llano, Texas.

Pennybacker, Mrs. Anna J. Hardwicke. *A History of Texas for Schools.* Rev. ed. Austin: Mrs. Percy V. Pennybacker, 1912.

Petmecky, William. *Legendary Tales—Easter Fires of Fredericksburg.* Fredericksburg, Texas: Fredericksburg Publishing Co., 1963.

Ransleben, Guido E. *A Hundred Years of Comfort in Texas.* San Antonio: Naylor Publishing Co., 1964.

Richardson, Rupert Norval. *The Comanche Barrier to South Plains Settlement.* Glendale, California: The Arthur H. Clark Company, 1933.

Roemer, Ferdinand von. *Die Kreidebildungen von Texas und ihre organischen Einschluesse.* Bonn: Adolphus Marcus, 1852.

——. *Texas. Mit besonderer rücksicht auf deutsche auswanderung und die physichen verhältnisse des landes nach eigener beobachtung geschildert von dr. Ferdinand Roemer.* Mit einen naturwissen-schaftlichen anhange und einer topographische-geonostichen karte von Texas. Bonn: A. Marcus, 1849; see also, Mueller, Oswald. *Roemer's Texas.*

Rosenberg, W. von. *Kritik der Geschichte der Vereins zum Schutze der Deutschen Auswanderer nach Texas.* Austin: 1894. Barker Texas History Center, The University of Texas, Austin.

Scheffel, Fritz. *Deutsche suchen den Garten der Welt.* Stuttgart: Union deutsche verlagsgesellsckaft, 1941.

Sealsfield, Charles. *Life in the New World; or Sketches of American Society* (translated from the German by Gustavus C. Hebbe and James MacKay). New York: J. Winchester, New World Press, 1844. Barker Texas History Center, The University of Texas, Austin.

——. *Nathan, der squatter-regulator, oder Der erste Amerikaner in Texas.* Vom verfasser des "Legitimen," des "Virey," w. s. w. Stuttgart, Verlag der J. B. Metzler'schen buchhandlung. Zurich: Friedrich Schulthess, 1835. Barker Texas History Center, The University of Texas, Austin.

Solms-Braunfels, Karl, fürst zu. *Texas, 1844–1845* (translated from the German). Houston: The Anson Jones press, 1936.

Sörgel, Alwin H. *Für auswanderungslustige: Briefe eines unter dem schutze des Mainzer vereins nach Texas ausgewanderten.* Leipzig: Expedizion des Herold, 1847. Barker Texas History Center, The University of Texas, Austin.

——. *Neueste Nachrichten aus Texas. Zugleich ein Hülferuf an den Mainzer Verein zum Schutze deutscher Einwanderer in Texas.* Eisleben: Reichhardt,

1847. Barker Texas History Center, The University of Texas, Austin.

Taylor, Nathaniel Alston. See McDanield, H., and Nathaniel Alston Taylor. *The Coming Empire; or Two Thousand Miles in Texas on Horseback.*

Texas State Legislature. *Journal of the Senate of the State of Texas, Fourth Legislature—Extra session.* Austin: J. W. Hampton, state printer, 1852–1853. Texas State Archives, Austin.

Texas State Legislature, Adjourned session (July 7–September 1, 1856). *Report on the building and furniture of the Capitol of the State of Texas.* Austin: Marshall and Oldham, state printers, 1856. Texas State Archives, Austin.

Thran, Jakob. *Meine Auswanderung nach Texas unter dem Schutze des Mainzer Vereins.* Berlin: E. Krause, 1848. Barker Texas History Center, The University of Texas, Austin.

Tiling, Moritz. *History of the German Element in Texas from 1820–1850, and Historical Sketches of the German Texas Singers' League and Houston Turnverein from 1853–1913.* 1st ed. Houston: Published by Moritz Tiling, 1912.

Treitschke, Heinrich Gotthard von. *History of Germany in the Nineteenth Century* (translated by Eden and Cedar Paul). 7 vols. New York: McBride, Nast and Co., 1915–1919.

Valentin, Veit. *The German People: Their Historical Civilization from the Holy Roman Empire to the Third Reich.* New York: Alfred A. Knopp., Inc., 1952.

Verein zum Schutze Deutscher Einwanderer in Texas. *Gesammelte aktenstücke . . . nebst einer karte.* Mainz: Victor von Zabern, 1845. University of Texas Archives, Austin.

Wallace, Ernest. See Hoebel, E. Adamson, and Ernest Wallace. *The Comanches, Lords of the South Plains.*

Webb, Walter Prescott. *The Texas Rangers: A Century of Frontier Defense.* Boston and New York: Houghton, Mifflin Company, 1935.

Weddle, Robert S. *The San Sabá Mission: Spanish Pivot in Texas.* Austin: University of Texas Press, 1964.

Weinheimer, J., Sr. "Erinnerungen aus den Kriegszeiten," *Fest-Ausgabe zum fünfzigjährigen Jubiläum der Deutschen Kolonie Friedrichsburg,* ed. and comp. Robert Penniger (Fredericksburg, Texas: Robert Penniger, 1896).

Wendler, Dr. Camillus. *Briefwechsel des Freiherrn Karl Hartwig Gregor von Meusebach mit Jacob und Wilhelm Grimm.* Nebst einleitenden Bemerkungen über den Verkehr des Sammlers mit gelehrten Freunden, Anmerkungen und einem Anhang von der Berufung der Bruder Grimm nach Berlin. Heilbronn, Germany: Gebr, Henninger, 1880. In possession of Irene Marschall King, Llano, Texas.

Periodicals

Anonymous. "Der Häuptling mit dem brennenden Haupthaar," *Kalender der Neu-Braunfelser Zeitung fuer 1905,* pp. 59–60.

"Berichte des Prinzen Karl zu Solms-Braunfels an den Mainzer Adelsverein," *Kalender der Neu Braunfelser Zeitung fuer 1916.*

Biesele, R. L. "The German Settlers and the Indians in Texas, 1844–1860," *The Southwestern Historical Quarterly,* XXXI, No. 2 (October, 1927), 116–129.

Bonnet, Rudolf. "Otfried Hans Freiherr von Meusebach, ein aus Nassau gebürtiger Kulturpionier in Texas," *Nassauische Heimatblätter*, XXX, No. 4 (October–December, 1929), 144–148.

Dielmann, Henry B. "Dr. Ferdinand Herff, Pioneer Physician and Surgeon," *The Southwestern Historical Quarterly*, LVII, No. 3 (January, 1954), 265–284.

Gruener, Claude Michael. "Rutherford B. Hayes's Horseback Ride through Texas," *The Southwestern Historical Quarterly*, LXVIII, No. 3 (January, 1965), 358–359.

Hermes, Wilhelm. "Erlebnisse eines deutschen Einwanderers in Texas," *Kalender der Neu-Braunfelser Zeitung fuer 1922*, pp. 18–30.

Huber, Armin O. "Frederic Armand Strubberg, Alias Dr. Shubbert, Town-Builder, Physician and Adventurer, 1806–1866," *West Texas Historical Association Year Book*, XXXVIII (October, 1962), 37–71.

Kalender der Neu-Braunfelser Zeitung fuer 1905. [New Braunfels, Texas]: Neu-Braunfelser Zeitung.

Kalender der Neu-Braunfelser Zeitung fuer 1914. New-Braunfels, Texas: Neu-Braunfelser Zeitung.

Kalender der Neu-Braunfelser Zeitung fuer 1916. [New Braunfels, Texas: Neu-Braunfelser Zeitung].

Kalender der Neu-Braunfelser Zeitung fuer 1922. [New Braunfels, Texas: Neu-Braunfelser Zeitung].

Kapp, Friedrich. "Lecture by Frederick Kapp delivered at Clinton Hall in Astor Place," New York *Daily Tribune*, Saturday, January 20, 1855.

Mueller, Esther. "How Fredericksburg Came to Be," *The Edwards Plateau Historian*, I (1965), 1–5.

Ramsdell, Charles. "El Sol Colorado," *San Antonio Express Magazine*, January 30, 1949, p. 7.

Reinhardt, Louis. "The Communistic Colony of Bettina, 1846–8," *The Quarterly of the Texas State Historical Association*, III, No. 1 (July, 1899), 33–40.

Schwartz, Karl. "Karl Hartwig Gregor von Meusebach, Lebensnachrichten" (Parts I–IV), *Annalen des Vereins für Nassauische Altertumskunde und Geschichtsforschung*, XXI (1890): Part I, pp. 41–52; Part II, pp. 53–76; Part III [separate series], pp. 1–13; Part IV, pp. 14–64.

Seele, Hermann, "Meine Ankunft in Neu-Braunfels," *Kalender der Neu-Braunfelser Zeitung fuer 1914*, pp. 36–43.

Tyler's Quarterly Historical and Genealogical Magazine, VIII (July, 1926).

Index